LADY MORGAN

■ **Mary Campbell** spent her early life working in the documentary film industry where she was one of the few women involved in writing, directing and editing films for the Central Office of Information and other official bodies. Marriage and children put an end to the life of going on location, but she continued to work as a freelance in film, television and radio. A stint in advertising was made bearable by the discovery that she could write for the printed word and, for the last few years, she has written for the Arts and Studies pages of *The Irish Times* as well as many other publications. *Lady Morgan: The Life and Times of Sidney Owenson* is Mary Campbell's first book.

PANDORA PRESS

Lady Morgan

Portrait of Lady Morgan, Courtesy of the National Library of Ireland

LADY MORGAN

THE LIFE AND TIMES
OF SYDNEY OWENSON

Mary Campbell

Michael – with love

Mary

29. 3. 1988.

PANDORA

LONDON SYDNEY WELLINGTON

First published in Great Britain by
Pandora Press an imprint of the
Trade Division of Unwin Hyman Limited, 1988

UNWIN HYMAN LIMITED
15-17 Broadwick Street
London W1V 1FP

Allen & Unwin Australia Pty Ltd
8 Napier Street, North Sydney, NSW 2060, Australia

Allen & Unwin New Zealand Pty Ltd
with the Port Nicholson Press
60 Cambridge Terrace, Wellington, New Zealand

ISBN 0-86358-203-6

A CIP catalogue record is available from the British Library

Set in 10 pt Sabon
by Columns of Reading
Printed in Great Britain by
Biddles Ltd., Guildford, Surrey

CONTENTS

ILLUSTRATIONS

INTRODUCTION

In the writing of prefaces one could do worse than to follow the example of Lady Morgan. She loved making direct statements to her readers, and produced new forewords for different editions of her books. Often these were political and patriotic manifestoes – more earnest than the actual content of the work in hand. She would state magisterially that Ireland was her vocation, and her constant theme. She would boast that her books on France and Italy were an affirmation of the radical spirit that had inspired the political events in those countries, and sometimes, even more boldly, she would make excuses for any faults that her readers might find in her latest four-volume confection hot off the press by saying that she had written the entire work in three weeks, that there had been no time to revise, but that she was confident that her readers' love and loyalty would make all acceptable. So, like her I have set out my ideological manifesto and claim that I was moved by her love for Ireland and her radical opinions to want to write about her in the first place, and if I have overstated her importance this fault is balanced by the unfair neglect and denigration that her reputation has suffered for decades. Unlike her, I cannot claim my readers' indulgence by saying that I tossed off this study of the lady in three weeks; she proved to be a totally absorbing subject, even though there was no new cache of letters or manuscripts to discover. But there was plenty of material. She mined deeply into the past, but she lived vibrantly in her own present, sharing all the political and social assumptions of the time. Any fresh insight I have had into Sydney Morgan has come from seeing her in that context, and assessing her in the terms of modern Ireland.

It is given to few lady novelists to be under the constant surveillance of the security police, or for the politics of a nation to be argued out in the rhetoric of her romantic fiction. But for a period in the first half of the nineteenth century, between the Act of Union which brought to an end the rule in Ireland of the Ascendancy, and the Famine, which brought to an end the old Gaelic peasant world, the novels of Sydney Morgan had a potency that affected such issues as Catholic emancipation, the Repeal of the Union, and the whole question of English rule in Ireland and made her the object of the attentions of the secret police, both in England and Ireland, and abroad. This might seem very heavy treatment for someone who claimed to make up 'tissues of woven air, in which I then clothed my heroines'. But out of these tissues she created the image of herself, so powerful that in the public's mind she took on the persona of her most original heroine – Glorvina, the Wild Irish Girl.

Sydney Owenson as she was then, was the daughter of an itinerant actor; forced by poverty to become a governess, she achieved a title on her wedding day and created an important social and literary salon in Dublin which she later transferred to London. She also created an eager and large readership for her novels of Irish 'national' life both in England and Ireland, and was the first woman writer to be given a pension – three hundred pounds a year – for her service to 'the world of letters'.

If she was well rewarded she was also widely reviled. All through her professional life she was attacked by powerful and influential critics, not so much for her literary lapses as for her Whiggish and Jacobin opinions. And all through her life she fought them valiantly, and they could dent neither her spirit nor her popularity. But now that she is dead, it is a very different story. Eminent literary historians since her death have either ignored her or dismissed her as a footnote in literature. And today she has more or less been written off. One Irish writer has recently – without giving evidence to support his claim – called her 'a trashy novelist'. These generalisations are as unfair now as was the criticism she suffered when she was alive – for having too much significance! For the sake of literary history it is necessary to understand why she was considered so important in her own time and, in spite of her relegation to the ranks of writers now deemed obsolete, how much she can still contribute to an understanding of the social, political and religious problems that still bedevil Ireland today. Her 'national' tales analysed the conflicts in Irish society then which led eventually to the troubles of all the ensuing years, and her advocacy of justice and tolerance might still be heeded with some better results.

Ireland is a country still regarded by many as outside the mainstream of the European literary tradition and whose unique romantic heritage has enhanced a literature dominated by folklore and fairies. The other side of the medal, etched by colder-eyed observers, is the Ireland of conflict, caricature, and prejudice that expresses itself eventually in the cruel anti-Irish joke. When Sydney Morgan started to write, this was the stereotype she had to break. She herself was the victim of racist and sexist prejudice on a horrendous scale, which she fought vigorously and successfully. In one of her fighting prefaces she reminded her readers that she wrote in an age 'when to be a woman was to be without defence, and to be a patriot was to be a criminal'. She was proud to be both a woman and a patriot, and endeavoured to raise the status of her country and her sex, even though as her friend and observer Mrs S.C. Hall remarked, 'Envy, malice and uncharitableness, these are the fruits of a successful career for a woman.'

Modern Ireland provides us with a prime example of an impressive literature brought into being by politics. After the trauma of the rebellion of 1916, the poet Yeats, overwhelmed with the responsibility of the artist asked anxiously, 'Did that play of mine send out – certain men the English shot?'

Lady Morgan was no Yeats. She would never win the Nobel Prize for Literature and there is no summer school in her name in the Ireland of today; her contemporary, Thomas Moore, another bright star of romantic nationalism, and once acclaimed as Ireland's national bard, is also out of favour. But in their time, in the days of their fame, they were responsible for an awakening of patriotic feeling and identity, which provided the dynamic for political action, and a completely new tradition of Irish writing.

Lady Morgan was the first Irish writer of the nineteenth century to express the passion and the commitment of those members of the Anglo-Irish who espoused the nationalist cause. Before her, writing in Ireland had been a colonial literature, written for English publishers and an English readership. She found themes that were deeply relevant to the Irish – themes of religion, racial heritage, and family loyalties in a broken society – and at the same time made these matters palatable and comprehensible to an English public. Thomas Davis, the chief poet of the Young Ireland Movement that took up the nationalist struggle in 1848, paid tribute to the influence of Sydney Morgan and wrote his own manifesto which might have been taken from one of her prefaces:

> Nationality is the summary name for many things. It seeks
> a literature made by Irishmen and coloured by our scenery,
> manners and characters. It desires to see Art applied to
> express Irish thoughts and beliefs. It would make our music
> sound in every parish at twilight . . . and our poetry and
> history sit at every hearth.

These ideas were taken up by other poets and writers, now
more honoured than the woman who originated them. They
may have been responsible for over inflated oratory, inferior
literature and unsuccessful revolution. They might have helped
to keep nineteenth-century Irish writing trapped in the nets that
James Joyce had to fly, in order to embrace the main issues of
European fiction. But they also inspired a great literature, the
Celtic Revival, the plays of the Abbey Theatre and the poetry of
Yeats. Modern Ireland was born out of these ideas, and Sydney
Morgan was there at the beginning. She tried to express her
vision through her writing. Her novels – if one is looking –
contain a key to the 'Irish problem'. To ignore her is to reject
the potency of literature.

CHAPTER 1

DEAR HARP OF MY COUNTRY

When Lady Morgan was in her prime, which in fact she was for most of her life, a literary critic, in the name of the public interest, set up a Royal Commission to find out how old she was. He even offered money for information. This ungentlemanly conduct was approved, and even emulated by others, for her critics were many and merciless. All through her long writing career they attacked her for so many things that offended their polite susceptibilities, yet they never could suppress her lively pen. So they went for the really sensitive question of her age. She seemed to have been around so long, they said. 'This female Methusaleh!', this *'jeune dame qui a été jeune si long-temps!'*; these are among the milder specimens of personal abuse to which she was subjected. But her self esteem which had supported her well through many a rough passage continued to protect her. In spite of about fifteen estimates of her date of birth, with discrepancies of more than ten years between first and last, she kept her secret, and they could not break it. Consequently we have only inspired guesses to work on, which give 1776 as the most probable date, and possibly Christmas Day, on the mailboat crossing from England to Ireland. Now, the Irish sea in winter is a notoriously stormy passage, and a natural parallel to the difficult, long relationship between the two countries in question, and to be born half way over seems a very appropriate place for one who was destined to play the living incarnation of one country for the entertainment of the other. Did it happen that way? With Lady Morgan who can tell? She wove the strands of her own origins and genealogy more skilfully than many of the plots of her novels. It was a portentous year in which to be born. The American Declaration of Independence had just been signed. Ideas of republicanism and the rights of man were circulating in England and even in Ireland, and consequently the forces of

1

reaction were closing their ranks fast. Lady Morgan was born at a time of struggle and change – when history was putting in the bill for unpaid debts.

Speaking specifically of Irish history, James Joyce said that it was a nightmare from which he was trying to awake. For Sydney Morgan history was the stuff of dreams out of which she made her novels. And because of the juxtaposition of the time she lived in and the past she recreated, her version of history took on the glamour of an archaeological discovery, like a gold cup found in the furrows of a ploughed field. She seized on such consoling images that the times needed, to lift the spirits of a humiliated and downtrodden nation. These images became the inspiration of a whole school of national romanticism in both literature and art. They not only sustained the Irish in dark days but influenced the way in which some of the English were to view Ireland and her problems from then until the present times.

For the English reading public, which up to then had not been particularly sensitive to the romantic aspect of Ireland, loved Sydney Morgan; from the very start her books sold. *The Wild Irish Girl*, written in 1806, went into seven editions in two years, in spite of the savage reviews that greeted it, and in fact were always to greet her work. The gentler critics said of her early work that she was in immediate need of a spelling book, and then, in the course of time she might acquire a pocket dictionary. They called her books 'flimsy Irish slip-slop'; but as the public continued to buy them they produced even fiercer epithets, like 'blustering virago', and 'Irish she-wolf'.

Why did the critics attack her so violently for books that were manifestly romantic fictions, soaked in sentiment as a sweetcake is soaked in tea? Why did Dublin Castle, the headquarters of government in Ireland, stalk her down and keep a file on her as though she was an Irish terrorist on the run? It was as if some modern queen-bee of romantic fiction were to be fingerprinted and phone-tapped by MI5, with special agents posing as literary critics paid to expose her.

But of course it was not only for her solecisms, her wobbly syntax, her improbable plots and impossible characters that Sydney Morgan was attacked, but for the 'national' sympathies that she expressed in her novels. Throughout her life, she took a 'dangerously' radical line in both religion and politics. She was an avowed liberal, and anti-clerical in outlook. With regard to Ireland, she supported Catholic Emancipation, deplored the Act of Union, the civil disabilities imposed on the Catholics, and the consequent degradation of the native Irish, which resulted from general misgovernment, absentee land-lords, grasping middlemen and double tithes. And she scattered these opinions, with copious footnotes, all over her novels, along with the wild scenery, the ruined castles, the graveyards, and the parted lovers.

The Wild Irish Girl was the first of her novels to make her opinions unmistakably clear. In 1836, thirty years after it was first published, she wrote in the preface to yet another edition:

> At the moment *The Wild Irish Girl* appeared it was dangerous to write on Ireland, hazardous to praise her, and difficult to find a publisher for an Irish tale which had a political tendency. For even ballads sung in the streets of Dublin had been denounced by government spies, and hushed by Castle 'sbirri' because the old Irish refrain of *Erin go bragh* awakened the cheers of the ragged, starving audience.

Here she went to the heart of the matter. The potency of popular music has long been acknowledged; how old emotions are stirred by the tunes which first evoked them. And in the same way, popular literature, if it touches the nerves or the heart, can energise the mind to effect both political and social change. The Victorian novelists surely had more influence in bringing about the Factory Acts, and improving the lot of little blacking boys or crossing road sweepers than any amount of Blue books or government reports. The authorities in Dublin castle, in their dark conspiratorial way, had always been aware of this public susceptibility. After all, from the point of view of the occupying force in Ireland, the enemy was within, locked inside the garrison. From the very start, laws had to be passed to stop the English settlers locked in with them from being seduced by Irish cajoling ways and witchcraft. To become more Irish than the Irish – *hiberniores ipsis hibernis* – was an occupational hazard so laws were passed in an effort to prevent it. It was forbidden to speak the language, marry the women, wear the clothes, or even adopt the flamboyant hair styles of these 'rug-haired kernes'. For a successful colonisation the Irish spirit had to be broken, as well as their land taken. It was made known, and soon became general knowledge that their language was barbarous, their religion idolatrous, their culture non-existent, and that civilisation only came to Ireland with the

Normans. David Hume, still regarded and even studied in some quarters to this day as an eminent historian, wrote in 1767:

> The Irish, from the beginning of time, had been buried in the most profound barbarism and ignorance; and as they were never conquered or even invaded by the Romans, from whom all the western world derived its civility, they continued still in the most rude state of society, and were distinguished only by those vices to which human nature, not tamed by education nor restrained by laws, is for ever subject.

There was so much of this kind of scholarly pronouncement on the ethnic unworthiness of the Irish that the English began to feel virtuous in their conquest, and the Irish kept their heads very low. It was important for the keepers of the garrison that everyone should stay that way and not be stirred up by the heady draughts of national sentiment purveyed by the like of lady novelists.

Sydney Morgan was indeed well worth watching. For in her time she was that most dangerous of propagandists, one who directly expressed for the hitherto inarticulate, what they were feeling, or half-feeling. She caught what was in the air, and brought it down to earth. Fearing neither the obscurantist scholars nor the closed-shop intellectuals, she made bold assaults on their citadels and raided them for all they were worth. She took the new continental ideas of liberty and egality and made a strange *mélange* with the romantic notions of a Gaelic past, more noble and desirable than the superimposed tyrannies of the present.

Today 'that most brilliant of Ireland's daughters', as her first biographer W.J. Fitzpatrick called her, is dismissed as light-weight and unreliable, a mere footnote to the received appreciation of Anglo-Irish literature. She was fashionable in her time and not fundamental, and fashions change. And with hindsight she does seem a mass of contradictions. Her public life and social career in many ways seem to run counter to the sentiments expressed so strongly in her work. She can be accused of social climbing, of sycophancy to the English aristocracy – one who danced a jig in the drawing rooms of the oppressor. Like Thomas Moore, her contemporary, and another fallen idol in the critical estimation of today, Sydney Morgan has been accused of taming the wild harp of Erin into a musical snuffbox.

The Irish no longer need Tom Moore, who was once their 'National Bard', and they have forgotten Lady Morgan this many a long year. But at the time when they were both writing and making their voices heard not only in Ireland but in England, they were the first, and for the time being the only voices to keep alive their country's grievous sense of loss:

> Dear harp of my country, in darkness I found thee
> The cold chain of silence had hung o'er thee long
> When proudly my own island harp I unbound thee
> And gave all thy chords to light, freedom and song

So sang Tom Moore, and every household that boasted a piano or a bookcase had a copy of his *Irish Melodies* – green and gold with harps and shamrocks, and embellished with engravings of minstrel boys and Irish kings wearing collars of gold, in every piece of available space; the very stuff of Sydney's stock in trade. It all seems tourist trade kitsch now, but sometimes she, as well as he, went much deeper. Out of these tentative evocations of a romantic past, out of their appeal to the sense of loss, came a number of important things. Artists who are regarded today as more interesting and more relevant to our times, from the poets of Young Ireland down to W.B. Yeats, took their cue from these themes and produced a new look at Irish history inspired with a fervent desire to revive the lost language and its literature; to revive Irish traditional music and establish a realistic political identity. Sydney Morgan may have made only a fleeting contribution to all this progress by being a part of the spirit of the age, but her nationalist novels, if read with an understanding of her times, can make us appreciate the way in which cultural and political myth was created in nineteenth-century Ireland. Issues of nationality and cultural identity, two of the problems that beset the modern world, are the substance of her 'insubstantial' novels.

But to understand her importance in the Ireland of her time, and the reason for her enemies' ferocity towards her, it is necessary to look back as she looked back, into that history. The eighteenth century, for all its enlightenment, was ending badly in Ireland. Not that the native Irish had enjoyed much of its 'civility' at any time. They still lived in their mud cabins, proscribed in their religion, language and land. Their poverty had shocked Swift into savage indignation, and objective travellers like Arthur Young had written in fury of their profligate landlords. But for the Anglo-Irish, enjoying the spoils, it had been the 'great century' of their achievement. In 1690 when two foreign kings faced each other across an Irish river to fight for the British crown, the unlucky Irish backed the Catholic James II, and were decisively beaten. Let the vanquished beware! After the Battle of the Boyne, the ferocious Penal Laws made it absolutely certain that the Protestant conquerors would possess all the power and privilege and most of the land. The native Irish gentry, along with old Norman families who had remained Catholic, were dispossessed of their estates, banished into the mountains and bogs or driven into exile. Their land and houses and everything that went with them were shared out among the conquering army. Many of these were long settled in Ireland, the descendants of the first English invaders, who were sent by Elizabeth or Cromwell; they still looked upon themselves as pioneering settlers, valued their English origins and disclaimed the name of Irishmen. Now they were joined by the Williamite soldier adventurers, many of them very new to the duties and responsibilities of landed property. Soldiers of fortune, or misfortune; merchants, carpet-baggers, entrepreneurs, and king's courtiers alike, they were given suddenly, by royal grant, great tracts of land to rule. Overnight they acquired high sounding titles. Sir Richard Boyle, of England, had already become the Great Earl of Cork, with all his sons ennobled. Mr Browne became the Earl of Kenmare, and Mr Smith the Earl of Bantry. It was heady stuff, and these new lords vied in magnificence and opulence with the older English grandees who now owned half Ireland, as well as great estates in England. For example, the Marquis of Hertford owned sixty thousand Irish acres, and had an annual rent from his tenants of £69,000. The Marquis of Downshire owned 75,000 Irish acres, with £73,000 a year rent coming in. In today's terms this was wealth indeed. In this extravagance of money and unbridled power lay the foundations for *Castle Rackrent* and the seeds of their own destruction as a class in Ireland.

But this extravagance and wealth also produced a brilliant society and a great flowering of the arts and architecture. Now that the Protestant gentry were firmly fixed in power they began to feel secure for the first time for centuries in a land no longer at war, and to rebuild Dublin as a capital worthy of their self esteem. The old town, founded by the Danes had been a huddle of Tudor timber framed houses, medieval walls, dark alleys, liberties and ancient churches, all dominated by the

1 *Charles Coote, 1st Earl of Bellamont* by Joshua Reynolds, National Gallery
of Ireland

feudal fortress of Dublin Castle. Now the city was laid out in a spacious classical style, with wide streets and fine squares; by the end of the century it had acquired a distinct character all its own, and taken on the air of a capital. Two hundred and fifty of the peerage, and three hundred of the House of Commons, with their families and connections built town houses in this Anglo-Irish stronghold. They employed the best architects in Europe for the exquisite façades of town, as well as for their country mansions. They patronised Italian stuccadores, and marble mantlepiece makers; they commissioned the best silversmiths, glassblowers and portrait painters that money could buy. The theatre and opera flourished, and Handel conducted the first performance of the *Messiah* in Dublin in 1741. Their carriages, their balls, routs and masques were as fine as any in London.

But the stucco ceilings and the ravishing fanlights were but a painted mask upon the tatterdemalion state of native Ireland. The Catholic peasantry who paid for all this were living, for the most part, on five or ten acres, with an average wage of about sixpence a day. Crushed and acquiescent under the Penal Laws, they held masses in rain-soaked fields, with their outlawed priests. Without churches, without schools, without the benefits of any organised society they were condemned to sink even lower. For no Catholic was allowed by this penal code to take part in any aspect of the life of the state. They could not vote, or enter Parliament, or go into any of the professions. They could neither buy nor inherit land. They might not teach nor go to the university or even send their children to be taught abroad. The main object of these laws was to keep the native Irish down. They must never again be strong enough to challenge the foundation of the power of the Ascendancy. It was hoped that as time went on the national ideals would fade, the Catholic faith be silently abandoned, the people lose their racial pride, submit to their masters, and become reconciled to English rule. There was no reconciliation. The most enterprising of the Irish gradually left the country to serve in foreign wars, or settle in America, and those who remained, without property or scope, sank into further poverty and ignorance. Jonathan Swift, outraged by all this poverty and injustice in the midst of sophisticated luxury, declared himself to be the passionate friend of liberty and wrote 'There is not an acre of land in Ireland turned to half its advantage, yet it is better improved than the people'. When a particularly bad famine

2 *Charlemont House, Dublin* by James Malton

struck the already starving countrymen he wrote his satire advocating that the people should eat their babies as a way out of the problem; his words were no more heartless than the general disregard for the state of the poor and hungry. And yet the people, creeping in and out of their hovels, as wretched a people as any in Europe, remained irreconcilable, retained their outlawed religion, and in their own despised and secret language made poems that kept alive, if only flickeringly, a sense of their history and pride of race:

Now I shall cease, death comes, and I must not delay
By Laune, and Laine, and Lee, diminished of their pride;
I shall go after the heroes, ay, into the clay,
My fathers followed their fathers before Christ was crucified.

Sydney Owenson was no peasant but she was Irish enough to know that all is not what it seems, and that in the old stories the hag throws off her tatters to reveal the true queen. The lost Gaelic past haunted her imagination. When she was a child she had her feet in two worlds – the newly built ultra-urban streets

3   Cutting turf on the bog

of Ascendancy Dublin, and the old impoverished Ireland of the West, where the banished order was still remembered and lamented. This was the land of the O's and the Mac's, her father's people, deeply woven into the tangled skeins of her genealogy.

Few countries have ever suffered such a total loss of native aristocracy as did Ireland after the Williamite wars. It was a shock from which they have probably not yet recovered, especially as so many poets and novelists throughout the years have chronicled the disaster, and helped them to remember the nature of what exactly was lost. From contemporary poets of the time like Egan O'Rahilly, remembering an old grey eye weeping for lost honour and renown, to Yeats, lamenting for Romantic Ireland, dead and gone, the mourning has gone on. 'The Wild Geese' was the name given to the men of the Irish army, twelve thousand of them, who sailed to France after the Treaty of Limerick, in 1691, to form the nucleus of the Irish Brigade. Colonel Charles O'Kelly, who went with them wrote:

And now, alas, the saddest day is come that ever appeared above the horizon of Ireland. The sun was darkened and covered with a black cloud as if unwilling to behold such a wofull spectacle. There needed noe rain to bedew the earth, for the tears of the disconsolate Irish did abundantly moisten their native soile, to which they were that day to bid the last farewell.

In the continental wars of that time, from 1691 to 1745, 150,000 Irishmen are said to have died in the service of France alone. Of romantic heroes there were no shortage, from Patrick Sarsfield himself, who died at the Battle of Landen, saying 'Oh, that this were for Ireland', while the Irish regiment cried 'Remember Limerick' as they made the English army run. And in the houses of her father's cousins, in Mayo and Sligo, the young Sydney Owenson would surely have heard the old wandering harpers, now forced to travel the roads 'playing to empty pockets', lamenting their former patrons and friends:

> At the Boyne Bridge we took our first beating
> From the bridge of Slane we were soon retreating,
> And then we were beaten at Aughrim too
> Ah fragrant Ireland, that was goodbye to you . . .

> And over the seas are Ireland's best,
> The Dukes and the Burkes, Prince Charlie and the rest,
> And Captain Talbot, their ranks adorning,
> And Patrick Sarsfield, Ireland's darling.

Let a child hear such songs of lost causes and brave men and its imagination is fed and its allegiance won 'The names that stilled your childish play', to quote Yeats, became accusing ghosts, demanding retribution. Some of Sydney's own contemporaries listened to those voices and tried to avenge them in actions that also ended with the emigrant ship, or the hangman's rope, while others wrote it out in a verse, or in a national tale.

In the process of mythmaking, it is not what actually happens that is important, so much as the creative energy that goes into the telling of the tale. Whatever the merits of the lost Gaelic world — and the revisionists and demythologists can quickly make what they want of that — future poets and patriots, and Sydney Owenson too, looked back on the Irish past as part of a Golden age of chivalry and honour, almost within living memory but irrevocably lost. It was this sense of

4 Irish peasant 'cabbin', drawn by Arthur Young

loss which inspired their imaginative nationalism.

But the wrongs of Ireland were far from being ancient memories, softened and sentimentalised by time. For some the present was too harsh to be borne, and there were still brave men and women who hoped to change the situation. Although the real rule of Ireland came directly from England through Dublin Castle, for a period in the last half of the eighteenth century there had been a spirit of national independence and patriotism growing among the more enlightened members of the Protestant ascendancy. Britain's conflicts with France and the colonies had spread her military resources perilously thin, and forced her to leave Ireland comparatively unprotected against foreign invasion. The Protestant nobility and gentry of Ireland stepped into this breach and formed yeomanry corps of infantry and cavalry. Bright uniforms and green sashes, and gold epaulettes were ordered for this army of volunteers, and when events did not call upon them to take the field, they were reluctant to put down their swords and put the splendid fancy dress away. Suddenly they realised that they were in an excellent position to argue their cause against English domination in all matters Irish, and started to rattle their sabres. A contemporary commentator, Sir Laurence Parsons wrote:

The whole nation in a few years were thus arrayed. . . . That is every Protestant capable of bearing arms. But their spirits rose with their armament, and discipline, and beginning only to assure themselves and proceeding to protect the country against France, they concluded by vindicating their constitution and liberty against the aspiration of England.

That is to say they refused to disband, and put an unexpected weapon into the hands of Henry Grattan, leader of the Irish House of Parliament, who had been fighting a lonely and seemingly hopeless battle there for some sort of Irish independence. Now, in 1782, he was able to win from London an unwilling concession of Ireland's right to self government. His announcement of this victory was in the language of archetypal 'Irish' oratory:

> I found Ireland on her knees. I watched over her with a paternal solicitude. I have traced her progress from injuries to arms, and from arms to liberty.
> Spirit of Swift, spirit of Molyneaux, your genius has prevailed. Ireland is now a nation. In that new character, I hail her, and bowing in her august presence, I say, 'Esto perpetua!'

Such eloquences was sure to be immortalised in future anthologies of Irish oratory! It was inspiring language to be heard by a girl already in love with words. But the beautiful rhetoric clothed a sham. The Irish 'nation' was an exclusively Protestant nation; the 'mere' Irish as they were called in Elizabeth's time, were still outside the Pale. Parliament remained unreformed – the majority of its members were place men who took bribes. The real management of Irish affairs stayed in the same cynical hands. But there were a few benefits. Some commercial restrictions were removed, bringing an increased prosperity for some Catholics who started to rise in the towns as a merchant class. For landowners with food to sell in a time of war, the money really came in, and they knew better than most how to spend it. Drinking, gambling and above all, duelling, were the recreations of the bucks, the rakes, the half-mounted gentlemen, the abductors of heiresses, the cabal of the Hell-Fire club; 'Does he blaze?' was quite a reasonable question to ask of a gentleman's habits. They were in a wild race to ruin, in their coaches and six and on their thoroughbred horses. The material was gathering for such plots, such characters, such botheration to fill the pages of a stream of future novelists specialising in Paddywhackery and to inspire stage Irishmen for generations to come.

More serious in intent, Maria Edgeworth published in 1800 her first and best novel, *Castle Rackrent*, described by her as 'an Hibernian tale, before 1782'. Though on the surface seemingly picaresque and comic, it is really an elegy for the rise and fall of the Protestant nation, which sought to rule Ireland by enlightened, but basically English and Protestant landlordism. The young Sydney Owenson, also, more intent on 'national' rather than 'hibernian' interpretations, was still absorbing the material that she would later produce to remind her readers what the 'nation' had meant to her.

And, as it was Ireland with all its conflicting loyalties, mixed up with the comic, the picaresque, the rhetorical, and the flamboyant, there was also an element of heroic tragedy. Some young men of the Protestant ascendancy, intellectually committed to the libertarian ideas of France and America, rejected the inflated oratory and double dealing of the Irish Parliament. Their ideas of a nation embraced the whole people. Wolfe Tone, a young lawyer, Lord Edward Fitzgerald, younger brother of the Duke of Leinster, and some of the rising class of Catholic tradesmen, founded the Society of United Irishmen to make common cause with the native Catholic Irish.

They had a plan and it was daring. It was for the Scots-Irish Presbyterians of the north to rise with the Catholic peasants of the south and, with the assistance of France, overthrow the government and establish a republic. Tone's words were just as eloquent as those of any other. He appealed to the men of no property 'in the common name of Irishman'. But spies and informers infiltrated their ranks; the French did not give the promised help, and the landlords with their instinctive siege mentality, even apprehensive of rebellion, moved in quickly and punitively – burning, torturing and gibbeting the brave but bewildered peasantry. The rebellion was put down, and not forgiven. The leaders of the United Irishmen had committed the ultimate crime of calling upon France against England. Wolfe Tone cut his throat, and Lord Edward died of wounds, and both entered into the pantheon of Ireland's hero-martyrs. What material for the burgeoning novelist! Many authors have since taken both these characters for their heroes. Their blend of aristocratic and radical sentiments seem irresistible, but Lady Morgan was the first to portray Lord Edward in the best of her novels, *The O'Briens and the O'Flaherties*, which she wrote in 1827.

But this was much later in her career. Now, in the year 1800, Ireland had to face the aftermath of the Rising and the Act of Union which followed it. For the dream of an aristocratic elitist Parliament governing a resigned peasantry was over. The consequence of the rebellion showed on what shaking sands the Protestant nation had been built. In spite of the splendid architecture, the Adam fireplaces and the beautiful *objets d'art*; in spite of the orators and the grand statues around Trinity College, in spite of the Royal Dublin Society and the balls and the masques; the great landowners and their hangers-on; the wits, the duellists and the squireens, who had lived like feudal barons, they all allowed themselves to be bought and sold, for many thousands of pounds, of course, and a great many impressive sounding titles. Grattan could do no more than exercise his much admired eloquence.

With the Act of Union the Kingdom of Ireland came to an end. The Irish Parliament was dissolved; their right to govern themselves given up. The beautiful Parliament buildings, like Handel's music translated into stone, were gutted and turned into the Bank of Ireland. The great century was over. And Sydney Owenson, now aged twenty-four, notebooks in hand, must have been eager to take the stage and create her own future.

CHAPTER 2

THE WEARING OF THE GREEN

But who was Sydney Owenson, the girl who was to turn into Lady Morgan – 'that most brilliant of Ireland's daughters'? With hindsight she could be called the lady's most carefully wrought piece of fiction. But first we have to cut through a century of literary conjecture, and try to establish her birth date. 'The date of her birth' said the *Athenaeum*, in a lengthy obituary, 'she would never tell.' Her attitude to dates is flung down like a gauntlet in her *Memoirs*:

> I take this opportunity to enter my protest against DATES
> . . . What has a woman to do with dates? Cold, false,
> erroneous, chronologic dates – new style, old style,
> precession of the equinox; ill-timed calculations of comets,
> long since due at their stations and never come! I mean to
> have none of them.

But the date which pins her down, as far as it is possible, is 1776. In that year a new name appeared on the bills of the Theatre Royal, Crow Street, Dublin, announcing the appearance of Mr Robert Owenson, from the Theatre Royal, Covent Garden. At that time the theatre was flourishing in Dublin, and that city could boast that plays were presented on its stages before they were seen in London. For the most part the Dublin theatre played for the English colony in Ireland and was a great social event. The Viceroy could fill a theatre with a command performance, attended by his whole camp following of Anglo-Irish courtiers. So it must have been a startling moment when the new importation from London began to enrich his speeches with phrases and songs in the Irish language – that barbarous tongue more or less proscribed in the capital of the Pale. For Mr Robert Owenson, although he was brought over from England 'at great expense' was, in fact, Robert MacOwen, from the barony of Tirawley, in the county of Mayo, the Irish speaking Kingdom of the West.

For the last five years he had been in England, trying his luck both in London and the provinces, without too much success. He had anglicised his name to Owenson, to please the English managements; he had married an English wife, and now at the age of thirty-two he was trying his luck once more in his native land. He came over on his own to test the market. He was a fine figure of a man, handsome, and with a good singing voice which, coupled with his knowledge of Irish songs and catch-phrases were enough of a novelty to make him immediately popular; so he summoned his wife to join him. Mrs Owenson was pregnant, and apprehensive about Ireland, but she booked her passage. On a rough sea crossing, in a small boat on Christmas Day, 1776, she gave birth to their first child, a daughter. Or so it is said, in the much worked-over legend of Lady Morgan. In later years Sydney claimed to be a trueborn native of Dublin, and described in her *Memoirs* with almost total recall, her nativity, when the bells of all the churches of the city, led by the great bell of St Patrick's, rang out for the birth of Jesus, and of Sydney Owenson. But it was a tradition among her father's fellow actors that she had been born at sea. Fact or fiction, it was metaphorically appropriate, for in her subsequent career she was always between two currents, in hereditary traits, in religion, and in politics; her father and mother in their different origins represented the conflicts that perpetuated the great divide. He, temperamentally was what is called 'typically Irish', exuberant and irresponsible, and his roots were in the old Gaelic Catholic Ireland. Jane Hill, her mother, was an English Wesleyan, devoted to order and cleanliness, and fundamental religion. Her mother seems from the start to have been overwhelmed by her husband's personality. It was one thing to have him in England where, surrounded by her own family, she could curb some of his excesses, but once in Ireland she took refuge in building a little wall of English reserve around herself. From her earliest days Sydney looked to her father for warmth and entertainment. He was the source of all her Irishness, and most of her contradictions. For the sake of having any kind of a career he had nominally turned Protestant in his youth, and this had made him acceptable to Jane but had not changed his character. As Sydney said of him:

In the course of my early life, and after years, it was a source
of infinite delight to hear him narrate . . . traits and incidents
of his story and of the times in which he lived mingled with
relations of habits, customs and manners still existing in
Ireland down to the close of the last century.'

By the time Robert Owenson's stories had been embellished
further by his daughter it is difficult to see him other than as a
character in one of her novels, rather than in one of his more
knockabout stage roles.

A love of genealogy, a preoccupation with pedigree, is a very
Irish trait. With such a history of dispossession, enforced
exodus, and exile it is not surprising that the Irish should have
suffered an identity crisis. In one generation Protestant settlers
were turned from soldiers, merchants, carpet-baggers and
adventurers into landed gentry, and Catholic gentlemen who
had held land and estates with kinsmen and tenants living
under a tribal paternalism, were turned into beggars and
outlaws. So it was often desirable to rewrite family histories.
The new lords had their new titles to justify, and worked away
at suitable family trees. The uprooted Catholics, on the other
hand, were in a state of utter confusion. Some to save the land
turned Protestant; others went down with the general ruin;
some, barred from public life, crossed and recrossed the seas,
fighting for different foreign armies. Some too old for
adventure, or too dispirited, hung their ancestors' swords on
the walls of their hovels, and looked back into the past, or into
a whiskey glass. The truth was that at the end of the eighteenth
century, when Sydney was born, Ireland was a rich stew of
class confusions. There was a great deal to cover up, and to
make up, and there were always those with very long memories
whose greatest pleasure was to sit around the ashes of the fire
'counting kin'. Sydney recalled how, as a small child, she had
sat on her father's knee listening with tremulous attention to
that species of rambling stuff – 'my inspiration and my theme',
called 'shanaos'. 'Shanaos', she explained 'is a sort of genealogy
chitchat, or talking over family antiquity, family anecdotes,
descent, alliances, to which the lower as well as the higher
order of the Irish in the provincial parts are much addicted.' In
fact, so addicted was she herself to this activity that in *The
Wild Irish Girl* she makes her heroine offer a visitor the
following irresistible entertainment:

Nay, if you please, you shall hear our old nurse run through

the whole genealogy of Fingal, which is frequently given as a
theme to exercise the memory of the peasant children:
'Oscar, MacOssian, MacFionn, MacCuil, MacArt . . .'. All
the way back no doubt, to the grand-daughter of Noah who
according to the *Annals of the Four Masters* arrived on the
coast of Ireland and started a dynasty!

For the ordinary people of Ireland who never had much land or
glory to lose, these stories of a better past, like patina on old
wood, helped to console their wretchedness. The more cynical
and brutalised city dwellers made a joke of genealogy, when
they bought broadsheets from the blind singer called Zozimus,
who stood in all weathers on the Essex Bridge over the Liffey.
Sydney knew this doggerel because she quotes it in her
Memoirs:

> St Patrick was a gentleman, he came from decent people,
> In Dublin town he built a church and on it put a steeple.
> His father was a Callaghan, his mother was a Brady,
> His aunt was an O'Shaughnessy, his uncle was a Grady.

Jane, her mother, had no sympathy at all for this tangled skein
of Irish family relationships. She was very sure in her origins,
and came from a prosperous Shropshire family, all fervent
evangelical Methodists, all convinced that the theatre was the
tabernacle of Satan. But Robert was very handsome and full of
the blarney, and Jane was getting on a bit, a little *passée* by the
standards of Shrewsbury society. Though hating the stage, she
fell in love with the actor. Her parents objected strongly; an
actor and an Irishman as well! – it could not be considered.
Robert arranged the perfect romantic elopement, and the
parents had to accept the *fait accompli*. Jane's father had the
discretion to die shortly afterwards, leaving her 'the mistress of
a moderate but independent fortune'. Sydney was always prone
to exaggerate the importance and wealth of her mother's
family, but the legacy was certainly large enough to allow
Owenson to take up an offer to go to Dublin, and manage the
Theatre Royal, and to buy a little house in the suburbs for Jane.
  With his wife's money to invest, and fatherhood in prospect,
Robert jumped at the chance to go back to Ireland. Jane
followed after, and when their first child was born they had her
baptised into the Church of England and called her Sydney.
Actors' children often have fanciful names, but Sydney's name
did not come out of a play but from her father's own romantic

background. It was his mother's name. Forty years earlier, according to his tale, a great hurling match was held by the landowners and farmers of Sligo and Roscommon, at which the elected Queen of Beauty was Sydney Bell, orphan grand-daughter of Sir Malby Crofton of Longford House, Sligo. The Croftons had been settled in Ireland since the days of Elizabeth, owing their estates and patronage to Sir Henry Sydney, governor of Connaught. They were widely related to other families of the West, and Sydney Bell could claim cousinage with Oliver Goldsmith, now making his name in London. The champion of the sports, a handsome young farmer called Walter MacOwen fell in love with the Queen of Beauty, and persuaded her to what the people of the country called 'an abduction', but the Crofton family counted a mésalliance, never to be forgiven.

MacOwen proved to be an irresponsible fellow, spending all his time at fairs, hurling matches and other rustic frolics, but beautiful Sydney Bell adapted herself patiently to her lot, and gained the name of 'Clairseach an Bhaile', or Harp of the Valley, because of her sweet singing and skill on the small Irish harp.

To be named after such a grandmother was the stuff of high romance, and Sydney later recalled in her *Memoirs* how the little girl, sitting on her handsome father's knee, listening to his resonant actor's voice, had begged for more stories. There seemed an endless store. He told her how he had inherited his father's strong physique and good looks, and his mother's artistic instincts and singing voice. He told her how his mother had persuaded both the Catholic priest and the Protestant rector to teach him, and thus he had learnt a little French and Latin, and something of the English classics as well as all the Irish songs. How did he get to England? Well, that was another high adventure. When he was about seventeen an absentee landlord called Joseph Blake, who had grown rich in the West Indies, came back to his family estates in Ardfry, Co. Mayo. He was what was called then an intellectual epicurean – a confirmed bachelor, with a penchant for personable young men, and to begin with he was enthusiastic towards his duties as a landlord. There was an old story that the Gaelic MacOwens were the original owners of the lands of Ardfry, and that the Norman Blakes were usurpers. The new landlord listened sympathetically to this story, especially as Robert was so personable, and his mother so persuasive, and to make some kind of amends Blake offered to take young Robert as his protegé, and educate him as a gentleman. Before long the intellectual epicurean grew tired of Irish country life, and returned to London taking Robert with him. They stopped over in Dublin, to smarten the young man up, in keeping with his newly anglicised name of Owenson. Sydney reports that 'The Connaught suit of genuine ratteen was exchanged for the fashionable costume of the day; his luxuriant black locks were transformed into the coiffure poudré, and ailes de pigeon which had succeeded the wigs of the preceeding half century.' He was enraptured furthermore, by a first visit to the Theatre Royal Dublin where he saw the Irish actor Henry Mossop in *Coriolanus*.

And then on to London. Blake took him to the musician, Dr Arne, who declared that the lad had one of the best baritones he had ever heard. And in Blake's house in Great Russell Street, where he had music lessons, did the accounts and carved the meat at dinner parties, Robert met with Garrick and Oliver Goldsmith who accepted him as a distant cousin and took him to theatre green rooms and to literary clubs. The young man found he had other talents with which to amuse. In the course of his musical studies he met Madame Weichsel, a popular vocalist, wife of the primo violoncello of the Italian opera. Though no longer young she was still beautiful. The handsome Robert helped her with the duets in Arne's opera *Artaxerxes* taking the role of her lover. Before long he found she was not averse to him assuming the same role in real life. We do not know how much of this story he revealed to the infant Sydney, but in her *Memoirs* she remembers how one day a mysterious lady came to see her father in Dublin; how her mother locked herself up in her bedroom and wouldn't receive her, and that the visitor was the famous soprano Elizabeth Billington, daughter of Madame Weichsel. Years later Sydney recalled how strong was Elizabeth Billington's resemblance to her father, and without any Victorian *pudeur* notes: 'If there was any foundation for the supposition which assigned to her a filial relationship it would be curious to trace her fine voice in musical descent from Harp of the Valley.'

The affaire did not please Blake, however, who dismissed his erstwhile protegé peremptorily. Owenson had long decided that he wanted to go on to the stage, and now tried his luck with Garrick in Drury Lane. Amazingly, with absolutely no real experience, he was given the leading part in *Tamerlane*. The critics were very harsh, declaring that to bring forward a young unknown, speaking as he did with a heavy Irish brogue, was one of the greatest insults ever offered to the town. And so it was that Robert Owenson left Drury Lane and the London stage forever, forced to start again in the English provinces, playing the stage Irishman.

It was not only with his own adventures that he enchanted his daughter. He claimed kinship with the whole thirteen tribes of Galway, the families that had once ruled that city, and he could expound the genealogies of them all. The stories were laced copiously with songs and the names of the bards who had composed them, and Sydney learned to honour the memory of Turlough O'Carolan, who had written so many of her father's favourites, and to weep on cue for the symbolism of 'Drimindu Deelish' which was an allegorical lament for some lost cause. Then getting into full voice, Robert sang the parts from the oratorios of Handel and Arne, and recited dramatic scenes ranging from Shakespeare to O'Keefe, until even the servants picked up the reverberating words. 'Shakespeare, Handel, Carolan the Irish bard' said his daughter 'were the three Dii Majorum Gentium of our household altars.'

This legacy of words was her heritage from her father. From her mother Sydney received very different gifts. The most she could say, when assessing her parents in later life, was that her mother – 'my poor distracted mother' – gave her the quality of commonsense to temper down the exuberance of imagination that was her father's ultimate downfall. With the customary coolness that she always showed towards her mother's memory she wrote: 'She had received as much education as women of her class receive in England and no more … she had no accomplishments, no artistic tendencies, but she was a good English scholar.' She reported that her mother hummed 'discordantly', and as she was 'an enemy of all slovenliness of habits, conduct or mind', she conceived an over-riding hatred for the dirtiness of the Dublin houses, and the equal dirtiness of the conversation in so-called polite society; for Dublin ladies were, in good Swiftian tradition, fond of bawdy. 'My mother's mater-of-fact disposition and natural truthfulness were distressed and perplexed by the lively brilliant exaggeration which was the prevailing trait of conversation and of daily life.' Poor Jane Hill of Shrewsbury, disapproving of the theatre and married to an actor, was forced to live in 'her penal settlement … hating both potatoes and papists with Christian inveteracy, and

5 *Carolan the Harper* by Francis Bindon, National Gallery of Ireland

culinary prejudice'. In retrospect, Sydney paid pious respect to her mother's memory, but psalm singing and moral homilies could not compete with the songs and stories on offer from her father.

And then there were the servants, always sources of influence upon a growing child, particularly in Ireland; they too were full of genealogical fervour:

They frequently made claim to participate in the affairs of

the family because they believed themselves related to the family. Pat Kavanagh could prove himself descended from the Kavanaghs, kings of Leinster; Thady O'Connor came lineally, and 'that not fifty years ago' from O'Conor, king of all Ireland, and Dennis Brian, 'if everyone had their rights' was the real O'Brien, king of Thomond.

The Owensons could only afford one servant, but Sydney met many of the type in the theatre and in the streets. Their own maid was Mary Cane, whose name her mother turned to Molly because she would have no papist mariolatry about her; Molly quickly became invaluable to her mistress and when a manservant was needed she introduced 'a follower' who named himself James the Butler. When Mrs Owenson discovered that they were both Catholics, commonsense proved stronger than prejudice, and they were not dismissed.

At first Owenson worked for the actor–manager who had brought him over from England. This was Richard Daly, famous for introducing dancing dogs to the Irish stage, and notorious for his duelling exploits, having fought nineteen in two years. Robert moved between the two main theatres in Dublin, Crow Street, and Smock Alley, also called the Theatre Royal. It is difficult to pick up plays of that era with Irish characters, without finding his name. He played Lucius O'Trigger in *The Rivals*, Major O'Flaherty in *The West Indian*; he played Callaghans, O'Brallaghans, and Teagues galore. A first hand account of him on the stage comes from Jonah Barrington:

> Mr Owenson was at that time highly celebrated in the line of Irish characters, and never did an actor exist so perfectly calculated in my opinion, to personify that particular class of people. Considerably above six feet in height, remarkably handsome and brave looking, vigorous and well shaped, he was not vulgar enough to disgust, nor was he genteel enough to be out of character. In the highest class of Irish characters he looked well but did not exhibit sufficient dignity, and in the lowest his humour was scarcely quaint and original enough, but in what might be called the middle class of Paddies, no man ever combined the look and manner with such felicity as Owenson.

John O'Keefe, the playwright, Owenson's famous contemporary, also praised him for 'his singing the Irish songs, being

6 *Smock Alley Theatre in 1789*, National Gallery of Ireland

the master of the Irish language', and no doubt cast him in his opera for those qualities. *The Shamrock, or St. Patrick's Day* is, alas, lost, with all its music and its glorious cast lists: 'With a great pageant and procession of Kings of Leinster, Munster and Connaught; Strongbow, de Courcy, Sitric the Dane, each attended by Druids, Bards, Footballers, Banshees, Leprecauns, Hibernians in their original state. To conclude with a song by Carolan, the ancient Irish bard (Mr. Owenson) and grand chorus.'

Robert tried to make Jane happy in her exile. They took a villa in Drumcondra, a pretty little village outside the city with a view of the Dublin mountains. But their true home was the theatre. Sydney was far happier with the sylvan scenery and the hermits' caves of the painted backcloths than with her mother's genteel domesticity. Owenson, flushed with optimism, had

7 *The Old Music Hall* by Flora Mitchell, National Gallery of Ireland

taken on the management of the Old Fishamble music hall,
scene of Handel's *Messiah* première in 1741, and now given
over to political meetings, state lotteries, magic shows, lectures,
riots and masquerades. It needed completely rebuilding after
the floor collapsed during a political meeting in 1782. He put
all Jane's money and his energy in to this enterprise to create

what he hoped would be a national theatre – for with all his professional ambitions he held sincere patriotic ideals. And it was a time of national resurgence. After all, in 1782 Grattan, leader of the Irish Parliamentary party and with an ineffable oratory worthy of any actor, had called the 'Irish nation' into being. The spirit of the age was, for the time, in favour of patriotism and the wearing of the green.

Up until this point political and social conditions had not been favourable to the development of any native Irish drama. For one thing it was not in the tradition – in fact there was no play performed in the Irish language until 1901. The religious impulses that brought the miracle plays into England and the European theatre were stifled in Ireland by the same Penal Laws that had ensured that there would be no public buildings, and no churches for the native Irish. The old tradition of epic poems recited by a bard, or a story told by the cottage fire, brought the only form of dramatic experience to the people. In these performances the fine word and its delivery were of the utmost importance. A good shanachie or storyteller, could fill a room, and eventually the silver-tongued orator, so valued in Ireland, took over from this tradition, and became a main source of dramatic entertainment, even though the purpose of the exercise might be political. In their manipulative eloquence these orators endlessly recounted the history of Ireland, with the Shan van Vocht, Cathleen ni Houlihan, and Dark Rosaleen, all poetical names for Ireland, playing the heroines of a never ending melodrama.

For these, and many other reasons, the theatre as an institution had little significance for the mass of the native Irish. It depended upon the patronage of the alien occupiers, reflecting their taste and manners, and taking its standards from London. But again, paradoxically, although plays and players came over from London, it became a two-way exchange, with Irish actors and playwrights contributing to the London stage.

With players like Garrick and Mrs Siddons coming over, the theatre in Dublin flourished, and with the growth of industry and trade, the native merchants and shopkeepers started to participate. The poorer classes, admitted for twopence, were crowded into the pit and galleries. Jonah Barrington in his *Recollections* gives a vivid account of the Dublin theatrical world at the end of the eighteenth century. His grandmother sometimes lent him her silver ticket of admission to Crow Street:

The performers would snuff the tallow candles that lit the
stage, on which stood soldiers with fixed bayonets to keep
order. The galleries were noisy and witty and called out
loudly for whatever tunes they fancied, whether in the play
or not, and hurled apples and oranges at the performers of
their choice; the boxes were models of decorum; the pits
filled with critics and respectable citizens who decamped
hastily if the Trinity students were having a night out.

Apart from the rowdiness of the upper gallery another nuisance
was the mass invasion of the stage and green rooms by young
men of fashion who obstructed the actors and pestered the
actresses. Thomas Sheridan, father of the famous playwright
who tried to manage Crow Street, said it was half bear garden,
half brothel, and he got rules passed to reform it, before it
finally defeated him. Such was the condition of the theatre in
Dublin when Owenson tried to make his name.

And in some of the larger provincial towns the removal of
many of the laws against Catholics and the increase in Irish
trade helped to create more prosperity. Theatres began to be
opened, encouraged by the fashion for amateur theatricals
which was flourishing among the gentry. Plays were acted in
country houses like Edgeworthstown, home of Maria Edgeworth
and her father Richard, and theatres were incorporated into
Dublin town houses. While the Fishamble street theatre was
being rebuilt Owenson, capitalising on this wave of enthusiasm,
led a troupe of strolling players through the West of Ireland
and, because of his connection with Blake of Ardfry, was
invited to manage an amateur theatre in Galway, set up by the
wealthy landowner Richard Martin. The latter had been known
in his youth as Hairtrigger Dick, because of his passion for
duelling, and in his old age as Humanity Martin, because of his
passion for the welfare of animals. This spell in Galway would
not be of any great significance were it not for a playbill which
is still in existence, showing that among the amateur actors
working with the professional Owenson was the twenty-year-
old Wolfe Tone, taking time off from his studies in Trinity
College, Dublin, to tutor the sons of Richard Martin. In this
way did Sydney, through her father's life as an actor, connect
with one of the great historical personages in Ireland's history;
for with all the stage Irishmen strutting the boards, the sham
fire eaters and hell raisers, here was the real thing – Theobald
Wolfe Tone, who was to lead and inspire the 1798 rebellion
and lose his life in the event.

At the THEATRE, KIRWAN's-LANE:

ON Friday Evening, the 8th of August, 1783, will be
presented the celebrated Tragedy of

DOUGLAS.

Douglas,	Captain NUGENT.
Old Norval,	Major TRENCH.
Lord Randolph,	Mr. TONE.
Officer,	Lieutenant MOOR.
And, Glenalvon,	Colonel MARTIN.
Anna,	Mrs. SOPHIA CHEVERS.
AND, LADY RANDOLPH;	Mrs. R. MARTIN.

To which will be added a Farce call'd

ALL THE WORLD's A STAGE.

Sir Gilbert Pumpkin,	Colonel MARTIN.
Captain Stanly,	Captain NUGENT.
Harry Stukely,	Lieutenant MOOR.
Simon,	Lieutenant COSTELLO.
Watt,	Lieutenant DALY.
And, Diggory,	Mr. TONE.
Miss Kitty Sprightly,	Mrs. SOPHIA CHEVERS.
And, Miss Bridget Pumkin,	Mrs. R. MARTIN.

By particular Desire of the Ladies and Gentlemen,

STAGE 1l. 2s. 9d.   PIT 4s. 4d.

Tickets to be had of Mrs. R. MARTIN; and of Mr. Owenson at the Theatre.

The Ladies and Gentlemen request that no Hoops may be
worn at the Theatre on the above Occasion.

To begin precisely at Seven o'clock.

GALWAY: Printed by B. CONWAY, at the Volunteer Printing Office.

8   Theatre bill from Kirwan's-Lane Theatre, showing Wolfe Tone and
Owenson's names, Hardiman Library, University of Galway

Life in the provinces, managing amateur theatricals for country gentlemen , was not really what Owenson wanted. On the other hand the lack of money in the professional theatre was acute. The English players were paid generously enough when they came over, but the Irish players had to resort sometimes to strong measures to get their pay. What with the unruly audiences, the natural extravagance of keeping a theatre, and the chronic state of political tension a manager's life was hard. But Owenson, backed by Jane's annuity, went to his newly decorated Dublin theatre with high hopes. As the Irish Volunteers' Congress was just then assembling, he enlisted some of the leaders as his patrons, including the prominent James Napper Tandy, and on 20 December 1784 held his opening night. The Volunteers in the audience came in their ceremonial uniform, making it a patriotic occasion. Sydney wrote of the opening night:

> The first performance was to be altogether national, that is
> Irish, and very Irish it was. My father wrote and spoke the
> prologue in his own character as an Irish Volunteer. The
> audience was as national as the performance, and the pit
> was filled with red coats of the corps to which my father
> belonged.

Naturally the new theatre became a political issue. It was supported by the patriots, but ridiculed and vilified by all the lackeys of Dublin Castle. Editors of the daily papers were subsidised and supplied with good paying advertisements if they would support government policy. The *Freeman's Journal* as well as impugning the ability of the actors, tried to discourage patrons by emphasising the dirt and vulgarity of the audience, the insecurity of the building, and to demolish Owenson on the basis of his Irishness. The paper described the opening night as

> A jumble of the greatest balderdash that ever insulted the
> stage. We would readily acknowledge that it might be
> worthy of the applause of critics from the wilds of
> Connemara, but never could imagine for the honour of a
> Dublin audience that even the chimney sweeps of the
> metropolis of Ireland would bestow a dust of approbation on
> trash that disgraces language and debases the drama.

Owenson's theatrical enterprise came at a very critical time, moving rapidly to the crisis of 1798. The government authorities could not allow a specifically Irish theatre, which could be used as a centre for nationalistic propaganda, to develop. A bill was passed to put him out of business. It decreed that only one theatre could be licensed in Dublin, and it was not going to be Fishamble Street. Daly got the license. Owenson rejoined the Crow Street Theatre as Daly's assistant manager, but he still had the lease of Fishamble Street on his hands, and had gone deeply into debt rebuilding it. He made what he could by renting it out for public meetings, and by turning the old vaults underneath into wine cellars. The young Sydney saw her father made bankrupt and humiliated for the crime of being a patriotic Irishman; she had her first lesson in the price demanded for going against established opinion.

And as for poor Jane Owenson, overwhelmed with bankrupt theatres, nationalist politics, Catholic servants, ladies who talked dirty and the mere fact of being in Ireland, she gave up the struggle and died from what was diagnosed as 'gout in the stomach'. Molly Kane handed Owenson his wife's wedding ring, in the Irish fashion, to tell him it was all over. While piously regretting 'my excellent English mother's death', Sydney repeats how disappointingly prim were her mother's reactions to the excitement of backstage theatre, and how intolerant she was to 'Ginger', the theatre cat. At the same time she vowed to look after her father. By our reckoning she was then fifteen or sixteen years old, though she always claimed to be younger.

In one year Owenson had lost his wife, her small income and his theatre. He had two motherless daughters to bring up; two other children between Sydney and Olivia had died in infancy. In order to make some sort of living for his family he had to go on tour again, and so the girls were sent to boarding school. Sydney's habit of interlarding everything with French phrases, sometimes wildly inaccurate, became in later years one of the traits her critics loved to satirise. Perhaps three years at Madame Terson's school in Clontarf was the cause. This school, 'the best school in Ireland . . . I may add in the United Kingdom', was a Huguenot establishment where all dinner table conversation had to be conducted in French. Here she learnt to sit straight with a backboard, endured cold seabathing and a plain diet, read the Bible, started a 'bit of authorship', and formed a high opinion of herself and her erudition. Formal education was rare for girls in Ireland, as indeed it was in England, and at Madame Terson's academy Sydney met the daughters of the statesmen Henry Grattan, and other privileged girls of that class. As well as French they were taught grammar, geography, writing, arithmetic and drawing. She did not learn Latin or Greek at school, but in later life she claimed to have picked up a bit of 'bog latin' from a hedge schoolmaster, that other source of education in Ireland where the children of the Catholic poor sometimes received haphazard lessons from a 'poor scholar', probably an ex-seminarian. For a few coppers he would conduct a makeshift school in a barn or outhouse – a very different establishment from Madame Terson, where the surroundings were elegant and the fees high. It meant a great deal of sacrifice for Owenson to send his daughters to such a school, but his wife had wished it, and he even managed to pay for extra music lessons for Sydney. She never forgot the debt she owed her father for this opportunity. They were with Madame Terson for three years; then she retired and the Owenson girls had to be transferred to Mrs Anderson's Finishing School in Dublin, where Sydney found both the French and the manners inferior. But they saw more of their father who took them out for walks, and arranged music and dancing lessons for them from some of his theatrical friends.

But even this was a struggle, for without his wife's income and her good influence over his extravagance and conviviality, any money he had left was soon used up. And as his nationalist sympathies provoked strong opposition in Orange circles, he was sometimes hissed off the stage when he sang his patriotic laments for old Ireland. Once more he decided to leave Dublin, and went down the country to manage a theatre set up by 'noble amateurs' in Kilkenny. This time both the girls went with him. Of this episode Sydney wrote: 'Change of scene, circumstance and society is the royal road to education, and cuts short the tiresome stages of school discipline. Every step forward from the dear early home of our childhood was a page in the history of our mental development!' Making the best of misfortune, Sydney now discovered the picturesqueness of ruins and the fascination of history. Kilkenny was the largest inland town in eighteenth-century Ireland and the centre of one of the most prosperous districts. It had long been the bastion of Anglo-Irish traditions since the Normans first landed there, and the castle of the Butler family, the Dukes of Ormonde, had dominated the town for more than five hundred years. This castle was one of the showplaces of Europe, 'rich on every side with marble and ornamented with many things so curious that those who have seen it say it surpasses many palaces of Italy'.

So wrote a French traveller in the seventeenth century. The Kilkenny Grammar School had a very high reputation and its roll included the illustrious names of Swift, Berkeley, Congreve and Farquhar.

Owenson was delighted to be invited to set up a theatre of 'aristocratic respectability' in this 'Versailles of Ireland' as Sydney, with characteristic hyperbole, described the small provincial town. The aristocratic families and the flourishing townspeople were hospitable to the actor and his daughters and Sydney was introduced to 'high art' in the picture galleries of Kilkenny Castle 'which awakened a passion for its noble powers which in after life broke forth in my life of *Salvator Rosa*, of all my works the most delightful to myself'. She was referring to her biography of the Italian painter of sublimely romantic scenery, whose images synthesised with the scenery of the West of Ireland in her landscape of the imagination. In this new circle of society she also met many dashing officers of the Irish Brigade who, when the French Revolution cut short their services in foreign armies, came home to Ireland. In this atmosphere of old families, ancient castles and brave soldiers of fortune, the stories and casts of her later novels, *O'Donnel* and *Florence Macarthy* were being assembled. For two seasons Owenson played in Kilkenny, bringing in star performers from Dublin, and taking many leading parts himself. The *Leinster Journal* (2 September 1795) reported that 'the beauty and neatness of the theatre, scenery, etc., far exceeded the most sanguine expectations of the public, nor shall we scruple to say that for its size it is not inferior to any theatre in this or the sister Kingdom . . . .' But although the same paper reported that 'a brilliant assemblage of beauty and first fashion of the county' often crowded into the new Kilkenny Playhouse, at the end of the second season Owenson was on the brink of financial disaster. Huge bills were unpaid, a mortgage was suddenly foreclosed, and none of the fine gentlemen who had encouraged him came to his rescue. All his own money was gone, and again he went bankrupt. The bailiffs took everything, including Jane's watch, which Sydney had worn hooked to her belt. The Owensons had to take to the road again.

As the Kilkenny enterprise had ended badly, the wine business in Dublin was wound up to pay the debts, and once more the actor–manager became a strolling player. The girls went back to Dublin with the faithful Molly, and as Sydney, pragmatic as ever, wrote: 'My character seems to have developed itself rapidly, for adversity is a great teacher.'

The years that followed are very poorly documented in her *Memoirs*. She either does not write them up at all, or juggles facts to obscure some of the many difficulties and humiliations the family had to endure. We know that on his tour of the provinces Owenson finished up in Sligo, in the regions of his own youth, and here he was taken up by his mother's cousins, the Croftons, who for the sake of his accomplishments and entertainment value conquered their old prejudices. Though the local gentry would not support his theatre, they condescended to invite him to dinner, where he sang – very well – for his supper. 'Give him a bottle of claret and a jug of poteen, and Owenson forgot all his care' – so reported a resident of Sligo who saw him in action. The Crofton cousins persuaded him to bring Sydney down to Longford House, where she met the old Connaught gentry and experienced at first hand life in the big houses of the West. W.J. Fitzpatrick, who wrote about her in the year of her death, 1859, found people still living in Sligo who had vivid recollections of the Owensons. Sligo was a garrison town 'full of military and militia, theatricals, balls, and so forth', and Sydney, now aged about twenty was courted by many and indeed loved by at least two of the officers stationed in the town. In her *Memoirs* she quotes extracts from letters written to her in the most exalted vein of sensibility; but nothing came of these courtships, and indeed one of the officers drowned himself in mid-correspondence. She never claimed that this was for unrequited love – but didn't disclaim it either.

But if Sligo was 'a wondrously gay place' the rest of Ireland was not. The revolutionary ideas of Europe were having their consequence in Ireland. Since 1790 Ulster had been agitated by political ferment. In 1791 the Society of the United Irishmen was founded in Belfast. Its objectives were supported by many well-born Protestants of liberal tendencies, who at first only asked for parliamentary reforms and democratic rights for Catholics. But by this time their leader Wolfe Tone had come a long way from the romantic young actor who had played in Dick Martin's theatre in Galway under Owenson's management. A letter from him, intercepted by Dublin Castle, showed just how far: 'My unalterable opinion is that the bane of Irish prosperity is in the influence of England. I believe that influence will ever be extended while the connection between the two countries continues.' Hitherto the radicals had wanted reforms under the British crown; here, now, was out-and-out talk of separatism.

In 1793 the French cut off their king's head, and the war between France and England started which, with small intermissions, was to last for twenty-two years. The old threat of a French invasion made Britain offer some measure of conciliation to the Catholics in an attempt to buy their loyalty; too little and too late, as always, and the idea that France would offer the Irish the liberty that Britain denied them became an attractive and growing political objective. How much of these intoxicating options were discussed in the green rooms of the touring players we do not know, but Owenson was notorious for his nationalist sympathies. And in the west of Ireland, where many of the smaller gentry were Catholics or undercover Catholics, it was always possible to dine with 'absolute and unavowed conspirators'. 'Connemara' it was reported to the government by one of their agents 'is the asylum of outlaws, deserters and persons escaped from justice; the stronghold of smugglers. There are at least two thousand stands of arms dispersed in cabins, and two battalions of deserters.' It was difficult for the legitimate theatre to thrive in such an atmosphere, and poor Owenson endeavoured to draw in the customers with knockabout comedy and songs.

Between the jigs and the reels, Sydney, with her dramatic sense, must have been aware of the dark divided heart of the so-called Irish nation. Travelling between Dublin and the West there was always danger. The French were actually in Bantry Bay in 1796. Wolfe Tone had persuaded Napoleon to invade, but the weather turned foul and a 'Protestant wind' blew the French fleet back to France. The threat of invasion brought on the reprisals that had been used to subdue Ulster. Floggings, torture and hanging were daily occurrences, and whole villages were burnt to trap a few rebels. The news from Dublin in the spring of 1798 would surely have reached Sydney, spending her time with her Crofton cousins; she would have heard that the United Irishman Lord Edward Fitzgerald had been arrested, only a few doors away from her father's old theatre in Fishamble Street. Lord Edward died of his wounds, and Dublin was proscribed; all households had to place a list of occupants on their front doors, and curfew imposed from 9 p.m. Meanwhile, in his theatre in Sligo, Owenson played once more to empty seats.

And then the French did invade. On the 22 August 1798, a French fleet under General Humbert landed troops in Killala, County Mayo, some twenty miles from where the Owensons were lodging. It was harvest time; some peasants working in the fields abandoned their crops and rode off to join the French; some gentleman patriots mustered small bands of countrymen together, and carried green branches, in memory of the early days of the French Revolution when Camille Desmoulins had plucked a leaf of chestnut in the gardens of the Palais Royal and, sticking it in his hat, had shouted '*Aux arms – citoyens!*' Trees of liberty appeared in little towns, and blacksmiths worked day and night making pikes. But it was not the full scale uprising that the French had been promised, for the movement was infiltrated by spies and informers and the government was well prepared. Half the peasants were already intimidated by the terrible reprisals which had been taken in Ulster and Leinster and the Republicans were divided. Some of the Catholics had also been conciliated with the right to buy land; they wanted the reforms for which the insurgents were fighting, but not revolution in the French style. The memory of Robespierre made them think again, and put their arms away.

But initially the suddenness of the French invasion brought amazing success. Twelve hundred Frenchmen under Humbert took Killala, unfurled a banner on which was inscribed '*Erin go bragh*', and gave arms and ammunition to the assembled country boys. Then this motley army marched through the almost impassable defile of the Mayo mountains, and surprised Castlebar. Incredibly, the Irish rabble made the English soldiers run! To celebrate the 'races of Castlebar', the French gave a ball and supper that very night. Numbers of ladies attended and an observer wrote 'decorum was strictly observed; they paid ready money for everything'. These were the hard men who had served in Italy and with the army of the Rhine. But soon the luck ran out. English reinforcements came up; the insurgent army was routed, and the rebellion was over. The French were treated like gentlemen and sent home. The Irish, peasants and gentry alike, were a different matter. They had committed treason, and were executed in droves; heads on spikes and bodies hanging on trees desecrated the landscape for months. Wolfe Tone was on one of the French ships that was captured. He was recognised by an English officer who had been at Trinity College with him as a student and taken to Dublin in chains, where he was sentenced to be hanged, drawn and quartered; but to escape his enemies, he cut his throat. He was thirty-five, and it was fifteen years since he had trod the boards in Galway in the farce 'All the World's a Stage – tickets to be obtained from the theatre from Mr. Owenson'.

Owenson's whole world was falling apart. Where was his national theatre now? How could he play the comic Irishman in such circumstances? The gibbet and the walking hangman overshadowed even his insouciance. Anyway there was no audience and no theatre. A week before the battle of Castlebar, his scenery, dresses and decorations were seized by the landlord in lieu of rent. Even his songs failed him. He knew the words, but did not want to sing the grim ballad that was now going the rounds: 'They're hanging men and women for the wearing of the Green'. His professional career seemed to be at an end. Sydney, in the meantime, unwilling to be a burden to him in the wake of such disaster, or dependent upon the kindness of others, had gone off to Dublin to look for some sort of employment.

CHAPTER 3

GOVERNESSES AND BLUESTOCKINGS

Necessity – the muse of women writers – was Sydney Owenson's driving force. For these were hard times, both for her family and for Ireland. Robert, with his theatre closed and his wine business bankrupt was at the end of the road. Dublin offered him little opportunity. Although it remained the seat of the vice-regal court, after the Act of Union it was little more than a provincial city. One by one the parliamentary peers, having made themselves redundant, returned to their affairs in England, and their big houses were turned over to other purposes. Some were taken over by lawyers and doctors, others fell into tenements. The days of balls and routs, and theatrical benefits were over – at least for the time being. Sydney's devotion to her father, and her admiration for his talents remained as strong as ever, but now she had to summon up all the hard-headed commonsense she had learnt from her mother. Her sister Olivia was only a schoolgirl, and though faithful Molly held them all together, they had no settled home nor reliable source of income. Sydney knew that she would have to take on the responsibility for all of them, and that she would soon have to earn some money.

As in England, there were very few occupations open to untrained middle-class girls at that time. Owenson wrote a few pathetic letters to former patrons on Sydney's behalf, but he found little response, and anyway she did not want patronage. There was no intention of allowing her to go on the stage; both she and her father had seen too much of the anxieties of that life. He often told the girls he would rather see them picking cockles on the seashore than being the first prima donnas in Europe. And to save them from the boards he had denied himself many luxuries in order to give them both a 'ladylike' education. This equipped Sydney at least to be a governess. She decided to look for a place for herself, but in order to keep his spirits up, she had an alternative plan. She had read of lady novelists who made money from their writing, and when she wrote to Robert about becoming a governess, she spoke also of her hopes of a literary career:

> Now dear Papa, I have two novels nearly finished. The first is *St. Clair*; I think I wrote it in imitation of *Werther* which I read in the school holidays last Christmas. The second is a French novel, suggested by my reading the *Memoirs of the Duc de Sully* and falling very much in love with Henri IV. Now, if I had time and quiet to finish them, I am sure I could sell them, and observe, Sir, Miss Burney got three thousand pounds for *Camilla* and brought out *Evelina* unknown to her father. But all this will take time. Meanwhile I want an asylum for myself and Olivia.

Owenson had good reason to feel that governessing was not what he wanted for his clever daughter. As in the time of the Brontës, the position was associated with humiliation and oppression. In England, it was customary for daughters of tradesmen to be sent to boarding schools where little attention was paid to health and many girls died or fell ill of the consumption known as the 'putrid fever'. Wealthy parents preferred a resident governess who could teach music and needlework, elocution and, most desirable accomplishment of all, French. A governess was neither a servant nor one of the family, though a great deal was expected from her. In *Letters to a Young Lady* a clergyman of 1789 wrote a manifesto for governesses: 'A Governess, in the first place should be a prodigy of virtue ... she should love her pupils as her daughters and possess great knowledge embellished with taste. She should always appear lovely and always inviting, knowing the best books.' The going rate for such perfection was between £20 and £40 a year, with keep.

The ideal governess, of course, was a girl from an upper-class or at least a genteel home that had been brought down by financial disaster. Then the surrounding families would fall upon the unmarried and impoverished daughters and carry them off like bargains at a bankruptcy sale. Important Anglo-Irish families, on the other hand, often looked to England for their governesses and sometimes picked up some very rare birds; Mary Wollstonecraft, for example, author of *The Rights of Women* was a most unusual employee for an Irish household. In 1787, when her father's business failed, she went over to be governess to the daughters of the Earl and Countess of Kingston. Even in that exotic Ascendancy society, the King family were remarkable, Lord and Lady King were cousins who had married when very young, in order to bring their land and fortunes together, and consequently were jointly the largest and richest landowners in Ireland. He aspired in a somewhat erratic way to be an improving landlord, and laid out Mitchellstown as a model town. Lady Caroline was beautiful and underoccupied, bathing daily in asses' milk, and living in a turmoil of 'satins and pet dogs', which she preferred to her many children. The great house in County Cork was newly built in the fashionable Palladian style, with twelve hundred acres of estate, enclosed by a thick wall, shutting out any view of the miserable cabins outside. Mary Wollstonecraft shared the squalid splendours of this Italianate castle, surrounded by miles of desolate bog, and was paid forty pounds a year. She maddened Lady Caroline with her airs and her opinions, considered quite unsuitable in a servant, and they maddened her, with their autocracy and assumption of their divine right to every pleasure. She left – with umbrage taken upon both sides – but also took with her her manuscript pages of her novel *Mary*, using the King family as her source material, to devastating effect. She also left her distinctive mark upon one of her pupils, Margaret King; this young girl was married off early by the family to Lord Mountcashel, a neighbouring landowner, but remembering Mary's teaching, left him for a man of advanced and republican opinions. 'Mr and Mrs Mason' eventually left Ireland, and joined Shelley, and Mary's own daughter Mary Shelley in their circle of free love and liberated politics in Italy.

Some of these Anglo-Irish aristocrats could be quite advanced in their attitudes to education. There were the Edgeworths who were very 'progressive' and eventually opened their own school. There was the Duchess of Leinster, mother of Lord Edward, who had actually invited Rousseau himself to come over to Ireland in 1760, to be tutor to her children. Of course, he didn't come, but in that family anything was possible.

Sydney Owenson was certainly not in this league in her qualifications to teach. Her mother's ideal of childrearing had been expressed in praise of a distant English cousin who had read the Bible twice before she was six, and could knit all the stockings for the family's coachman. Sydney had other skills;

she had her Clontarf French, and had learnt music and dancing from her father's friends in the theatre. Eventually, John Fontaine, a French dancing master domiciled in Dublin, got her a job with a former pupil of his own, Mrs Margaret Featherstone of Bracklin Castle, as governess and companion to her two daughters. The Featherstones were not grandees like the Kings or the Fitzgeralds, but were typical landed gentry settled for many generations in county Westmeath in the Irish midlands. James Featherstone was High Sheriff, and his wife Margaret was the daughter of Lady Steele of Dominick Street, Dublin, who in her youth had been one of the reigning beauties at the viceregal court of Lord Chesterfield. This formidable old lady, now ninety years old, interviewed Sydney for the position, and turned her down because she was too young and skittish. However, Mrs Featherstone wanted Sydney for being as she described 'so merry and musical', and engaged her to come down to Bracklin Castle, 'a large handsome mansion of white stone' surrounded by woods. Oliver Goldsmith, her father's cousin, also came from this part of Ireland, and describes the landscape in his poem 'The Deserted Village'. Here he also set his most famous play, for it was a real life Squire Featherstone upon whom he based the theatrical Squire Hardcastle, in *She Stoops to Conquer*.

Sydney does not tell us anywhere in her journals or *Memoirs* how she prepared herself for her first job – whether or not she packed Maria Edgeworth's *Practical Education* or *The Parent's Assistant* in her luggage. Neither does she give any impression of the stereotyped, sad demure governess with her dark clothes, and 'pale despondent looks of her class'. No one ever seems to have patronised her or sent her to the servant's entrance. In fact her whole experience appears to have been remarkably pleasant. From the first moment she arrived in the stage coach from Dublin to Bracklin, in her new pink satin slippers and white muslin dress, having come straight from what she described as a 'bal d'adieu' (farewell party to ordinary mortals), she was treated as one of the family, encouraged to sing and dance a jig, and was generally petted.

The picture that she always gives in her letters to her father as the belle of the ball wherever she might be is, of course, typical of her determination to keep up her own self esteem, and to help him maintain his. Her story-telling ability started to develop in this way. She regarded her own life as her source material, to be edited to the best imaginative effect, and her account of the time with the Featherstones leaves out all the longueurs and slights which must at times have attended her ambiguous position.

And later on she made good use of these experiences, for when she published *O'Donnel* in 1814, a governess was featured as a romantic heroine for the first time in English fiction. This was the enigmatic Miss Charlotte O'Halloran, who through the vagaries of plot turns into the lovely, irresistible Duchess of Belmont, and eventually marries the hero. She is early in a long line of glamorous governesses in nineteenth-century fiction.

Bracklin was a gracious house with the civilised domestic charm that many of the Anglo-Irish created for themselves. But in her visits to other families in the countryside Sydney must occasionally have entered the ramshackle world of the country squireens described by Arthur Young, the English agricultural-ist, in his *A Tour in Ireland 1776–1779* some twenty years before. Writing of a gentleman in that same Westmeath countryside he said:

> His hospitality was unbounded, and it never for a moment came into his head to make any provision for feeding the people who came into his house. While credit was to be had, his butler or housekeeper did this for him; his own attention was given solely to the cellar, that wine might not be wanted. If claret was secured, with a dead ox or a sheep hanging in the slaughterhouse ready for steak or cutlets he thought all was well. He was never easy without company in the house, and with a large party in it would invite another of twice the number. One day the cook came into the breakfast parlour before all the company; 'Sir, there's no coals' . . . 'Then burn turf' 'Sir, there's no turf'; 'Then cut down a tree.'

That was Anglo-Ireland at the turn of the century. It ran the whole gamut from pastiche Versailles to profligate Castle Rackrent, and Bracklin was decently in between. Remembering it in later life, Sydney wrote with affection in her *Memoirs*:

> The order and propriety which marked the economy of the house, the regular and easy hours gave me impressions of domestic discipline which are not yet effected from my life and practice. It was just the epoch when 'the tide in the affairs of men' had taken that turn which introduced a high

domestic civilisation into the homes of mere country
gentlemen unknown to the Irish nobility of other times.

Sydney found to her delight that there were good books in the
library, and Mr Featherstone, a man of some intellectual
pretensions, engaged her in grave discussion such as she had
never before encountered. If her formal education had been a
bit sketchy, she was now acquiring knowledge fast. She had
always devoured books, copying out any pieces that appealed
to her. When she was barely sixteen her name had appeared
with those of five other women in the original subscription list
of the ambitious literary magazine *Anthologia Hibernica* which
during its two years of existence had published the first
youthful effusion of Thomas Moore, and the precocious poems
of Thomas Dermody, an infant prodigy befriended by her
father. No book was ever too erudite to frighten her. She read
the philosopher Locke, and was fascinated by the problem of
innate and acquired ideas. She became seriously interested in
chemistry and studied the work of the French chemist
Lavoisier, as well as the writings of the eccentric Irish scientist
Richard Kirwan, whom her father had known as a young man
in Galway. She was intrigued to find that old Lady Steele was
connected with the family of Sir Richard Steele, editor of the
London literary journal the *Spectator*. When the old lady died
her house in north Dublin was left to her daughter. In the early
eighteenth century Dominick Street, though now a dilapidated
slum, had been one of the most beautiful streets in the city.
Sydney, helping to clear the house, found that it was an
unaltered, albeit fading, monument to the taste of that earlier
time, the marble chimney piece reached halfway to the ceiling,
and was surmounted with carved Etruscan vases; the curtains
were of crimson silk; there was Chinese paper on the walls, and
Turkey carpet on the floor. A large table in the centre of the
room was covered with folio books. While she was sorting
these treasures the butler needed papers to put round the
candles. She had to search through an old coffer in the garret,
and found among the waste paper letters from Alexander Pope
and Jonathan Swift, which she was allowed to keep. Sydney
recognised the exalted company she was in, even if now they
were only dusty ghosts. She was determined to keep her own
end up in such society, and it is certain that when she first came
to Bracklin, with whatever governessy material was provided in
the way of copy books, instructive manuals, illustrated card

games and geography globes, first and foremost there would be her own notebooks and unfinished manuscripts. She later complained that she was overworked as a governess, but nevertheless the opportunity 'to snatch some hours from congenial duties in voluntary pursuits' helped her to finish her first book. Her father vigorously canvassed subscribers for this, and in 1801 there appeared *Poems dedicated by permission to the Countess of Moira* – 'a tiny book by a tiny author'. She herself later referred to this first book as *Poems by a Young Lady between the age of twelve and fourteen* claiming for it a rare precocity, and at the same time obscuring the question of her age. The poems, all forty of them, are for the most part facile imitations of eighteenth-century favourites – with all the attendant vocabulary of 'pensive thought', 'bowers' and 'cots', yet underneath all the poesy there is the unmistakable voice of one who although no poet, could reproduce a fair imitation of what was in vogue. The frequent allusions to her father show how strongly he had claimed her. His 'expressive eyes' and 'smile benignant'; his 'tears of affection' and 'muscular embraces' are the subjects of poems of whole-hearted adoration. A poem suggested by his portrait bears a strong resemblance to Cowper's verse on his mother's picture, but nevertheless it is Robert Owenson she is looking at:

> Dear shade of him my heart holds more than dear,
> Author of all that fond heart's purest bliss,
> Dear shade, I hail thee with a rapturous tear,
> And welcome thee with many a tender kiss!
>
> This brow indeed is his, broad, candid, fair,
> Where nature's honest characters are wrote;
> But o'er the beauteous transcripts morbid Care
> And Time of late their ruthless fingers smote . . .

And so she goes on, for another seven verses in the same vein. The references to other men are few and unemotional, and apart from her father, and verses on the death of her mother, practically all of the poems deal directly or allusively with the chief subject of her sensibility, herself. In a piece addressed to *Myself* she begins:

> Ah, little maid, how blest the day
> When with the frolic hours you gay and careless roved.
> Thro' life, from woe, from trouble free
> Nor thought you e'er could parted be, from those you
>   loved. . . .

9   *Thomas Moore* by Martin Archer Shee, National Gallery of Ireland

While this book was in preparation she met another young poet who was beginning to rise fast. The Featherstone girls were taking music lessons from John Stevenson, one of her father's old friends, who often stopped behind after class to sing or play for the little governess. One day he enchanted her with a new song:

> Friend of my soul, this goblet sip,
> T'will chase away that pensive tear;
> 'Tis not so sweet as woman's lip,
> But oh, 'tis more sincere . . .'

The sentiment vastly appealed to her, and Stevenson told her that the words were by Thomas Moore, whose verses he was setting to music. He arranged for her to go to a musical party given by the Moores for their idolised son. And so the poet who was to make Regency society in England weep for the sad fate of the Minstrel Boy met the novelist who would make the same people climb on chairs to get a glimpse of the Wild Irish Girl. But for the moment they were just two young hopefuls, taking tea in the room over his parent's grocery shop in Aungier Street, Dublin.

In the meantime, Sydney's father, still without a theatre, was moving from one set of lodgings to another, first in Dublin and then in the small towns of Ulster, where he took on the management of a travelling repertory company. Her appointment with the Featherstones came to an amicable end, and Sydney joined her father and sister in Coleraine. In spite of her longing for their society which she had expressed so feelingly in her verse, she quickly grew tired of the tedium of a small provincial town, particularly in dingy lodgings, and looked for another situation. Her second engagement as a governess was with the Crawford family of Tipperary, and once again she found herself treated with respect and consideration. 'Here I am', she wrote to her sister, 'almost the subject of idolatry among the servants, and caressed by all ranks of people.' Once more she sang and danced in the evenings at dinner parties, to great applause, and in the leisure hours worked on her 'bit of authorship'.

Now in 1801 in spite of all her evasion of dates and descriptions of herself as 'a child', 'a dear little girl', and a 'little maid', she was a young woman of twenty-five or so; her relationship with men had been controlled by her passion for self-improvement and her commitment to help her father. She was witty, agreeable and vivaciously good looking, and as such drew admirers and even adorers to her side. There had been the two young ensigns in Kilkenny, one who courted and one who stood back in platonic friendship; there had been the boy poet Tom Dermody, who like the young Chatterton in England had made a great stir, and then dropped away from favour. Throughout their adolescence these two had exchanged poems and letters of high-flown sentiment, but were both too thoroughly self-centred to mean a word. Meanwhile she poured all her romantic notions and received ideas of love into her writings. It was this channelling of emotion into words that had kept her out of mischief when she was very young, and exposed to all the seedy glamour of a fit-up theatre. This precarious way of life, with her mother gone, her father often away on tour, and only old Molly to guard and chaperone herself and her sister had made her, so ingenious and open on the surface, really very wary. She was certainly no beauty, but she was able to persuade some people that she was beautiful. In her youth she was slight and graceful, with black curly hair, cut short in the Regency style; 'crops are all the rage', she wrote 'as savage as possible'. She had large luminous eyes, set slightly unevenly, or with a squint, according to whether it was friend or enemy describing her. She had learnt backstage how to make the best of herself. In her childhood she had watched and listened to those goddesses of charm and seduction Mrs Billington, Mrs Siddons and Dorothy Bland, a young protegée of her father's, who later as Mrs Jordan was successful enough on the London stage to become mistress to teh Duke of York, and mother of his ten illegitimate children. She learnt from experts how to dress dramatically on very little money, and how to paint her face. Eventually she was able to present herself as skilfully as she learnt to present her fictional heroines.

Her first novel *St. Clair* was published in Dublin in 1802. The publisher's name is unknown and it is said she received four copies of this book as payment. Written as a series of letters after the fashion of the time, it was a short idyll of romantic passion, modelled as she had once promised her father, on Goethe's *Werther* and Rousseau's *Nouvelle Heloise*, which masterpieces, in the novel, are constantly in her lover's hands. Its theme, the unconscious growth of love out of platonic friendship between a young man and a girl who is betrothed to another, relates to both those works, and also to the declaration of love she had received from one of her young subalterns in Kilkenny. The exquisitely stilted way in which he had expressed himself in his letters certainly met with her own ideals of style. The two distinctive features of the plot are the lively character of the heroine, Olivia Desmond, and the serious treatment of Irish scenery, music and legends. The heroine of course is based on herself, and the scenery is that of Sligo, that archetypal landscape of limestone and precipitous waterfalls, where an Atlantic gale will blow the water back against the cliff, so that (as W.B. Yeats – himself a Sligo-man, wrote later) 'the cataract smokes upon the mountain side . . . that cold and vapour turbanned steep.'

St. Clair is very much the work of a novice, but the combination of romantic sentiment and learned information remained her hallmark throughout her later novels. Sydney had such strong passions for acquiring knowledge that she could not resist displaying it. The editor of her *Memoirs* states:

> In all her early works her heroes and heroines indulged in wonderful digressions, historical, astronomical, and metaphysical, in the very midst of the most terrible emergencies, where danger and despair are imminent and impending; no matter what laceration of their finest feelings they may be suffering, the chief characters have always their learning at their finger ends, and never fail to make quotations from favourite authors appropriate to the occasion.

And so it is in *St. Clair*. Before the lovers die, one killed in a duel by a jealous rival, and the other of a broken heart, they lend each other books, discuss music and philosophy, all the while suppressing the love that is growing between them. St Clair wrote to a friend: 'It is now an hour past midnight, And I am going to read *Werther*. I had almost forgot to tell you – Olivia lent it to me and the passages marked by her pencil give me the most flattering conviction of the coincidence of our tastes.' The situation between them has reached boiling point when she asks him: 'Was it not Eristratus who discovered the secret malady of Antiochus by comparing its symptoms with Sappho's description of the effects of love?' He gives her an appropriate answer, and their fate is sealed.

It is very easy to make fun of *St. Clair* – it certainly was not written for the taste of the last half of the twentieth century, but it was successful enough in 1803 to be reissued in London, and was well received by the English public. They liked the spirited heroine, and the Irish setting was a change. The *Monthly Mirror*, no doubt misled by the name 'Sydney' reviewed it seriously: '*St. Clair* is obviously the production of a man of distinguished abilities, and though many of its sentiments may perhaps be justly considered as exceptional, it affords on the whole a most useful lesson.' The *Monthly Review* hoped that 'the children of unsophisticated virtue will doubtless close the eventful recital with conformed resolutions of guarding against the seducing influences of romantic sensibility, while they drop a tear over its ruined but amiable victims.'

Now that she was an authoress, Sydney wanted more than the slightly amused praise of her provincial patrons. She wanted to break into the society of serious intellectuals. The Countess of Moira, who had sponsored her little book of poems, and Lady Steele, that old woman who had known Swift and Pope, must have told her of the English bluestockings that they had known in their youth, women who pursued knowledge instead of fashion, and instead of card-playing and other frivolities, held evening assemblies 'where the fair sex might particulate in conversation with literary and ingenious men animated by a desire to please'. The 'Queen of the Blues', the undisputed leader of this circle at that time was Mrs Elizabeth Montague, who made her house the social centre of intellectual society in London in the mid-eighteenth century. Other women, some married to rich men, and others who were often parsons' daughters gathered around her and formed what Horace Walpole called 'the petticoterie'. Some of them were considerable scholars and raised public opinion regarding the intellectual capacity of women. Hester Chapone published a very much admired *Letters on the Improvement of the Mind* in 1773, and Elizabeth Carter, whose clergyman father had taught her Latin, Greek, and Hebrew, as well as housewifery, was praised by Dr Johnson, who said 'My old friend Mrs. Carter could make a pudding as well as translate Epictetus from the Greek.' For the most part these women were well provided for, and did not have to write for money. Many of them expressed their talents for social comment and observations, which might have gone well into successful novel writing, in long letters to each other, producing between them an enormous amount of correspondence, and it is from these letters that we can best learn what they stood for. For the most part they deplored the extravagance of fashion; as well as overstated romance and passion. They disapproved of marriage by barter, declaring it a crime. They held exalted opinions about friendship, as being the highest emotion of human nature, and most revolutionary of all, they believed that there should be one and the same moral standard for men and women. They were at the height of their influence in England in the 1780s, but as their leaders grew old or died, their movement was increasingly satirised for being overprecious and artificial. The Age of Enlightenment was giving way to the Romantic Movement. 'The Princess of Parallelograms' was Byron's unadmiring epithet for his mathematically inclined wife; very different from Dr Johnson and Boswell who had thought the 'Blues' most admirable women.

But in Ireland, where fashion is always decades behind, there was still a circle of Blues. Sydney could never penetrate into the high aristocratic society of women like the Duchess of Leinster and her sisters, where the possibility of employing Rousseau as a tutor was taken as naturally as a dish of tea; with the Duchess the upper air of intellectual life was warmed a little by her collection of spotted cows, à la Marie Antoinette, her diamonds worn in the afternoon, and French horns playing at every meal. This was very high style in Ireland.

The reputation and example of the more austere Mrs Delany, however, would still be influential in the Dublin circles to which Sydney aspired, and a direct link to the bluestocking tradition. Mrs Delany was an English aristocrat, sister of Lord Granville, who had married an Irish clergyman, and had lived a life of such sense and sensibility as to be an example for all young ladies with intellectual aspirations. She had been the friend of Handel and had corresponded with Swift. She was called by Hannah More a 'living library of knowledge' and by Edmund Burke the 'highest bred woman in the world'. In England she had been one of the 'petticoterie' but she found that 'exclusively feminine company, no matter how intellectual, was poor diet for one who loves a plentiful meal of social friendship'. Mrs Delany died in 1788, but there was always Maria Edgeworth to be admired, issuing her regular treatises on high thinking and plain living from her large estates in the county Longford. Miss Edgeworth was a bit unapproachable to someone of Sydney's background, but they were very aware of each other. Maria was no romantic, hating both sentimentality and overt feminism. 'Of late years we have heard more of sentiment than of principles: more of the rights of woman than her duties.' Thus she spoke from her heights of rectitude.

10   Carton, home of the Duchess of Leinster

Sydney approached the Dublin coteries by seeking out their most attractive 'blue', Mrs Alicia Lefanu, sister of Richard Brinsley Sheridan, and daughter of Thomas, the actor–manager and friend of her father. Later she acknowledged her debt to this lady by writing in her *Memoirs*:

> The most literary house then open in Dublin was that of the charming sister of Sheridan, Mrs. Lefanu, the author's earliest and dearest friend. It would be want of pride and gratitude not to boast of the advantages she then derived from the attentions and hospitality of the distinguished families of Charlemont, Leitrim, Charleville, Cloncurry and Tighe on her first entrée upon life and literature.

Here was the combination of upper-class society and liberal learning that she loved, 'ton' and intellect together. In this circle she made friends with accomplished women older than herself, who would influence her and sustain her through many difficult times. Even when she was away from Ireland, she corresponded copiously with them. Mary Tighe was the youngest; she was the wife of a Kilkenny landowner, who aspired to be a classical scholar and had based a long and rather limp poem called *Psyche* on the story as told by Apuleius. It was popular enough to have been reprinted eight times. Mary Tighe was fey and delicate and died young; but her fame was such that a tomb carved by the fashionable artist Flaxman was erected to her memory in an obscure churchyard in Inistioge. Lady Charleville, on the other hand, was a very tough old dame, living to be over ninety, with houses in London and in Dublin where she held literary salons, and Sydney deferred to her opinions always. She had been educated in France, and was considered to be an authority on practically everything. Alice Lefanu also became Sydney's friend for life. She encouraged her and introduced her to useful people, and having praised *St. Clair*, with certain reservations, gave her advice on the danger of too advanced opinions. She warned her against becoming too rarified a bluestocking, recommending the 'useful virtues' against the 'splendid', and advised her to cultivate the 'everyday qualities' of good humour and tolerance. Sydney, anxious to dispel the impression which she had apparently made by her first attempt to shine in a Dublin literary coterie wrote back

> I entirely agree with you that *some women* in attaining that intellectual acquisition which excites admiration and reverence forfeit their (oh, how much more valuable) claims on the affection of the heart . . . I must tell you, my dear madam, I am ambitious, far, far, beyond the line of laudable emulation, perhaps beyond the power of being happy. Yet the strongest point of my ambition is to be every inch a woman. Delighted with the pages of Lavoisier, I dropped the study of chemistry . . . lest I should be not a very woman. Seduced by taste to Greek and Latin, I resisted lest I should not be a very woman. And I have studied music rather as a sentiment than a science, and drawing as an instrument rather than an art lest I should have become a musical pedant, or a masculine artist.

Having thus renounced the role of bluestocking in favour of being every inch a woman, Sydney nevertheless indulged and increased her research into old Irish archaeology and literature, and the instinct to show off her learning, in her own writing if not in the salons, remained very strong. So pedantic is she that, in some of her books, footnotes take up more space on the printed page than does the text. The antiquarian movement which was developing strongly by the end of the eighteenth century was virtually a rediscovery of the language and ancient lost culture of Gaelic Ireland, and along with the songs which she had learnt from her father, she started to read deeply in old

11   *Mary Tighe* (author of *Psyche*), National Gallery of Ireland

12   *Pilgrims at Clonmacnoise* (the discovery of Gaelic Ireland) by George
Petrie, National Gallery of Ireland

Irish history and poetry. At first it was the old music that captivated her. She began a correspondence with scholars like Joseph Walker, author of *Historical Memoirs of the Irish Bards*; Charlotte Brooke, whose *Reliques of Irish Poetry* translations published alongside the original Irish, appeared in 1789, was another great influence. And there was Edward Bunting's collection of *The Ancient Music of Ireland* which first appeared in 1796, greatly stimulated by a unique gathering in 1792 of nearly a dozen Irish harpists in the fiercely Presbyterian city of Belfast. One of these harpists, Art O'Neill, was ninety-seven years of age, and claimed to have once played for Bonny Prince Charlie. Here was a movement which gave scope for her patriotic sentiment as well as her love of learning. Following on her praises of Irish music in *St. Clair* she published two of her versions of old Irish songs – 'Ned of the Hills', and 'Castle Hyde'.

Dublin, starved of diversions after the Act of Union, was always avid for a bit of scandal or daring slander. In 1804 there appeared a series of six anonymous satires in which the talents of favourite Irish actors and managers were submitted to sarcasm and invective. It was an open secret that the author of *Familiar Epistles on the Present State of the Irish Stage* was John Wilson Croker, an ambitious young barrister, with high Tory affiliations, and probably on the pay roll of Dublin Castle, who was trying to launch himself on a political career. The malicious town was shocked and delighted by these impertinent barbs, and one actor is reported to have died from the ridicule, or so it says on his tombstone in St Werbergh's churchyard. An answer to this 'assassin of reputation' came out in a bold attacking pamphlet, signed by one 'S.O.', and Croker, with the rest of Dublin, eventually identified these initials as those of Sydney Owenson. By taking him on so wholeheartedly, she brought comfort and relief to the theatrical world, but she gained his implacable enmity for the rest of her life. To the personal grudge he held against her, he added a political one, which he demonstrated years later when he became editor of the influential *Quarterly Review*. Sydney's early biographer, W.J. Fitzpatrick, said of him at the time of the pamphlets 'This was the barbed pen which sixteen years later stabbed Keats to death, and sought to fasten itself in Sydney Owenson's heart.'

Her pamphlet in defence of the theatre and many of her father's friends was only a sideline to the main work in hand at that moment. In Inniskillen, in northern Ireland, staying for a while with Robert and Olivia, she finished the novel of *The Novice of St. Dominick*. Originally it ran to six volumes, for as she said herself 'in those days one volume or six volumes was alike to me'. However, no publisher would handle six volumes, particularly in her notoriously bad handwriting. But she had attached to herself another infatuated young man – a young chemist's apprentice in Inniskillen, called Francis Crossley, who copied out the whole wild gallimaufrey in a beautiful and legible hand. As a reward for this devotion, Sydney recommended books for him to read, refused his offers of marriage, and encouraged him to join the army and go to India, which he did. Her father moved his troupe on to Derry, and Sydney went with him. Having exhausted the popular novels in the local circulating library, she resumed her work on old Irish music, employing a young woman to take down the melodies as her father played them on his fiddle. She was also getting her six volumes ready to send to England for publication.

St. Dominick was the other novel that she had dreamed up to rescue herself from a life of governessing. It differed from its predecessor in length, in scene and in action. Where *St. Clair* had been almost static, this one was full of adventure. It had a sense of reality instead of Gothic fantasy; it anticipated the new type of historical fiction to be perfected by Sir Walter Scott. France at the end of the sixteenth century had been researched conscientiously with many footnotes. But the chief interest again centres in the character of the heroine. Imogen starts her career as companion to a pretentious literary lady; later she wanders across France disguised as a troubadour, and has hairbreadth escapes from robbers. When she inherits great wealth, she studies languages, art, music and dancing, and entertains the king and his court in her own salon. Bankruptcy and illness finally lead to the triumph of true love over ambition and religious prejudice, all recounted in the language of sublime pedantry. The refined feelings and personal charm of the heroine contribute to Sydney's own image of herself, and point the contradictions of her nature, for while she is dancing and singing and wasting her money on false friends she is the child of Robert, but when she discovers the follies of fame and flattery, and turns to the joys of good works, she is the daughter of Jane. And although she is writing about France, a country not yet known to her, she makes it all applicable to Ireland.

Now with her manuscript beautifully copied out by the adoring Francis Crossley, she decided to make a personal approach to the English publishers. Writing about this she said 'Without one friend to recommend, when I wished to publish "The Novice" I took in a newspaper for a publisher's name. I saw R. Phillips, and wrote to him.'

Phillips wrote back, and encouraged her to come to London. Whether by luck or intuition she had picked on one of the most enterprising publishers in England, and one who would be sympathetic to her work. Phillips had been a radical bookseller in Leicester, where in 1792 he had been imprisoned for publishing a cheap edition of Tom Paine's *Rights of Man*. There were harsh laws against the distribution of seditious literature in England at that time, as well as in Ireland. Later, when he set up in London, he was more discreet, but his printing shop was the meeting place of reformers and radicals like William Godwin and Joseph Priestley. By shrewd practice he grew rich, and eventually became a sheriff of London. So discreet and shrewd did he become that eventually he was knighted. He was notorious both for his militant vegetarianism, and for his meanness towards his authors, one of whom said of him 'Notwithstanding his refusal of animal food, Phillips has no objection to feeding on human brains.' It was to this tough old entrepreneur of literature that Sydney brought her novel. Travelling alone, and as cheaply as possible, enduring the terrible sea voyage, and the long coach journey from Holyhead to London, she succeeded in charming Phillips into acting completely out of character. He paid her at once for the book although he insisted on having it cut down from six volumes to four. He invited her to dinner to meet some of his authors, including, Godwin – the widower of Mary Wollstonecraft, who had died in 1797, giving birth to Mary Shelley. Sydney stayed only a few days in London, but made arrangements to have most of her earnings sent on to her father. With what she kept for herself she bought an Irish harp and a black cloak. She had started to create her image. Her new publisher, realising that he had found a property, sent after her lots of good advice, useful to a fledgling writer:

The world is not informed about Ireland, and I am in the situation to command the light to shine . . . I assure you that you have a power of writing, a fancy of imagination and a degree of enthusiasm which will enable you to produce an immortal work if you will labour it sufficiently. Write only on one side of your paper, and retain a broad margin.

Sydney had found her publisher, and her subject. From now on she would write about Ireland, and for Ireland. Later, in the character of one of her heroines – the novelist Lady Clancare in *Florence Macarthy* she sums up this relationship between her patriotism and her ambition most honestly:

> Possibly you have heard that I am, by divine indignation, a sort of an author . . . and it is quite true. With Ireland in my heart, and epitomising something of her humour and her sufferings in my own character and story I do trade upon the materials she furnishes me, and turning my patriotism into pounds, shillings and pence, endeavour at the same moment to serve her, and support myself.

CHAPTER 4

LET THE LIGHT SHINE THROUGH

When Phillips the publisher told Sydney Owenson that the world was not yet informed about Ireland, and that he would help her let the light shine through, he might have been demonstrating his radical sympathies, but he was also acting on a shrewd commercial hunch. Maybe it was time for a new approach to the whole question of Ireland; an English publisher might very profitably set the trend, particularly as the Irish ones could or would not. There was nothing new, however, in the idea of English publications being destined for Ireland. Throughout the eighteenth century all intellectual, cultural and fashionable life was dominated by England, or rather London, which threw a long shadow over provincial England as well as Ireland. Dublin newspapers and magazines were filled with material taken from English journals; most of the works sold by Irish booksellers were produced by English authors. As we have seen, the Irish theatre looked to London, and all fashion came from England. It was said that the Irish were so governed by England in everything, taste as well as politics, that they seemed absolutely afraid to give the stamp of approbation to anything in the first instance, and hesitated to have an opinion of its merit until they had been guided by an English review.

In the troubled atmosphere of the last ten years, homegrown literature had sunk to a particularly low ebb. The editor of *Anthologia Hibernica* a 'superior' literary monthly which only lasted a year, wrote in 1793: 'Were the abilities of the Irish to be estimated by their literary productions they would scarcely rank higher than those nations who had just emerged from barbarism.' The silence of nationalist authors was understandable. Habeas Corpus had been suspended when the Act of Union was passed. The government, therefore, had a free hand to deal with anyone who got out of line, and Irish publishers were thoroughly emasculated by a system of bribes and threats.

When Byrne, the Irish publisher, advertised the text of the trial of Hamilton Rowan, the United Irishman, he was warned by the Lord Chief Justice, Lord Clonmel: 'Take care, sir, what you do; I give you this notice, if there are any reflections on the judges of the land, by the Eternal God, I will lay you by the heels.' It was well to take such warnings seriously.

In such a climate of political repression Sydney started to plot out *The Wild Irish Girl*. Writing of this time, much later, she recalled:

> Graves were then still green, where the victims of laws
> uselessly violated were still wept over by broken hearts; no
> work . . . of fictional narrative, founded on national
> grievances, and borne out by historic fact had yet appealed to
> the sympathies of the general reader, or found its way to the
> desultory studies of domestic life! *The Wild Irish Girl* took
> the initiative; in an experiment since carried out to perfection
> by abler talents, and it was no small publishing moral
> courage on the part of the most fashionable English
> bibliopolist of the day.

So she paid homage to Phillips who had encouraged her to break through the prejudice, and made a generous bow in the direction of those Irish writers like the Banim brothers, Gerald Griffin and William Carleton who, following her example, were to write novels from an Irish national point of view.

For all her ingenuous airs of 'little miss', Sydney was a shrewd political operator, though she said herself 'politics can never be a woman's science, but patriotism must naturally be a woman's sentiment'. In her first two novels, her sympathetic understanding of the Irish problem was secondary to the romantic nature of her plots, but her first visit to England changed that emphasis. The contempt and indifference to everything Irish that she found there made her rage, as she put it to 'bog-heat'. She was determined to combat what she considered the gross misinterpretation of her country. She wrote:

> I came to the task with a diffidence proportioned to the
> ardour which instigated me to the attempt; for as a woman,
> a young woman, and an Irishwoman, I felt all the delicacy of
> undertaking a work which had for the professed theme of
> its discussion, circumstances of national import, and
> national interest.

Yet, despite her feelings of diffidence and inadequacy, and all the political disasters of the time, the image of Ireland as a culturally distinct nation was beginning to take definite shape. In an amateur and dilettante way to begin with, the old Gaelic past was being disinterred. In 1785 the Royal Irish Academy was founded, and eccentric theories about the language and the existence of such mysteries as Round Towers and the old dolmens were expounded. Country gentlemen of a scientific turn of mind occupied their rural isolation with antiquarian studies, archaeology, linguistics and history and built up a new kind of cultural nationalism – even if such studies were more attainable to the Anglo-Irish than to the natives. If this semi-mythological past of bards and warriors could create a genuine diversion from the growing political and radical ideology which was causing so much trouble, then the Ascendancy, which had but recently crushed the rebellions of Wolfe Tone, and Robert Emmet (those two young renegades from the Protestant middle class) would be only too glad to support it.

Just a few years earlier, Robert Owenson had been criticised for 'groaning out the guttural chant of savages', and hissed off the stage for his Gaelic 'howls'. Now it was beginning to be appreciated that these too were part of the national heritage. Both Sydney and the rising young poet Moore had come into the new national movement through music. She had already published two old songs, transcribed from her father's repertoire. Now a London publisher, Preston brought out a further collection, *Twelve Original Hibernian Melodies*. When, shortly afterwards, Tom Moore began to write his own *Irish Melodies* he used this collection as a model, and honourably acknowledged his debt to Miss Owenson. Today, Moore is regarded by some as a minor poet of sugary sentiment – in fact his major work has been punned as 'Irish Maladies', but in his time he was a phenomenon of political as well as poetical importance; in those early days of romantic nationalism the daring concept of an Irish identity had to be made palatable to those who had formerly ignored or denigrated its very existence. Moore, who was certainly no rebel, had nevertheless been a college friend of that Robert Emmet who had been executed as a traitor in 1803. Five years after that abortive rebellion, Moore wrote a poem about Emmet, put it to music and sang it at fashionable parties in London and Dublin. On the gallows Emmet had said 'Let no man write my epitaph until

my country has taken its place among the nations of the earth.'
Moore softened this into:

> Oh, breathe not his name, let it sleep in the shade
> Where cold and unhonoured, his relics are laid;
> Sad, silent and dark are the tears that we shed,
> As the night dew that falls on the grass o'er his head.
>
> But the night dew that falls, though in silence it weeps,
> Shall brighten with verdure the grave where he sleeps;
> And the tear that we shed, though in secret it rolls,
> Shall long keep his memory green in our souls.

'It is easy to sleep on another man's wound' says an old Irish
proverb, and it is fashionable today to condemn Moore as a
weeper of crocodile tears. But in those callous days it was at
least something to make some of the conquerors weep for their
victims.

But the real Establishment did not weep. Dublin Castle kept
up its hard line and its surveillance. No Dublin publisher dared
to touch *The Wild Irish Girl* in 1806. Even Phillips, in London,
for all his radical swagger, panicked. 'The sentiments enunci-
ated' he said 'are too strongly opposed to the English interest in
Ireland, and I must withdraw from my original offer.' He was
also jibbing at the money that she wanted. Sydney, who
professed not to know anything of the London scene, then went
straight to the other publisher who would be sympathetic to
her views. Joseph Johnson, friend and patron of Mary
Wollstonecraft, and inclined to be both radical and pro-
feminist, offered her three hundred guineas for the copyright.
When Phillips heard of the deal with Johnson, he wanted his
'property' back, and in a crossfire of letters won the right to
publish, and paid up. He wrote to her in triumph: 'Dear
bewitching and deluding siren – not able to part from you, I
have promised the three hundred pounds. *The Wild Irish Girl* is
mine, to do with her as I please!' So he gloated like the villain
in a melodrama, but the triumph belonged to Sydney. The
novel came out in three volumes that year. Delighted with her
victory over one of the toughest operators in English publishing, she had achieved more than she knew. She had created the
first 'national tale' – a new category in Anglo-Irish literature.

Of course there had been stories dealing with the condition
of Ireland before, that had received circulation in England. In

1801 Maria Edgeworth had published *Castle Rackrent*, a sardonic fable portraying the ruin of an aristocratic family through their own irresponsible behaviour. But Maria's approach is very different. *Castle Rackrent* is set in 'former times', and the implications are that with good behaviour and right attitudes on all sides, these times need not return, and Ireland will be redeemed, still maintaining the same relationship of land and tenant. Maria was bound by birth and allegiance to the landowning class and, like her father Richard Lovell Edgeworth, was humane and 'improving'. She was in spirit always a child of the eighteenth century, rational in all things. Wild scenery was as distressing to her as wild behaviour. She saw the solution for the Irish problem in a benevolent landlord system, working in a patriarchal union with England, where the Protestant ethos would automatically prevail; Catholics would be tolerated, but certainly not encouraged. *Castle Rackrent* has been called an elegy for the Protestant nation of Grattan, that short lived ideal of political elitism which disappeared with the Union. Sydney Owenson, much closer to the changing nature of post-Union Ireland, owned no great estates nor did she hold any partisan religious beliefs. Her idea of the Irish nation would bring together Catholic and Protestant alike, that dangerous union advocated by Wolfe Tone, 'in the common name of Irishman'.

Both writers used plots as pegs on which to hang their different kind of hats. *The Wild Irish Girl*, and Edgeworth's *Ennui* and *The Absentee* have broadly similar story lines. They deal with the impact of Ireland upon a young man hitherto unsympathetic and unaware of the real state of the country; but there the similarity ends. The lessons to be learnt are different. Maria's young gentlemen discover responsibilities to land and tenants from a landlord's point of view; Owenson's hero discovers the way of life of a departed world, from the view of the dispossessed Catholic Irish holding on for dear life to the bare rocks of Connaught. For it was to Connaught – or to hell – that Cromwell banished the last of the Gaelic chiefs, hoping to hold native Ireland as a kind of penal colony. There were still pockets where these families survived as best they could; a few claimed lineal descent from the old Irish kings, like the O'Conor Don, and the O'Donogue. Arthur Young, on his tour in 1780, met such a one. He wrote:

Another great family in Connaught is MacDermott, who

calls himself Prince of Coolavin. He lives at Coolavin, in Sligo, and though he has not above one hundred pounds a year, will not admit his children to sit down in his presence. Lord Kingsborough, Mr. Ponsonby, Mr. O'Hara, etc. came to see him, and his address was curious:- 'O'Hara, you are welcome! Sandford, I am glad to see your mother's son (his mother was an O'Brien); as for the rest of you, come in as ye can!'

Twenty years later, staying with her father's cousins in Sligo, among the ruined abbeys, broken battlements and lashing seas, Sydney met this supreme example of romantic atavism, Myles McDermott, the Prince of Coolavin himself. He became her Prince of Inishmore, last of the endangered species of Milesian nobility and father of Glorvina, the Wild Irish Girl.

The novel is written as a series of letters, in the manner of *St. Clair*. It concerns the experience of a young Englishman, Horatio Mortimer, sent to Ireland by his father, the Earl of M. to recover from the affects of 'vitiated dissipation'. The family estates, originally won by conquest under Cromwell from the Inishmore family, are in the West of Ireland. The young man is full of typical English prejudices against Ireland, but soon the grandeur of the scenery overwhelms him; he sees it in terms of Italian painting, in the style of Salvator Rosa, with 'impervious glooms', 'stupendous heights', 'savage desolation' and 'rich ruins'. A simple goodhearted Irish guide takes him into the heart of the country, introducing him to equally simple and generous peasants, who all give him lessons in social economics, the landlord system and the wickedness of the middlemen. Soon he learns the real lesson of the novel – that Ireland is a very ancient country, with a civilisation much older than that of the usurper on her soil; and that the old Gaelic world is not extinguished completely, but lives on, albeit secretly and impoverished, in the person of the Prince of Inishmore, with his ruined castle, and his ragged court. His daughter, the Lady Glorvina then comes on stage. She is 'fairylike in stature', with 'locks of living gold on a brow of snow'. She speaks Latin and Greek, as well as Irish. She cures the sick, sings and plays the harp, and has 'an effulgency of countenance'. Horatio is soon attracted to her, but asks himself what can he, an experienced educated man, expect from this 'wild' Irish girl – (wild, as in artless, untutored). He soon finds out as she gives him unending dissertations on Irish music, the

13 *The Frightened
Wagoner* by James Arthur
O'Connor, National Gallery
of Ireland

harp, topography, ancient Irish orders of custom, chivalry and genealogy, and everything else a young man suffering from the effects of dissipation might want to know.

Sydney Owenson's natural pedantry made her waste nothing of all the information she had amassed from her reading, from Walker's *Essay on Irish Dress* to the latest transactions of the Royal Irish Academy, and from a regular correspondence with equally doctrinaire scholars. The vocabulary of *The Wild Irish Girl* is exotic to say the least, 'eleemosynary', 'superogatory', and 'exility' being just a few examples, and everywhere there are French, Italian, Latin and Shakespearian quotations. The footnotes climb all over the pages. But apart from endless discussions and harp playing, there is little development of plot. Eventually the Prince dies, and Mortimer marries Glorvina. England and Ireland are brought together, and the book ends with a plea for the reconciliation of all such differences.

It is certainly not for its plot that *The Wild Irish Girl* can claim to break new ground and start a new literary genre. Of course, the whole thing is an intensely imagined fantasy. Inishmore is MacDermott of Coolavin, but he is also Robert Owenson, who had been driven out of his rightful place through his fierce loyalty to all things Irish – who had dreamed of establishing national theatres throughout Ireland, like martello towers defending his country's threatened heritage. She describes the Prince in old age, with loving concern, as she saw her father in his physical decline:

A form also gigantic in stature, yet gently thrown forward by evident infirmity; limbs of Herculean mould, and a countenance rather furrowed by the inroads of vehement passions, than the deep traces of years; eyes still emanating the ferocity of an unsubdued spirit, yet tempered by a strong trait of benevolence, which like a glory irradiated a broad expansive brow; a mouth on which even yet the spirit of convivial enjoyment seemed to hover.

Many an old drinking companion of the ever convivial actor–manager would recognise him in that portrait.

Glorvina is, of course, an idealised Sydney. An elfin girl, passionately devoted to her father; incredibly well educated, she is a harpist beyond compare, whose young prince will admit her, in all her Irish simplicity, to the highest circles of English nobility. But the fantasy has connotations. Sydney, without any profound knowledge of Gaelic scholarship, but

Ensign Dighton Pinx.   Jr. Godby sculp.

Miss O'wenson?

14 Portrait of Sydney Owenson as Glorvina, Courtesy of the National Library of Ireland

with a strong love of the old traditional music, had invented a very potent name for her heroine when she called her 'Glorvina'. A favourite form of the old songs was called an 'aisling', or a vision, in which a patriotic theme under the guise of a lovesong was concealed. The vision was usually of a beautiful maiden, who represented Ireland – alone, defenceless and robbed of her rightful inheritance, and the poem promised that an avenging husband, sometimes Napoleon or James II would come and restore her lands, and marry her. The maiden is variously named, sometimes Cathleen ni Houlihan, dark Rosaleen, or Granuaile, and Glorvina, elusive and mysterious, clearly represents that tradition. Her name is made by taking the Irish words 'glor' – meaning voice, and 'binn' meaning sweet, and making Glorvina 'the sweet voiced one'. In this way Glorvina belongs to the old Gaelic poetic tradition, and with her harp and 'wild' aspect embodies the iconography of Ireland as it was known at the end of the eighteenth century.

But with all her pedantic scholarship and antiquarianism, Sydney was also in touch with the poor and dispossessed people of Ireland, who were still singing songs in the street about the death of Emmet:

> Despair in her wild eye a daughter of Erin
> Appeared on the cliff of a bleak rocky shore
> Loose in the wind flowed her dark streaming ringlets
> And heedless she gazed on the dread surges roar
> Loud rang her harp in wild tones of despairing
> And time passed away with the present comparing
> And in soul thrilling strains deeper sorrow declaring
> She sang Erin's woes, and her Emmet no more.

So went the street ballad, and for the singers of patriotic songs, Sydney's image of 'a daughter of Erin' was like their own. Yet, why was the novel such an enormous success in England where such sentiment was not appropriate? Hepworth Dixon, the editor of her *Memoirs* tried to explain:

> It conveyed in a vivid and romantic story curious
> information about the social conditions, the manners,
> customs, literature and antiquities of Ireland. There was in
> it a passionate pleading against the wrongs and injustices
> to which the country and the people were subjected. The
> work dealt with the false ideas about Ireland which
> prevailed in England at the period of misconception and

misrule. As these pleas were put forward in an interesting form they were eagerly read.

So eagerly, in fact, that the book went into seven editions in less than two years. *The Wild Irish Girl*, which seems now a light-weight piece of confection, was popular in England just because it helped liberal consciences, sharpened by the recent events in America and France, to come to terms with their confusion and misgivings about the way in which Ireland had been governed. It gave them something new to think about. While it had seemed quite a good thing to have tried to bring 'civility' to a savage race with a mumbo-jumbo language and a religion based on superstition (as they had been told so many times), it was quite another matter to have tyrannised an ancient civilisation with a strong cultural identity superior in many ways to that of its tyrant. Now, in the form of popular fiction, *The Wild Irish Girl* mixed up all the harsh realities with the new enthusiasm for bardic 'reliques', Gothic scenery, pride of race, and tragic destiny, slipping in warm humanitarian pleas for religious tolerance and alleviation of social and economic hardship. The pill was sweetly sugared, and proved highly palatable. 'The harp that once through Tara's halls' was much more easy to contemplate, through a haze of sentimental tears, than the 'gun peal and slogan cry' which was the other side of the coin. Neither Sydney nor her audience knew what kind of a time bomb she was handling. She was pleading mutual understanding and reconciliation in plots that were as flimsy as any in her father's ramshackle repertoire. It was fit-up scenery and 'tissues of woven air' straight out of the property basket. But the authorities thought differently. Liberal consciences played no part in their scheme of things. They saw her as a dangerous subversive, bringing aid and sustenance to that old canard – the claim to an Irish national identity.

The approach of Dublin Castle, stronghold of such authority, to Sydney was simple. They were most concerned in the short term with her influence upon the Anglo-Irish in Ireland, particularly those of liberal tendencies who were in the pay or patronage of the Castle, but had begun to be indulgent to the idea of 'old' Ireland. How could they suppress the passion for all things 'native' that the book had inspired? Ladies in the vice-regal court were now wearing their hair held in place by golden bodkins, as worn by Glorvina. Dublin jewellers were competing with each other in turning these out, and thus

putting up the price of Irish gold. The drapers were advertising
the 'Glorvina' mantle, a scarlet cloak, as a companion for the
ornament. All this was adding to her fame. They had to
damage her credibility and ruin her reputation – and they
thought they had just the man. This was John Wilson Croker,
her old enemy, author of the *Attack upon the Irish Stage* which
had so agitated Dublin society; to the new political grudge he
could add the personal one he held against her. Though he
wrote anonymously, he had a style that was immediately
recognisable, full of moral superiority and undiluted vitriol.
This is how he reviewed her little book of romantic fiction:

> I accuse Miss Owenson of having written bad novels and
> worse poetry – volumes without number and verses without
> end. Nor does my accusation rest upon her want of literary
> excellence. I accuse her of attempting to vitiate mankind,
> of attempting to undermine morality by sophistry, and
> that under the insidious mask of virtue, sensibility and
> truth . . . such are the charges.

The *Freeman's Journal* in which this criticism appeared, was
supposed to be the paper of popular tendency but, like other
leading Dublin newspapers, it received large sums of money
from the government for the insertion of Castle proclamations,
and was, therefore, open to articles of this type. Croker, always
willing to exercise his talent for demolition, was an eager
contributor. A fortnight later he returned to the assault at
greater length:

> I will be accused of having attacked with coward pen a
> helpless unprotected female; of the atrocious attempt to
> injure infant fame and delicate sensibility; every eye will shed
> a crystal tear for the martyred authoress. I will be accused
> with the elegant lavishness of sorrow, and all the fashionable
> volubility of woe. I will be impeached in every sigh, and
> sentenced in every whisper.

Having thus forestalled opposition he made a further attack on
the young author's potential bad influence on the young:

> I call upon the parental or the appointed guardians of youth.
> I require them to peruse the work, and then pronounce their
> unequivocal judgement on its merits. If they find one page
> which will act towards the increase of moral rectitude,
> one voluntary contribution to virtuous feeling, or

uncontaminated truth, I will not only qualify my assertions
with doubt, but retract them with denial.

Now it was *The Wild Irish Girl* which provided matter for the
same absurd political battlefield that her father had experienced
in the theatre, piloried for his songs about little brown cows
and old Irish feasts. The book, ostensibly attacked for its errors
of style and taste, was really the target of the virulent anti-
nationalist strain in the Ascendancy party, and divided the
ruling class of Ireland into the two strands that always ran
through Anglo-Irish government, expressed either in coercion
or conciliation. Such was the see-saw Sydney had set in motion.

Had she organised all this herself in order to publicise the
book, she could not have done better. A torrent of letters and
poems in her defence flooded in to the *Freeman's Journal*
which, incidentally, was only a four-page production, usually
paying no attention at all to literary topics. By this time Croker
must have realised that he had over-reached himself, and that
instead of squashing Miss Owenson, he had helped to inflate
her reputation. He answered her defenders:

> Let them beware, unpalatable as my former communications
> may have been, the succeeding ones may acquire some
> additional acidity . . . I will not recede from the prosecution
> of the undertaking until I shall have convinced the public of
> the correctness of my original assertion as to the tendency of
> Miss Owenson's work . . . No threats shall have power to
> frighten me into silence while I can render up my humble
> mite to virtue by pointing out vice concealed under her
> trappings, with the semblance of feeling and the mimicry
> of truth.

Whatever his other faults, Croker was always consistent;
throughout his life he kept his pen sharp for Lady Morgan, and
he became ever more powerful as a Tory polemicist when he
left Ireland and the *Freeman's* humble columns, and was able
to spread himself in the influential *Quarterly Review*. But these
attacks only helped to bring her name before the Dublin public,
exactly where she wanted it to be. She even received a letter
from Richard Lovell Edgeworth, father of Maria, which
contained a slight hint of sisterly advice from the more
established novelist:

> As a sincere and warm friend of Ireland, I return you my
> thanks for the just character which you have given to the

lower Irish, and for the sound and judicious observations which you have attributed to the priest. The notices of Irish history are ingeniously introduced and are related in such a manner as to induce belief among infidels . . . . Maria, who reads (it is said) as well as she writes has entertained us with several passages from *The Wild Irish Girl* which I thought superior to any part of the book I had read. Upon looking over her shoulder I found she had omitted some superfluous epithets. Dare she had done this if you have been by? I think she would have dared, because your good taste and good sense would have been instantly her defender.

Neither praise nor criticism could stop her now. As well as arousing the interest of the great Maria, the publicity also brought her unexpected patronage from the very heart of the vice-regal court. The persecution of *The Wild Irish Girl* was typical of the anti-nationalist policy that dominated Castle rule, which permanently administered Irish affairs; but the attitude of the vice-regal court fluctuated with changes in central government. It happened that the Whigs now in power in England had embarked on one of the periodic courses of conciliation in Ireland, and had advised the lord lieutenant of the day not to be so heavy handed. *The Wild Irish Girl* had the sort of literary and social implications which could be accommodated. Miss Owenson was known to be working on a comic opera, and it was hinted that if it was ever produced, it could count on the viceroy's patronage.

It is surprising that with all her father's theatrical connections and her own love of singing, she hadn't tried her hand before at such a project. To show how impromptu the whole thing was, she called it *The First Attempt, or Whim of a Moment*. It was set in Spain, with lots of clandestine wooings and trapdoor escapes. The *Freeman's Journal* of 11 March 1807, changing its tune with the political climate, announced to the public that Miss Owenson had paid £85 for the expense of hiring the Theatre Royal, with thirty guineas for Mr Tom Cooke, the director of the orchestra, for the musical composition, and added 'It requires therefore all the support and countenance of her friends and the public not to let her be a sufferer for contribution to our public amusement.'

Although the background was Spanish, the chief comic character was one O'Driscoll, an Irishman, a part expressly written for her father who had not played on the Dublin stage

for ten years. Her devotion to him was recorded in the
Prologue, written by Joseph Atkinson, a popular playwright of
the time. He reminded the audience:

> That an old favourite of the Thespian art
> Appears this night to take a daughter's part
> That all her powers of filial love engage
> To prove the comfort of a Father's age;
> Hearts formed as yours can such endearments boast
> And those who feel them can applaud the most.

And reminding them also of the recent Crokerisms, he ended:

> Snakes in the grass may hiss and critics hector,
> But she's a woman, and you'll all protect her.

The snake in question was in the audience on the first night,
and even he was forced faintly to admire the play. Then he
turned to his old tack: 'It may damp the pleasure which Miss
Owenson's friends would otherwise derive from my approbation to hear that *The Wild Irish Girl* is not forgotten. Some
circumstances have hitherto prevented a continuation of my
former critical observations upon that subject which will be
immediately resumed.'

But for the moment the resumption of hostilities had to be
postponed, for John Wilson Croker departed from the Dublin
scene to take his seat in the English parliament as member for
Downpatrick. His efforts on behalf of the establishment were
being rewarded. With her chief enemy otherwise engaged, all
was praise and admiration for Sydney. Dublin society took her
up, and she was invited everywhere to sing and play her harp at
parties. Her resemblance to the heroine of her novel was
marked by her being universally called 'Glorvina'. In later years
she wrote about her early popularity without illusions,
remembering that she was only tolerated because she was taken
up by the ladies of the vice-regal court, in a period of
relaxation, and when they were looking for amusement in their
tour of official duty. And as for the permanent 'establishment
society' in Dublin, she knew exactly where she stood with
them:

> As for the Irish Protestant Ascendancy dames, the Mrs. Chief
> Baron This, and the Mrs. Chief Justice That, Mrs.
> Commissioner of Wide Streets, and Mrs. Secretary of the
> Paving Board, she might have perished in the streets in want

15   *Lady Morgan (The Wild Irish Girl)* by Samuel Lover,
National Gallery of Ireland

of infamy, before one of their Ascendancyships would have
stretched forth a finger to save her from either.

The First Attempt was still running when Phillips brought
out a collection of her poems under the title *The Lay of an Irish
Harp*. She, at least, did not seem to take these verses too
seriously as she insists in the Preface that they are but 'metrical
trifles . . . bagatelles . . . vers de societé' put before the public
only because the publisher offered her a good price, and she
needed the money. They are frankly autobiographical and on
the subject of love she documents at least two distinct affairs of
the heart, and pleads for unimpassioned friendship, 'sentiment
and sense', because love has injured her.

Towards the end of the year, Phillips published her *Patriotic
Sketches* written in Connaught. These were much more
revealing of her serious views on political and social problems.
She now faced these more openly than in her novels, diagnosed
the causes of discontent, and suggested remedies with an insight

that later events did much to justify. She tackled the injustice of double tithes, the system where the Catholics had to pay to maintain the Protestant church; many years of bloodshed were to elapse before the importance of this grievance was finally admitted. The other source of discontent, in her opinion, was to be found in the 'middle-men', the agents and overseers of absentee landlords, who were often corrupt and cruel, sometimes fomenting trouble in order to increase their temporary importance. For the rest of her life she attacked the tyranny and officiousness of this class of her own countrymen. While admiring the generous sentiments and sincere feelings for the Irish poor expressed in this book, her biographer W.J. Fitzpatrick cannot help complaining about the excess erudition:

> Of footnotes we have what many readers would be inclined to regard as more than enough. Every sketch abounds with them, and it would seem that the fair author had yet to learn that such illustrations except when unavoidable, completely break up the flowing beauty and encumber the sense of literary composition. The reader in the midst of the most beautiful details is suddenly hurled to the bottom of the page by a falling star!

In this wonderful year of 1807 her opera was repeated several times, and her father was so revitalised that he prepared a farewell benefit on the old marathon proportions. It was to be definitely his last appearance. The theatre bill read:

MR. OWENSON'S NIGHT

On this evening the 27th May, 1807, will be presented a prelude called THE IRISH ACTOR or the RECRUITING MANAGER. Phelim O'Guffinocarrollocraneymacfrane, the Irish actor Mr. Owenson, in which character he will sing first a new characteristic song, written for the occasion called *An Irishman all the world over*, and *Drimunduh* or the Poor Irishman's lament for the loss of his cow. To conclude with a comic occasional address, in the character of the Irish actor, by Mr. Owenson; after which will be performed a comedy called *The West Indian*. To which will be added the admired opera of *The First Attempt*.

So Robert Owenson, the supreme stage Irishman, with his shillelagh under his arm, appeared for the last time on the boards. He played Major O'Flaherty, the role that first introduced him to Dublin, and finished up with O'Driscoll, the role created especially for him by his adoring daughter.

CHAPTER 5

THE ROCKY ROAD TO LONDON

Sydney's opera was well subtitled *The Whim of a Moment* for it was a very flimsy piece. With her customary blunt honesty, she was in no doubt of its lack of worth, for she wrote about it afterwards: 'The success of my little opera was not due to its merit. It was piéce de circonstance, upheld by a party.'

But the enthusiasm with which it was taken up, both socially and critically, showed how much Dublin needed entertaining, and how thin was the competition. The public mood was still low key and depressed. For the time being the dreams of a free and united Ireland were dead. Parliament had been bought and sold; of the members of the Irish House of Commons who voted for the Union not more than seven, it is said, were unbribed. The transactions carried through by Castlereagh had cost Britain nearly a million pounds in secret payments. And in this divided society the scars of the Rebellion were barely healed. Memories of the young men who had ended their lives on the gallows or in exile were still very close to the surface. People from very different ranks of society mourned not only the ill-armed and badly led country boys who had died, but their own friends and brothers. Jonah Barrington in his *Memoirs* recalled how he had dined with seventeen gentlemen in the town of Wexford on the eve of the Rebellion and how, three months later, everyone of that company, barring himself and three others, had been executed, their blackened heads stuck on pikes. Lady Charleville, one of the 'Irish-minded' liberals of the Ascendancy, who had left Dublin for London in the first exodus, writing to Sydney on a more or less literary subject, commented on the impossibility of taking any novel seriously: 'Alas!' she said, 'Our poor Emmet hanging so recently in our streets does not suffer us to enjoy our miseries·in any fiction for years to come.'

There was no immediate danger of further insurrection but

16 *Trinity College, Dublin, seen through the portico of Parliament House* (now the Bank of Ireland) by James Malton, National Gallery of Ireland

'law and order' was punitive. Publishing was chiefly confined to the 'production of devotional and moral tracts, the printing of handbills and plays'; no doubt some of these were for *The First Attempt*. Sydney, with her unique capacity for being in two places at once, took whatever social delights came her way, and at the same time kept a vigilant eye on the political situation. She wrote letters to the papers about the sufferings of the poor, and the state of debtors' prisons. These letters still make powerful and persuasive pleadings, anticipating Charles Dickens's similar concerns by some thirty years. For a young woman who had so recently and painfully got a footing on the social ladder, it took courage thus to force the miseries of the poor upon the conscience of her prosperous and well fed new friends. But everything she did was praised; in those dull times it was amusing to invite this lively young authoress of popular books, who was also willing to play the harp and entertain generally. She was invited to country houses where she had once been as a poor relation or a governess, but came now as an honoured guest. Even in the wilds of Sligo she continued to hear of the praises that were being lavished on her book. 'As much news of that kind as you will' she besought her old pupil, Margot Featherstone. 'I can take flattery in anyway; lay it on with a shovel, or administer it out of a gallon, I can open my mouth and gulp it down.' The *Freeman's Journal*, which had treated her as fair game when Croker was writing for it, now published three adulatory poems addressed to her, and added its own tribute:

> It may justly be said that this young lady is one of the
> greatest ornaments our country could ever boast of: she
> moves in the very highest circles, courted and admired as
> well for her unrivalled talents as her elegant and unaffected
> manners; she is realising we hear a noble independence by
> the exertion of her own highly cultivated and expanded mind.

Another piece of flattery, the most sincerest form, was paid to her by the very eccentric young clergyman, the Reverend Charles Robert Maturin, who borrowed so much from her that he called his first novel *The Wild Irish Boy* and made his main character a proud old chieftain maintaining the ancient glory of Ireland.

All this approval was very gratifying, but Dublin now seemed a dull and provincial place. More interesting attention was coming from over the water. With pressing invitations from Lady Charleville, and other absentees, she made plans for another visit to London.

For someone whose natural position was halfway across the Irish sea, the journey from Dublin to London should have been an easy undertaking, but in 1808 it was a most hazardous journey. First of all there were the sixty odd miles of rough sea crossing to Holyhead. This, with fair weather, could be a trip of about twelve queasy hours, but ships sometimes lay held up by storms for a week or more in the harbour. Once across, there were the twenty-seven miles of the perilous old Anglesey road to the Meni Straits; then the dangerous ferry to the mainland; through the precipitous passes of North Wales into England, and more than two hundred miles – and six days of hard driving – to London. For centuries this route had been trodden flat, sometimes in footprints of blood, by the comings and goings of chainmailed Normans, Elizabethan adventurers, Cromwellian soldiers, horses, cattle, strolling players, poets, playwrights, statesmen and highwaymen. Jonathan Swift, who had himself spent many a weary hour riding horseback from London to Holyhead, left traces of his presence in epigrams written with his diamond ring upon the window panes of wayside inns. He tried to explain why the Bishops of Ireland, all of them appointed in England, were such a villainous lot. It was, he affirmed, that although honest men were sent in the first place, these were always waylaid by footpads and highwaymen on the Holyhead road, who stole their clerical vestments, and forever afterwards impersonated them. He once had the misery of being holed up in Holyhead by wind and weather for several days and described this experience for all travellers everywhere: 'Whoever would wish to live long should live here, for a day is longer than a week, and if the weather be foul, as long as a fortnight!'

But Swift's travels had been in the early 1700s, and when Sydney made her first journey to the metropolis, in 1805, with all the hazards of wind and weather, and perilously steep roads, there was at least a regular coach service between Holyhead and London, with plenty of coaching inns and fresh horses stabled on the way. On that occasion, young and unknown, she had arrived at the 'Swan with Two Necks' in the city of London, too worn out and impecunious to do anything but sit down on her trunk in the yard and fall asleep. Now, though still short of money and luggage, she was nevertheless coming as a celebrity, armed with introductions both for the journey and the metropolis. Not for her this time the 'muddy ale and mouldy bread' of Swift's inns, but an invitation to break her fast at the 'fine old Welsh mansion' of the Dowager Lady Stanley of Penrhos in Anglesey. Lady Stanley had read *The Wild Irish Girl* with admiration, finding it entirely in keeping with her own refined taste for Rousseau and Madame de Staël and she had written a fan letter to Sydney, thus starting a long and rewarding friendship. Sydney, breaking her journey with this new friend, wrote home to Sir Charles Ormsby overwhelmed by the luxury of it all:

> All here is stamped with a character new and impressive to my fancy . . . we sat up till two this morning talking of *Corinne*. I have found a harp and piano here . . . they have loaded my dressing box with perfumes, and such simple things as you know I like . . . the flattery . . . the kindness addressed to me here!

This was just a foretaste of things to come. More flattery and kindness awaited her in London. The Anglo-Irish ladies who had taken her up in Dublin now prepared the way for her entrée into a world outside any of her former experience.

Regency London was the gayest, most flamboyant and the most fashionable city in Europe. The Prince of Wales, though not actually designated Regent until 1811, had long taken over from his ailing father; his style had dominated the look of London and high society since the start of the century. The upper class with money to burn had a sure belief that the English nation was second to none, and the Regency was a triumphant expression of this confidence. In the Season the streets of the West End were crowded with elegant carriages, all outdoing each other for spit and polish and well turned out flunkies. The rows of Hyde Park were thronged with equipages and riding horses belonging both to ladies of '*haut ton*' and to the current favourites of the *demi-monde*, like Harriet Wilson, who could be seen again in the evening with feathers in their hair and rouge on their cheeks in the boxes of the Royal Opera House and the Haymarket Theatre. In Pall Mall, St James and Piccadilly, the centre of 'the world', the dandies and the 'voluptaries of fashion' strolled up and down in their skin-tight 'trowsers', and high white 'starchers', to see and be seen before going on to Whites or to Crockfords, their exclusive clubs, where they played all night at the gaming tables. Then there was Almacks, the very inner temple of exclusiveness, where a ball was held every Wednesday night throughout the Season, and only those approved by a cabal of aristocratic patronesses could get tickets of admission. Not to be admitted to Almacks was social death. The fashionable world was a very narrow circle; nobody of 'ton' ever went to the barbarous outlying areas of London; never, for instance, as far east as Charing Cross. Beau Brummell, it is reported, when asked to dine in Bloomsbury, asked if he would have to change post horses *en route*. Of course, all around there was always the sprawl of old London, the narrow lanes, the gin palaces, the rookeries, the dives, the stews. But fashionable London, gripped by a passion for building, was spreading out in all directions into neo-classical squares and terraces, with far more domestic comfort than the old Georgian style. Regency households could benefit from the products of the new industrialisation. In 1808 Sydney would see the first gas lamps illuminate the streets; her soirées would be lit by gasoliers, and in the houses where she was a guest rudimentary air conditioning and central heating were starting to be installed.

Gambling, racing, eating and fashion dominated the attention of the dandies and fashionable set immediately around the Regent, but in more intellectual circles, political and social issues were livelily and controversially debated. The American and French wars had caused the deeply-rooted old conservative attitudes to be questioned, and defended, with a new fervour and clarity. Publishing and the Press were relatively free for the time being, and issues such as religious toleration, Regency immorality versus evangelical puritanism, and English liberty versus Napoleonic tyranny were eagerly debated, as well as all the immediate and new problems brought into focus by rapid growth of population, urbanisation and social dislocation everywhere.

New schools of writers were developing. Romanticism was on the horizon; Blake and the Lakeland poets, Thomas Campbell and Sir Walter Scott dominated the new poetry, and Byron and Thomas Moore had just started to publish. Maria Edgeworth was the best known Irish writer, and Sydney was the new name. In the language of the Regency, the 'world' meant fashionable society, but literature, politics and fashion were inextricably mixed. The drawing rooms of the great hostesses – their salons – were the entrée into this world, and one of the ways into those hothouses was to become a literary lion. This was the powerful milieu that Sydney dared to confront. Arriving in London at the height of the Season, the little Irish Miss, who had learnt very early in her poverty stricken youth how to play many parts, was now on a very different stage. She knew polite Irish society both from the lowly position of governess and then as the pet of the Dublin grande dames, but she was clever enough when she came to this citadel of exclusivity, the very pinnacle of London society – to play it 'au simple'. She wrote years later:

> I was freshly launched from the bogs of Tireragh and had
> dropped at once into the very sanctuary of English 'ton'
> without time to go through the necessary course of training
> in manner or millinery, for such an awful transition; so with
> no chaperon but my incipient notoriety, and actually no
> toilet but the frock and flower in which not many days
> before I had danced a jig on an earthen floor with an
> O'Rourke, Prince of Breffny, in the county of Leitrim,
> I stepped into my job carriage at the hour of ten.

One of the first people she met was the bearer of a great Irish title, the Countess of Cork and Orrery, who was so much entertained by Sydney's talk that she invited her to her next rout. This placed her right in the middle of 'the world', for the old bewigged and bedizened Countess was one of the keepers of the shrine of high society. When Sydney met her she was well over sixty, and had known everyone worth knowing for forty years. When she was a girl Samuel Johnson, Sheridan, Joshua Reynolds, Edmund Burke and Horace Walpole had constantly visited her mother's house, and Mrs Siddons had been her closest friend. Aspiring in those days to be a bluestocking, she had been told by Johnson 'Dearest, you're a dunce', but with all the affection in the world. Now, in her own fantastically furnished mansion, surrounded by pet animals and birds, 'Corky' held receptions at which the guests were sure of meeting whoever was most conspicuous, for whatever reason, at the moment. Her receptions were categorised by colours – pink for the exclusives, blue for the literary, grey for the religious, and no colour at all for the all-sorts. For her first rout Sydney Owenson was herself the main attraction. She describes how she was exhibited:

I found myself pounced on a sort of rustic seat by Lady Cork. I was treated 'en princesse' and denied the civilised privileges of sofa or chair, which were not in character with the habits of a 'wild Irish girl'. So there I sat, the lioness of the night, exhibited and shown off like 'the beautiful hyena that never was tamed' of Exeter Change, looking almost as wild and feeling quite as savage!

Among the 'high sounding titles of princes and ambassadors and dukes and duchesses announced long before my own poor plebeian Hibernian name puzzled the porter', she caught a glimpse of Byron! 'As we stood wedged on the threshold of fashion my dazzled eyes rested for a moment on a strikingly sullen-looking handsome creature, whose boyish person was distinguished by an air of singularity, which seemed to vibrate between hauteur and shyness. He stood with his arms crossed and alone, occupying a corner near the door, and though in the brilliant bustling crowd was "not of it". "How do, Lord Byron", said a pretty sprite of fashion. I was then ignorant that the young and beautiful inheritor of the historic name was to give it greater claims to the admiration of posterity.'

The two young exotic creatures, brought there to be stared at, stared at each other, and then passed on. Other claimants to the admiration of posterity were also invited to meet her, including the famous actor Kemble, who was 'much pre-occupied and a little exalted'; in other words he was drunk and, being a connoisseur of theatrical perukes, struck his claws in her dark cropped and curly hair, asked her in deeply sepuchral tones: 'Little girl, where did you buy your wig?' Having been persuaded to let go of her hair, he then drew forth a volume of *The Wild Irish Girl*, and 'reading with his deep emphatic voice one of the most high-flown of its passages, he paused, and with the look of Hamlet addressing Polonius he said: 'Little girl, why did you write such nonsense, and where did you get all these damned hard words?'

Most people in London, however, treated her with the utmost respect. She lapped up all the flattery, but let her publisher know all about it, hoping it would bring her better terms for her next book. William Gell, a leading archaeologist of the time, suggested that she might write about the cause of liberty in Greece. At a party at Lady Donegall's they had a long discussion about this, and he drew her a plan of Athens, and suggested books to study. Lady Charleville, who wasn't at all

17   *The Ladies of Llangollen* (Eleanor Butler and Sarah Ponsonby), Courtesy
of National Library of Ireland

averse to being compared with the French savante Madame de
Sevigné, lent her some prints and views of Greece, and
encouraged her with benevolent patronage, and endless letters:

I am delighted that your last effort promises a fair superiority
over your former productions. You should think so, that it
may in fact attain it. A person gifted as you are with fancy,
taste and feeling, requires only a correct attention to the

language and the ripening hand of time, (to prune away
juvenile exuberance, and consolidate the judgement) to write
well. A woman's writing too should ultimately forward the
cause of morality and virtue, and I believe the novel writer
can do more in that way than rigid spirits allow.

Suppressing her 'juvenile exuberance', Sydney now embarked
on the book which was to become *Ida of Athens*. But she had
one more visit to pay before she left England. On her way
home through Holyhead she stopped off at Llangollen, where
lived two remarkable women, whose fame was as strong at
home in Ireland as it was here. For it was from Ireland that
Eleanor Butler and Sarah Ponsonby had come originally.

No doubt Sydney's much admired friend in Dublin, Mary
Tighe the poetess, had given her an introduction to the 'Ladies
of the Vale' as they were called, for Sarah Ponsonby was
related to the Tighes and, before her flight to England, had
lived in Woodstock, the Tighe's country house in Kilkenny. By
1808 the 'Ladies' were famous – the 'most celebrated virgins in
Europe', so Prince Puckler Muskau, the German travel writer
called them. (Incidentally, he was to be as banal about Sydney
herself, many years later.) They had left Ireland long ago, in
1778, to the bewilderment and rage of their aristocratic
families. Eleanor Butler was thirty-nine, and Sarah Ponsonby
was twenty-six. Both of them had firmly refused suitors and
marriage, desiring only the companionship of each other. This
'unnatural' friendship horrified their families and they were
kept apart. They managed to 'elope' but were hounded down
and recaptured, trying to catch the boat for England. Sarah had
nearly died of grief; Eleanor was threatened with incarceration
in a French convent. They escaped again, dressed as men, and
with a faithful maid Mary Caryl, left Ireland for ever. From the
boat, they took the stagecoach, meaning to get to London but
their money had been cut off, and they could not afford to go
further than Llangollen, where they found a cottage to rent;
here in 'Plas Newydd' they settled down to lead a life of
extraordinary domestic intensity for nearly half a century. In
the early days the scandal and recrimination that followed them
made them notorious. Irish outrage turned to English disapproval. Their constant wearing of mannish riding habits and
black beaver hats was considered immodest. The word
'sapphism' was used. Mrs Piozzi, Dr Johnson's friend, wrote in
1795: 'It is now common to suspect impossibilities (such as I

think 'em) whenever two ladies live too much together.'

But in time most people merely recognised the existence of what was a more acceptable relationship altogether, that of romantic friendship, and Sarah and Eleanor, with their passion for country retirement, good works, intellectual pursuits, French novels, gardening and the single state, became an international cult. Their guest books registered not only royal visitors, but soldiers and inventors, philanthropists and men of letters. The Duke of Wellington came to call; Wordsworth and Southey composed under their roof. Josiah Wedgewood lectured them on rock formations, and Wilberforce and Sir Humphrey Davey asked for their advice. Yet they always retained their deep desire for seclusion, declaring that they never spent a night away from their own home; their private life was lived among a group of close and devoted women friends, and their private life was their own affair.

Among the famous names in the visitors' book was one that must have stirred Sydney, because it was very close to her own experience of Ireland's recent tragic history. This was an entry in 1792, for the visit of Madame de Genlis, and her accomplished 'adopted' daughter Pamela. Stephanie Felicité du Crest de Saint Aubin, Comtesse de Genlis, was a very influential writer of educational theories. She had been governess to the children of the Duc d'Orleans, Philippe Egalité, and lived to see her former pupil, Louis Philippe, on the throne of France. She had been the mistress of Philippe, and Pamela was said to be really their child. As Pamela later married Lord Edward Fitzgerald, who died in the Rebellion of 1798, Sydney knew all the tragic circumstances of this family, for Lord Edward was one of her great heroes, and she used him as a character in her novel, *The O'Briens and the O'Flaherties*. But here, in the little oak panelled cottage parlour, among the Aeolian harps, the Gothick lanterns, china, gold initialled books and all the profusion of gifts and tributes brought to them by admirers, the 'Ladies' relived the horror of the Rebellion and Sydney, in view of the high Ascendancy views of her hostesses, no doubt kept her nationalist sympathies under control.

Because of their mutual interest in the protagonists, they must have told her how in 1798 Llangollen was buzzing with rumours brought over by the Irish travellers on the Holyhead road. One day, in May of that year, the landlady of the local inn 'The Hand' had stopped them to say that she suspected

18 *Lady Pamela Fitzgerald and her daughter* by Mallry,
National Gallery of Ireland

Lady Edward Fitzgerald was in her house. They found that it was indeed the same Pamela, who had visited them six years before with her 'adopted' mother. They asked Pamela to call on them, for her rank was as high as their own, although she now was tainted in their eyes, with the sin of republicanism. Pamèla Egalité was not quite the same as the gentle protegée of Mme de Genlis. There was a brief ten minute meeting, and both ladies burst into tears at the plight of the poor fugitive and her two babies. For Pamela, with Lord Edward lying mortally wounded in Dublin, had been ordered to leave the country. She was trying to escape to Hamburg, hoping her husband would recover and join her there. Sarah Ponsonby remembered 'She had an idea of passing the day here, but we persuaded her principally for her own sake, and a little for our own, to proceed as fast and as incognito to London, the mind of the people in this country being so exasperated against the Cause in which she was, I fear, deeply engaged, that one dreaded her being insulted.' So they let poor Pamela go, and settled down again into their own chosen, comfortable exile. Sydney must have listened to the story with mixed feelings, before she packed her bags to go back to Ireland.

When she eventually arrived home she had to face some of the realities of her own life. She was now over thirty; she had no real settled home but lived in comfortable lodgings. Molly Kane looked after her father and sister. They all depended on what Sydney could earn from her writing, every penny of which had to be negotiated, in hard terms, with each book. Her younger sister was delicate, and needed care and comforts which her father could not supply. Sydney found Olivia a job as a governess with one of her own patrons who she was confident would not work her sister too hard, and would give her a good home. She herself slipped back into the long-running affair that she had been conducting with a prominent Dublin barrister, Sir Charles Ormsby, who was a widower, and quite a lot older than herself. It might have led to marriage; his letters found among her papers were certainly those of a lover, and on a package of her letters, together with a ring that she had given to him, she wrote 'One of the most brilliant wits, determined roués, agreeable persons, and ugliest men of his day.' For several years they were regarded as a pair, but he was always in debt, and involved in other dubious commitments. They had begun to quarrel long before she left Dublin, and her visit to London was the occasion for a more than usually violent disagreement from which their intimacy never really recovered. And now her sister had found a follower.

Olivia had been governess to the Brownrigg family for only a short time when she met one of those professional wits and flaneurs who were a feature of Dublin life now that the high society had gone, and doctors and lawyers dominated the smart set. Olivia's Dr Clarke was a physician to the navy and highly regarded in his profession. He was quite an oddity. 'A dwarf in height, a buck in dress, a wit, a musician, a man of science, a lover of quips and anecdotes . . . , such was the tiny, seductive and most respectable gentleman who proposed to the charming governess of General Brownrigg's children.' Not exactly the most romantic of lovers to capture the heart of a young girl, but he offered a good house in fashionable Great George Street, a carriage, the means to keep her in comfort, and most of all, a home for her father and old Molly. In addition he was agreeable and intelligent, and Olivia accepted him gladly. Soon, having cured the Lord Lieutenant of some skin complaint, he was knighted 'for public services', and old Owenson, comfortable and settled at last, had the pleasure of hearing his younger daughter addressed as Lady Clarke. Sydney continued to keep her own apartments, and independence, but whether through overwork, or too much of the demanding social round, or slight envy at seeing her sister not only married but addressed as 'your ladyship' as well, she gave way to what she called 'that internal oppression which at intervals preys upon me so heavily'. Her unsatisfactory affair with Ormsby was over; she was receiving unaccustomed criticism from Phillips for the work she had in progress, and for once her ability to put a good face on everything failed her. She wrote an admission of dejection to Lady Stanley, that kind old woman in Anglesey who had admired her and given her hospitality:

> I feel that young as I am, I have lived long enough; my existence, made up of epochs, has given a high and false tone to my feelings which calls for that excitation no longer to be obtained. I live in a state of torpor, nothing touches me, and I resemble some unfortunate animal whom experimental philosophy has placed in an 'exhauster', with this difference, that it is still susceptible of vital powers, but that I am beyond the possibility of renovation. This will all seem romance to you, and you will laugh; but were I sitting with you over the fire, I could make you understand me.

'The excitation no longer to be obtained' had become the drug that she would crave for the rest of her life.

She picked away at her book about Greece, but filled up most of her time with a round of visits, a prey to all the lion hunters in Ireland. In October, when all fashionable Dublin moved to Kilkenny for amateur theatricals, she accepted an invitation to spend three weeks at Kilkenny Castle, that stonghold of the Butlers from which Lady Eleanor had escaped so many years before. The gaiety was feverish; a large dinner party every day, and a play or a concert every night, with a ball and late supper to follow. 'Meanwhile, the poor book lies by', she confessed to Lady Stanley, 'Heart still taking the lead of the head in the old way.' But in spite of the social demands, she managed to knock off three volumes, and sent them to London, but the old fox Phillips, discerning the haste and distractions under which they had been written, turned them down, and she had to look elsewhere for a publisher. The novel was accepted by Longmans, who nevertheless remonstrated against some parts of it. They objected to her 'promulgating deistical principles', and 'being tainted with the philosophy of the new school of French moralists'. She defended herself with her deeply held conviction that organised religion is irrelevant to intrinsic human virtue, and the man who promotes the happiness of his fellow creatures is a virtuous man, which in effect was more or less agreeing to the charge. In Ireland, divided by sectarian religion, that made her a very brave soul indeed.

But in *Ida of Athens* she was also taking up another difficult cause – the defence of her own sex in a male-dominated world. In each of her three previous stories the central female character had been drawn much more distinctly than that of the man; she was influenced even more in this direction by Madame de Staëls novel, *Corinne*, published in 1807. This work had become the talking point in the correspondence between Sydney Owenson and thoughtful friends like Lady Stanley and Lady Charleville, who had started to call her 'the Irish de Staël'. This was a very high horse for her to ride, for Germaine de Staël was everything she admired. For one thing, she spoke and wrote in French. She was the daughter of Jacques Necker, the finance minister of Louis XVI, and as such she had lived all her life at the centre of á circle of brilliant and important men. She wrote as boldly and as authoritatively as any of them on matters of politics, education, literature, science and, most significantly for Sydney, on the status of women. To Germaine de Staël this was always highly relevant to the condition of literature, as well as indicative of the standard of morality in the community. The Greeks, she said, did not permit women to perform their natural function of elevating morals and taste. 'Concern with private affairs', she argued, 'depends entirely upon the role that women play in a country.' So Sydney, emulating her example, set herself consciously to expound the innate merits of the feminine character. She defined these attributes in her Preface to Ida: 'that almost innate propensity to physical and moral beauty, that instinctive taste for the fair ideal, and that lively and delicate susceptibility to ardent and tender impressions which should distinguish the character of woman in its purest and highest state of excellence!'

Ida is a beautiful and intellectual Greek maiden whose lover has had to flee the country after an unsuccessful revolt. A cynical and self-indulgent English aristocrat, travelling in Europe, falls in love with her, proposes to make her his mistress, and cannot understand why she, with a mixture of affection and disdain, refuses him. The scene moves to London where Ida, after suffering as a refugee, suddenly inherits a fortune and is taken up by London society. She wastes herself and her money on sycophantic guests only to discover their basic insincerity. At the end, her dissipated suitor, in a burst of untypical nobility, reunites her with her true love, who is now a Russian general plotting another Greek revolt. Sydney's passion for civil and religious liberty found full scope in this story of Greek struggle, but Ireland's woes were also remembered in the analogy of usurping barbarism subjugating native religion and culture. Wearing her 'de Staël' hat, she ranges over definite theories of education, religion, and ethics, and Ida is revealed as a perfect idealist, tolerant and advanced, deriving all her beliefs from the laws of nature, rather than from human dogma.

The book came out in four volumes in 1809, and in a Preface of ineffable naive egotism, she laid herself open to her enemies. To cover up any deficiencies in her material, she claimed that she had written it in three months, that she never corrected a proof sheet, and that she was supremely confident of its acceptance through the love and indulgence of her public. Too much flattery had obviously distorted her customary common-sense. Miss Jane Austen reacted with gentle satire: 'We have got Ida of Athens by Miss Owenson', she wrote in a letter, 'which must be very clever, because it was written, as the authoress says, in three months. We have only read the Preface yet, but her Irish Girl does not make me expect much. If the warmth of her language could affect the body, it might be worth reading in this weather.' Perhaps Miss Austen derived some satisfaction, as the book came out usefully enough in December.

It happened that a new political and literary periodical, the *Quarterly Review*, had just been launched to maintain Tory principles by ruthlessly attacking anyone who wrote with other political affiliations. *Ida of Athens* had the distinction of being the very first victim of this new policy of literary terrorism, and Gifford its editor had a new colleague to help him with his 'slashing' reviews. Though anonymous, the attack on *Ida* bore all the marks of her old enemy, J. Wilson Croker. The plot is pulled to pieces, the Preface is ridiculed, her language is described as 'an infatuated jargon composed of terms picked up in all countries, and wholly irreducible to any ordinary rules of grammar or sense'. Her sentiments are condemned as 'mischievous in tendency and profligate in principle, licentious and irreverent in the highest degree'. She is advised to buy a spelling book, and a pocket dictionary and to take lessons in 'joined-hand', and then she is treated to this astonishing piece of advice:

If afterwards she could be persuaded to exchange her idle raptures for commonsense, practice a little self-denial, and gather a few precepts from an old fashioned book, which although it does not seem to have lately fallen in her way, may yet, we think, be found in some corner of her study, she might then hope to prove, not indeed a good writer of novels, but a useful friend, a faithful wife, a tender mother, and a respectable and happy mistress of a family.

Croker was on safer ground with the *Quarterly* than he had been with the *Freeman's Journal*, for the former did not publish protesting letters. But for all his misogynism and personal grudge he still failed to do Sydney any harm.

The other reviews were more sympathetic. The *Monthly Review* preferred *Ida* to *Corinne*, finding the heroine attractive and the story more probable, although it warned her against 'the strange phrases which swarm in these pages'. Lady Charleville sent her a long and detailed letter, giving the reaction of her fashionable friends:

I find particular ingenuity in the novel attempt to interest us for a woman who loved two: . . . and for each of the lovers the episode was happily contrived in this plan, and executed with great taste and wit . . . . I do heartily reprobate your putting off the period of polishing and purifying your language for pique to those censors, who, after all may be the best of friends, if they point out a path so attainable to fame.

Thus she received her usual mixture of praise and blame. But her compassionate picture of the plight of the Greeks under Turkish rule appealed very much to the sentimental nationalism then in the air, for Greece and liberty were top of the list with young romantics. As Byron sardonically put it in a letter to Thomas Moore:

> When a man hath no freedom to fight for at home,
> Let him combat for that of his neighbours.
> Let him think of the glories of Greece and of Rome
> And get knocked on the head for his labours.

In 1811, Byron, in character very like her own dissipated and disillusioned English aristocrat hero went off to Athens, and eventually got 'knocked on the head for his labours'. He obviously had read *Ida of Athens* for he discusses it in a note to *Childe Harold's Pilgrimage*, and though his tone is bantering, he gives it quite a puff.

CHAPTER 6

MISS O BECOMES MILADY

The mixed reception given to *Ida* both sobered Sydney and slowed her down. She was not Mme de Staël after all, not even an Irish version. Neither was her private life all it seemed. The infant prodigy was now over thirty. Her bluestocking women friends, for the most part older and more settled than herself, continued to treat her as a talented child, and to send her presents of dress materials – 'a bit of black velvet for a warm winter garment; 'tis only English velvet as you will see, but it looks nearly as well as the best by candlelight', was one such offering from Lady Stanley, as well as a few cast-off 'gowns'. She responded gratefully, and played up her 'greenest youth' and her 'young, gay and giddy spirit'. There was always a string of male admirers who liked to write to her as if she were the very young and fairylike Glorvina. They called her their 'volatile little girl', sent her 'elegant trifles', and were glad to 'execute little commissions for her', but they all had some fatal impediment as far as marriage was concerned. Some had invalid wives who persisted in lingering on; others had mountains of unpaid debts. Her young sister Olivia called this court of middle-aged widowers, or near widowers, reformed rakes and clergymen with literary leanings 'Sydney's army of martyrs'. From her earliest girlhood she had cultivated romantic flirtations – they were the dress rehearsals for her fictions, but they never turned to real love affairs, apart from the half denied, much conjectured relationship with Sir Charles Ormsby, her *'bien aimé'* for many years. He was the most persistent of her widower following and the one who came nearest to suiting the worldly, pragmatic side of her nature. But there was no engagement. He was considerably older than Sydney, with a family of grown up sons; successful enough to have earned a knighthood, he was nevertheless too typical of the Dublin smart set of the time; always in debt and a bit raffish. She was charmed by his wit and his worldliness and he certainly didn't treat her as a 'dear little girl'. But her well developed sense of her own worth made her hold back. Writing later about this time she remembered the dangers of her situation, living alone in her own apartments, a most emancipated thing to do in that city of mischievous gossip and backbiting. 'Inconsiderate and indiscreet, never saved by prudence, but often rescued by pride; often on the verge of error, but never passing the line.'

She no longer had family responsibilities for her father who was settled comfortably with Olivia and his son-in-law. Robert Owenson now spent convivial evenings with old cronies and young Trinity undergraduates, one of whom William Maginn, when later he became editor of the English magazine *Frasers*, conjured up the memory of the old man:

> Your goodly figure rises in whiteheaded, rednosed beauty
> before our mental optics, fresh as a daisy in the Spring. Still
> ring in our ears the glorious chorus of your songs – amatory,
> convivial, political, jocular, in all the dialects of Ireland, from
> the antique Milesian down to the disguised English of
> Connaught – nor can we take it upon us to assert that 'we
> ever heard you sing the praises of water!

To the people of Dublin, however, Sydney was still the golden girl with the Midas touch. Her books and her name were constantly before them; her letters to the paper on behalf of the little chimney sweeps or the homeless poor had give her a reputation for warm-hearted philanthropy. She was a patriotic Irishwoman who yet was clever enough to make money in England, and have the ear of the powerful ruling class. Such was her fame that when a poor Dublin postman named Barnaby Fitzpatrick was found guilty of stealing a money order from a letter and sentenced to death, in despair he wrote from his cell and begged her to use her influence to save him. She was sufficiently moved by his faith in her powers to canvass around energetically on his behalf, but her most influential friends told her that the case was hopeless. Then she made an appeal to Ormsby although they were in one of their periodic estrangements. 'Seriously and without sentiment' she wrote, 'my dear friend, rally your deceased feelings in my favour. I depend on you; for once forget yourself and remember me.' His feelings for her were sufficiently alive for him to answer her appeal and he helped her to approach the Viceroy's wife. Such was the power of life and death of this otherwise ordinary lady that they got the sentence lessened to transportation. The man went to Australia with his family, and henceforward lived a happy and useful life. With no ulterior motive but with the same energy and courage with which she had kept her own beloved father afloat, Sydney had saved the life of this pathetic man and his family.

But when the excitement of this particular campaign had died down she was again low in spirits. Again she confided to her diary: 'I am in possession of all the fame I ever hoped or ambitioned; I wear not the appearance of twenty years; I am now, as I generally am, sad and miserable.'

But she was still extremely vivacious in public. What she called her 'flimsy, fussy, flirty Celtic temperament' was irrepressible.

The desire to please was as strong in her as the desire to perform in public must have been to her father, but her stage was the *salon* and the *boudoir* of high society. Here she played her harp and danced for the entertainment of those Ascendancy lords and ladies who professed to love the quaint Irish customs. She had already created her role model of the idealised Irish colleen in one of her earlier ballads, published in 1805, which she sang on many occasions:

> Oh did you not hear of Kate Kearney
> She lives on the banks of Killarney
> From the glance of her eye
> Shun danger and fly
> For fatal's the glance of Kate Kearney.
>
> For that eye is so modestly beaming,
> You ne'er think of mischief she's dreaming
> Yet, oh I can tell
> How fatal's that spell
> That lurks in the eyes of Kate Kearney.

Kate Kearney, or Milady? This strong dichotomy in the character of Sydney Morgan has confused her critics for generations and damaged her reputation, particularly in Ireland where she has been dismissed by more than one critic, with the arrogance that comes from received opinion rather than personal study, as a 'trashy novelist'. She has been forgotten for her real worth, and remembered more for her personality and social gifts – which is an occupational hazard for the Irish

19 *Kitty Kearney going to market* from *Hall's Ireland*

even to this day. So many talented Hibernians have, through the years, either from choice or necessity, danced a jig to amuse the 'quality'. Sydney was very good at this – and was well rewarded for her trouble. But the best part of her, her sincere patriotism and intellectual honesty, always were reflected in her writing where she dared to be controversial, even unpopular; but such was her background and nature that she could not help playing up – not to the gallery – but to the great and famous. Their applause marked the measure of the distance she had placed between Miss Owenson, the famous authoress, and the two forlorn little girls left in shabby lodgings, in the care of old Molly, with no money to meet their expenses. To the end of her life she thought of her position in society as a battle won. The titles and wealth of her conquests were as so many bouquets of flowers tossed on to the stage after a successful performance.

For one who remembered so clearly 'seeing a father frequently torn to prison, a mother on the point of beggary with her children'; for one who had been evicted from shabby theatrical lodgings with her little sister, and their one friend, their maid, the invitation that now came to her to join the household of Lord and Lady Abercorn must have been impossible to refuse. For the Marquis and Marchioness of Abercorn – if it were scalps she was after – were indeed splendid trophies to add to her collection.

Not only to Sydney but to the rest of society, John James Hamilton Ninth Earl, and First Marquis was the embodiment of the aristocratic ideal. With the blood of the Stuarts in his veins he was a peer in the three kingdoms, and cousin to many of the noblest families in all three. He was rigid with protocol and high breeding and no novelist would have dared to invent him. He had been married three times and had been the centre of a wretched and romantic divorce, in which he had lost custody of several of his children. Always formally dressed, he wore all his decorations, Star and Garter and all, on the hunting field, and showed no emotion in public about anything. He moved in stately procession, with his third wife Jane-Anne and many assorted children, between his thousand acre estates in Northern Ireland, Scotland and the great house at Stanmore Priory in England. The Marquis was genuinely convinced that people of lower orders were of a different nature, even differently put together. His groom of chambers had orders to fumigate the rooms used by the family after liveried servants had been in them, and the chambermaids had to wear white kid gloves when making his bed. At this time of history this type of the English aristocrat, no matter how personally charming, was probably the most arrogant in Europe. After all, only a few years earlier in France his counterparts had had their heads cut off for less lordly behaviour.

Lord and Lady Abercorn had met Sydney in London at some grand party, and her reputation as a writer of fashionable books had caught Lady Abercorn's attention. The latter was a restless, febrile personality, always looking for diversions, who thought it would be amusing to have Sydney as a live-in lady companion, a sort of writer in residence; it would bring a cachet to the household, as distinguished perhaps as having a hermit living in an ornamental grotto in the grounds. Lord Abercorn was handsome, sarcastic and a roué. He flirted heavily with Sydney, called her his 'sweet Glo', and his 'dear little fool'. She needed all her vaunted commonsense and early radical indoctrination to withstand his attentions. The Marchioness, however, helped her constantly to remember that 'she had no place in the society upon which she now looked but that which whim had accorded or charity bestowed'.

Lady Abercorn was as much of a *monstre sacreé* as her husband. Sydney later used her as model for the spoilt and petulant Lady Llanberris in her novel *The O'Donnel* and paid back a few scores, for Jane-Anne was full of the divine right to be amused and obeyed. 'Goodnatured, and inconsequent, she took people up warmly and dropped them easily; she was incapable of permanent attachment except to those belonging to herself', so Sydney described her fictional character, and her real life employer. When the invitation came to join the Abercorns Sydney was 'resting', not engaged either emotionally or creatively in anything engrossing. This lull in her life was pleasant enough, with plenty of friends, her own apartments, and an amusing social round. She was reluctant to give it up for Lady Abercorn's patronage for if she did, she would have to cut herself off from Dublin completely. The Abercorns were far too grand for what they considered a second-rate provincial city. But her Dublin friends, perhaps more conscious than she that her life had reached an impasse, encouraged her to go for the sake of the social opportunities that the new life offered. Perhaps she might even find a husband. The Abercorns wanted her to commit herself to them indefinitely, but her friends advised her to keep her options open and return to Dublin when she had had enough of grandeur; on these terms she accepted.

Her letters to her three closest friends, Lady Charleville, Lady Stanley and Mrs Lefanu, tell the story of this period of her life with all her customary resolution to make the best of her situation. She reported how much she was loved and appreciated: 'I am at the moment the best lodged, best fed and dullest author in his Majesty's dominions', she wrote to Mrs Lefanu.

> What is it to you that I live in one of the largest palaces in England, and that the sound of a commoner's name is refreshment to my organs, wearied out with the thrilling vibrations of 'Your Royal Highness', 'Your Grace', and 'Your Majesty'. The house is no house at all for it looks like a little town, which you will believe when I tell you that a hundred and twenty people slept under the roof during the Christmas holidays, without including the upper servants.

She was, in effect, a sort of upper servant herself, though the Abercorns treated her with kindness; almost, if not quite, as one of the family. She was always addressed in correspondence by Jane-Anne as 'dear Miss O', and called 'Glorvina' in conversation. She extolled the glories of the palace to some of her correspondents, but sometimes she dared to criticise:

> I hear of nothing but politics and the manner in which things are considered give me a most thorough contempt for the 'rulers of the earth'. I am certain that the country, its welfare or prosperity never for a moment take a part in their speculation; it is all a little miserable system of self interest, paltry distinctions of private pique, and personal ambition.

But still she stayed. Partly to justify her position as 'writer' and partly out of boredom she started on a new novel. The travelling court was now encamped at Baron's Court in the north of Ireland where social life was not nearly so intense as in England. With her usual flair for anticipating trends, she now moved into the exotic realms of the Orient, already taken up by some French novelists, and as Sir Charles Ormsby had a library of books about India she made peace with him long enough to borrow what she wanted about that country. She called the work in progress *The Missionary*, and as an after dinner diversion from cards and gossip she read out to the assembled company what she had written during the morning.

The Marquis declared it was the greatest nonsense he had ever heard in his life, while Lady Abercorn yawned over it 'very dismally', but the other guests, for want of better sport, clamoured for more. When the book was finished she made arrangements to go over to England to see to its publication, and took the opportunity to dally in Dublin on the way. Lady Abercorn, who had a passion for ordering anything she had heard of or read about which seemed to be amusing, gave her a long list of commissions: she asked for harps, for books, for romantic Irish jewellery, 'on approval' as she always disliked or grew tired of these objects. Sydney took orders for numerous 'glorvinas' for Jane-Anne's stepdaughters and friends, and a small, ten-guinea Irish harp, all of which Jane-Anne asked her 'dear Miss O', on receipt, to change, 'as I know you do not mind trouble'.

Sydney so much enjoyed being in Dublin again that she sent her book on ahead to Phillips, her regular publisher. But, as usual, they quarrelled over terms, and after setting up the first volume Phillips refused to proceed. The Abercorns, in their stately round had now moved to England, so Lady Abercorn undertook to negotiate with a new publisher for her protegée; as she said of the book: 'Though I never wished to hear it read ten pages at a time, I am very impatient to see it all together.' But the great lady soon got tired of this new game of negotiating with publishers, and Sydney had to come over to England to see to matters herself. In complete contrast to the remote seclusion of Baron's Court, situated as it was in the wilds of rural Ireland, Stanmore Priory was a centre of high political and fashionable life. Close to London, it was easily accessible for weekend visits and, in spite of the Marquis's ultra Toryism, its doors were open to guests from both political parties – so long as the members were rich and famous. Sydney was amazed at some of the antics of the weekend guests:

How often have I seen Whigs and Tories united round the splendid hearths in the great drawing room, innocently playing their 'small games', having played through the preceding week their great games on the opposite side of the two Houses. How often have I seen the ministerial red box scarcely deposited in the hands of the diplomatic owner before it was suddenly jerked up in the air by the playful ingenuity of a romping peeress, and its mysterious contents scattered on the floor.

If one of the reasons for her having left Dublin in the first place was to advance her social position, it had certainly been justified. Now she had enough confidence to break finally with the not very satisfactory Ormsby. A letter to him found in her papers after her death was endorsed in her own handwriting:

> Last farewell letter to Sir C. Ormsby, returned with the rest of my letters and my ring after his death which took place in 1816: 'I am told you have had the kindness to call more than once since our arrival in town at my door. It is with inexpressible regret that I am obliged to decline your visits. I have no hesitation in declaring that I prized your society beyond any enjoyment within my sphere of attainment, and that in relinquishing it for ever I do a violence to my feelings which raises me in my own estimation, without reconciling me to the sacrifice I have made. At least do not withdraw from me your esteem; it is the only sentiment that ever ought to subsist between us. I owe you a thousand kindnesses, a thousand attentions; my heart is full of them. Whilst I exist, the recollection of all I owe you shall form a part of that existence. Farewell!'

So old lovers were dismissed, and old enemies reassessed. Lord Castlereagh – who for ten years she had regarded as a heartless villain, the architect of Ireland's wrongs; whose Act of Union she had repeatedly and forcibly denounced as 'corrupt and calamitous, atrocious in its principles and abominable in its means' – often spent weekends at Stanmore, and she found, to her surprise, that he was 'one of those cheerful, liveable, give and take persons, who are so invaluable in villa life, where pleasure and repose are the object and the end. His implacable placidity, his cloudless smile, his mildness of demeanour, his love of music, his untuneable voice and passion for singing all the songs in the Beggars' Opera, and the unalterable good humour . . . rendered him most welcome in all the circle'. And this charming companion was the man of whom Byron wrote:

> So Castlereagh has cut his throat – the worst
> Is that his own was not the first.

and Shelley added his tribute:

> I met murder on the way –
> He had a mask like Castlereagh.

With her Irish patriot's hat on, Sydney would have agreed with these verdicts, but for the moment she was on a different stage, with all the wealth and prowess of Tory England as her supporting cast. The role was irresistible. She wrote to Lady Stanley:

> I have been involved, engaged, dazzled, and you who are a philosopher and see human nature just as it is will account for and excuse this and say 'she is not ungrateful nor negligent, she is only human'. My entreé here was attended by every circumstance that could render it delightful or gracious to my feelings . . . . I hold my place of first favourite, and the favour I formerly enjoyed seems rather increased than diminished.

Lord Castlereagh proved more than amiable; he was useful; he would listen courteously to her laments on the sorrows of her country – for part of her amusement value to the Abercorns were her vehemently expressed nationalist sentiments. It was entertaining for them, in the safety of their own stronghold, to profess tolerance for their 'little rebel'. Castlereagh's favourite comment was 'No one cares for Ireland but Miss Owenson and I.' His lordship was perhaps the greatest admirer of *The Missionary* which could be tolerated, even admired for its liberal tone, as it was not about Ireland. He offered his carriage to take her to London to see her publisher, and allowed the meeting to take place in his own cabinet office. Overwhelmed by the grandeur of the surroundings and the presence of the Foreign Secretary, Stockdale the publisher promptly accepted the book and agreed to pay four hundred pounds. With Sydney backed by such patronage it is not surprising that Sir Thomas Lawrence, the most fashionable portrait painter of the day volunteered to draw her. 'He painted it of his own free will and choice, gratuitously', she wrote long afterwards (turning a sketch into a painting with her usual hyperbole), 'and that too when rival duchesses were contending for the honour of reaching posterity through his agency, all ready and willing to remunerate this talent with princely munificence.' The drawing was originally intended to form the engraved frontispiece for *The Missionary*. Leaning back on a *fauteuil* with as much nonchalance as any duchess, Sydney is dressed in a white muslin robe, with short petticoats and a shorter waist; her forehead concealed by a short fringe; looking more like a heroine of fiction indeed than her own confection – the lovely Brahmin princess Luxima; but when it came to publication, for

20 *Miss Owenson* by Sir Thomas Lawrence, Courtesy of the National Library of Ireland

some professional reason of his own, Lawrence would not allow his name to appear on the frontispiece drawing.

The fact that *The Missionary* was any good at all is remarkable. She worked on it in the mornings, but when it was read after dinner the distinguished guests all made their contributions which they expected the authoress to incorporate. In plot it resembles *St. Clair* with its simplicity of structure and concentration on the psychological states of two idealistic young people who fall in love, without being aware of it. Sydney had read up a great deal of Indian customs, history, and antiquities and many French novels on similar themes. The missionary, Hilarion, is a Portuguese priest, a nobleman of course, who goes to India to convert the heathen. Her first biographer, W.J. Fitzpatrick admiringly summarised the plot:

> Great success attends his labours at first but in an evil hour a Hindoo lady of surpassing beauty whom he had addressed in the language of fraternal charity brings her rich black eyes charged with amatory power to bear with deadly aim upon him. The struggle between duty and inclination which follows is in the highest degree terrific. In the course of a short time the lady is borne to eternity by an epidemic fever. Even the bed of death does not allay the unholy torment which rages within the Missionary's breast. He casts away his breviary and stole, and lives a sort of anchorite life in the recesses of a gloomy cave, his sole companion a pet fawn which had often been caressed by the beautiful Luxima.

It is very easy to send this book up. Even Fitzpatrick sees its comic potential and comments: 'We can say as Sheridan said when the servant threw down a china plate with a great crash without breaking it:- "You rascal, how dare you make all that noise for nothing!" ', and a contemporary critic coined a generic phrase for such novels, alluding to the 'amatory ladies of the Owensonian school'. But Miss Owenson herself, to the last moment of her life, attached some importance to it, and was engaged just before her death in completely remodelling this novel and seeing it once more through the press. The book also made a deep impression on Shelley, who was reading it at the time of his first attachment to Harriet Westbrook. He compared the graceful Luxima, gliding in and out of grottoes 'like a disembodied spirit', to his own love, pure, gentle and kind as well as beautiful ... 'The changing tints of her complexion resembled the dissolving tints of an iris'. He wrote to his friend Hogg:- 'It is a divine thing ... Luxima the Indian princess, were it possible to embody such a character is perfect. *The Missionary* has been my companion for some time.' He goes on, in an extravagance of praise: 'Since I have read this book I have read no other.' Such praise of Luxima, excessive to the point where he expressed his wish that she might be a living person for him to love, helped him to disguise his growing passion for Harriet, which he was not yet ready to admit to Hogg.

Byron was less impressed; at least he did not identify any of his current mistresses with Luxima. Although he was now living in Italy, he must have received it in his mail, for in letters to Moore and to Murray, giving an account of his current reading, he comments in doggerel verse:

I read the *Missionary* – Pretty? Very!

and Moore may well have soaked himself in it to boost his oriental lore. His description of the Vale of Cashmere in 'Lalla Rookh' is more than somewhat reminiscent of Miss Owenson's.

But all this admiration, indeed adulation, could not disguise from Sydney the fact that she was really not much more than she had been when she was a governess, and that her role here was to sit in the crossfire between the Marquis and his third wife's humours – to calm them down when they were ruffled, and to brighten them up when they were dull with her own good spirits and sprightly conversation. She was also in the firing line for his lordship's inclinations for exercising his '*droits de seigneur*'. She could cope easily with his world weary and cynical attempts at seduction, but her situation irked her nevertheless. All that she had won for herself through talent and hard work was insignificant when compared with the hereditary power and consequence of this family. She wrote to one of her 'martyrs' about 'the cold, tame nature of my present feelings, my disappointed heart, my exhausted imagination'; but at the same time she was immensely stimulated by being in the middle of all the political rumours and intrigues, and was able to send the same correspondent a confidential list of the cabinet changes that would occur when the Prince of Wales became Regent.

If it was fashionable for the men invited to Stanmore to pretend to be enchanted by the Wild Irish Girl, the women took a cooler view. A fellow guest, Miss Charlotte Clavering, wrote to her friend the Scottish novelist, Susan Ferrier, and gave her view of the family pet:

Miss Owenson has been living here these three months. I've had rather a surfeit of her. However I cannot in honour pass her over entirely. First to speak of her merits she is perfectly different from what I had fancied her from her works. Though vain of her works and fond of talking about herself I don't think her affected. She is extremely goodhumoured, likes to talk nonsense, loves to have men quiz her, and is

never affronted at being laughed at . . . she does everything
to make society agreeable, always ready to play, dance or
sing, none of which she does well. I expected she would
speak nothing but Greek or Latin; instead she never intrudes
pedantry upon one and never speaks of wise things, which is
quite proper, as I take it she does not understand them in the
least. She has not a better head than thousands of people
who never thought of writing a novel. As for her person I
thought her pretty at first, and now I think her frightful. Her
eyes would be pretty if they did not squint. Her figure is not
the better for being obtrusively crooked and her head is
ornamented with a frightfully ill-cut crop.

Her eyes always attracted comment, and so did the slightly
crooked shoulder; in later life Lady Morgan attributed this to
her habit of leaning on one side while writing or playing the
harp. She still had very little money for clothes and had the
good sense to avoid overdressing. She described her usual
costume at this time as a white muslin frock with a flower at
her bosom; she wore, of course, her red Celtic cloak wherever
she could, and did her hair by brushing her cropped curls with
a wet brush. But this simplicity of toilette did not stop her from
going up to London for the Season, and attending all the best
parties. Here she met all the best people:

> This party turned out to be one of the most agreeable I ever
> was at in my life. I spent the evening seated on the second
> flight of stairs, between Lady Caroline Lamb and Monk
> Lewis. On the landing place beneath squeezed, sauntered, or
> halted many a dandy or top sawyer of fashion, who received
> our grapeshot, or gave us a baterie d'enfilade in return as
> they crushed on. At two in the morning Lady Caroline Lamb
> proposed that we should go and sup snugly and return to
> waltz when her Grace's rooms should thin – and so we did.

This was indeed something to write about about – supper in
one duchess's house, and dancing the new, rather scandalous
waltz in another's. Furthermore that evening on the staircase
was the start of an enduring friendship with Lady Caroline
Lamb who, being related to both the Melbournes and the
Devonshires, had associations with Ireland that linked her to
Sydney. Her father, Lord Ponsonby had estates in Kilkenny,
and Caroline had lived as a child in Woodstock, the home of
Sydney's beloved friend Mary Tighe, and the very house from

which Sarah Ponsonby, one of the ladies of Llangollen, had escaped to become the companion of Eleanor Butler. Scandal had not yet touched Lady Caroline. She was still a 'pattern of conjugal affection' to her husband William and the fatal affair with Byron was still in the future. She was nevertheless always wild and unbiddable to the point of self-destruction, and yet her affection for the hardworking and shrewd Sydney was genuine, and their friendship survived through all the later stresses and strains.

One of the chief amusements of the Abercorns was to conject and conspire over Sydney's army of suitors. Lord Abercorn, not able to get very far with her himself, admired the way she played with her mixed band of swains – the good middle-class, professional men, widowers, clergymen, reformed rakes – whom they thought suitable for her. They did not expect her to contract a marriage for rank or fortune as they would for one of their own kind, but they were anxious to see her settled. Now that the affair with Ormsby was absolutely over, Lady Abercorn found what she thought was the ideal suitor, and one that would keep Sydney still within the Abercorn circle. For while Sydney was dallying in Dublin, the Abercorns had brought into the Baron's Court household a young English doctor as family physician.

An invitation to join the Abercorn household implied that the invited one would be distinguished, fashionable, or useful. Thomas Charles Morgan was a surgeon and general medical practitioner in an English provincial town. Passing through this town on his procession from one great mansion to another the Marquis met with an accident – and Surgeon Morgan was sent for. The young doctor attended his noble patient for more than a week, and under his skilful treatment the Marquis recovered. In gratitude he invited the doctor to visit Baron's Court where Jane-Anne was about to organise some splendid *fêtes champêtres*. So useful and charming did he prove to be that he was invited to join the household as doctor in residence, along with all the other assorted jesters, writers and favourites they held in luxurious captivity.

At the time of his 'capture' Charles Morgan, doctor of medicine, was thirty-one years old; he was a widower with one small daughter, as his wife had died in childbirth after one year of marriage. He had been educated as a classical scholar at Eton and Cambridge, and then took a good medical degree, and entered heart and soul into the controversies that took place when his friend Edward Jenner advocated vaccination. Handsome, witty and a good musician as well, he was just what Lady Abercorn needed to divert and amuse her, and she decided that he would make an ideal mate for their other favourite. She wrote glowing accounts to the absent Sydney of Morgan's learning and splendid qualifications, and equally puffed her up to him – her genius, her charm and general fascination, so that – not surprisingly – he worked up an immense prejudice against her. He was sitting one morning with the Marchioness, when the groom of the chamber announced that Miss Owenson had just arrived. Dr Morgan sprang from his seat, and there being no other way of escape, jumped through the open window into the garden below. Not being used to this kind of reception, Sydney was challenged and set out to captivate him. She had considerably more success than she had either desired or designed, for he fell deeply in love with her. She wrote her first impressions to Mrs Lefanu:

> We have got a most desirable acquisition to our circle in the family physician; he is a person of extraordinary talent, and extensive acquirements, a linguist, musician, poet and philosopher, and withal a most amiable and benevolent person; he is in high popularity, and he and I most amazing friends as you may suppose.

Sydney had long been used to flattering courtship by men amazed at the wisdom and erudition of such a 'slip of a girl'. Her emotional energy had gone into her romantic books and her practical care for her father. She was not seriously looking for a husband. If she married it would have to be a more brilliant match than an ordinary doctor of medicine, with an income no higher than her own, could offer. She certainly did not wish to be plain Mrs Morgan. Her ambivalent attitude to the situation in which she found herself is revealed in the letter she wrote to her father telling him about Morgan and his courtship:

> My dearest Dad, August 20, 1811 . . . I am at a loss how to begin to tell what am going to ask you – which is your leave to marry Dr. Morgan, whom I will not marry if you do not wish it. I dare say you will be amazingly astonished; but not half as much as I am for Lord and Lady Abercorn have hurried on the business in such a manner, that I really don't know what I am about. They called me in last night and

more like parents than friends begged me to be guided by
them – that it was their wish not to lose sight of me, which,
except I married a friend of theirs they might, as they never
would acknowledge a Dublin husband, but if I accepted
Morgan, the man upon earth they most admired and
approved, they would be friends to both for life – that we
should reside for one year with them, after our marriage
or if they remained in Ireland two years. . . . He is also to
continue their physician.

Her letters to her other friends at this time demonstrate her
indecision and lack of ardour for the state of marriage.
Acceptance of Morgan seemed to be acceptance in perpetuity of
the Abercorn's patronage. It meant that she would never again
be able to live in Dublin – yet above all, she was an inveterate
Dubliner. She had played the role that so many Irish have had
forced upon them by circumstance – that of smiling and
beguiling, and dropping a curtesy to 'his Honour', while at the
same time keeping the cold unforgiving heart, that resents the
patronage as much as the tyranny. After all, in her book
Glorvina was the daughter of the Prince of Inishmore, and her
genealogy went back before the Flood, when the Abercorns
were just painted savages!
  But her blarneying, conniving charm had completely captivated Morgan. He fell in love with her 'Kitty Kearney' persona
as well as appreciating her intellectual power. He was no fool –
a handsome, intelligent man whose independence of mind
could match her own in its acceptance of bold, modern
opinions. He was quite different from her usual run of suitors –
not a cynical witty Dubliner like Ormsby, nor a scholarly
clergyman to flatter her on her knowledge or half-knowledge of
everything under the sun. He was a widower, indeed, like so
many of the others, but a young widower, ardent and even
passionate about her. She used to say in later life how little
aware she was of the blessing that had come to her, and how
near she had been to missing it through her own perversity. The
affair with Ormsby had been made completely impossible
through her lack of real intention, and what her friends accused
her of, her inability to stop flirting with other men, and she was
still unable to take Morgan's courtship seriously. She wrote to
Mrs Lefanu:

The licence and the ring have been in the house these ten
days – all the settlements made; yet I have been battling off,

from day to day and hour to hour, and have only ten minutes
back procured a little breathing time. The fact is the struggle
is almost too great for me; on the one side engaged beyond
retrieval to a man who has frequently declared to my friends
here that if I break it off he will not survive it! on the other
the dreadful certainty of being parted for ever from a country
and friends I love, and a family I adore, to whom I am linked
by such fatalities that my heart must break in breaking them.

She further confided to Lady Stanley: 'I have refused and
denied him over and over again, because if it is not in worldly
circumstances a very good match for me, it is still worse for
him.'

One of her objections was soon overcome. Dublin was not
for nothing known as 'the city of deadful knights'. Anyone who
did a favour for the court could have a favour back. After all,
Dr Clarke, Olivia's husband had been knighted merely for
doing his job – curing the Duke of Richmond of a skin
complaint. Now the vice-regal entourage were guests at a
shooting party in Baron's Court. It was put to the Duke that Dr
Morgan might be raised to the same rank as Dr Clarke, and he
goodnaturedly obliged. Lady Abercorn reported this event to
another writer that she honoured with her patronage – the yet
to be famous Sir Walter Scott. A correspondence had started
between them because he had given a bad review to Sydney's
last book, and now wanted to make amends. Lady Abercorn
wrote:

Miss Owenson is now in Dublin and will not be here until
after Christmas, when she is to be married to Dr. Morgan,
who (you may have heard) the Duke of Richmond knighted
when he was here three months ago. It was thought that it
would be an advantage to him in his profession to have
dignity; and little Owenson, whose great talents do not
prevent her from being as vain as possible, liked better to
be Lady Morgan than Mrs Morgan; and to gratify them
both I asked the Duke to knight him, which he did.

But 'little Owenson' was still in Dublin. She had not yet
decided to give up her single state, in spite of the title, the ring
and the licence which lay waiting at Baron's Court, and the two
weeks leave stretched into three months. The affianced couple
wrote to each other practically every day, his letters full of
reproaches, her's full of excuses; her father's and her sister's

health was bad; she was ill herself; the loneliness of Baron's Court in winter would get on her nerves.

She did not spare him reports of the parties and pleasures of Dublin. He replied angrily, writing:

> Do not think me cruel . . . in reminding you that you have lost one husband by flirting, and that makes me feel that it is just possible you may drive another mad. I cannot give you to the amusements of Dublin. God knows (if he takes the trouble to know) this 'pile' is dreary enough without you, but it makes me curse the hour I threw away my love on one so incapable of returning it, when I see you looking forward to a solitary winter in it; trust me, dearest, a little natural philosophy will make time pass pleasantly enough, never fear.

He was willing that she should remain in Dublin as long as her family needed her, but not an hour more. He lamented:

> If you knew what love was it is impossible you could wish it. But I fear you are a stranger to love except as it affects the fancy. You may understand its picturesque effects; but of the anxious, agonising alternations of doubt and confidence, joy and despair, of all that is tender, of all that is heart in it, I fear you are utterly ignorant.

Sydney was somewhat shaken by the force of his letters, and sometimes replied with conciliatory pathos:

> Yes, Morgan, I will be yours, I hope and trust; God give me strength to go through with it; My poor father! I am very ill . . . the fatigue added to a bad cold and a settled cough has produced a horrible state of exhaustion and nervous lowness. You distrust me, and whether I marry or reject you, my misery is certain. Still I love you, oh! more than tenderly. I lean my aching head upon your heart, my sole asylum, my best and dearest friend.

He responded to such cajoling, called himself a 'beast' and her 'his darling injured love', but soon lapsed into the old reproaches when she showed no signs of coming back. She replied with spirit:

> Great God, is there no end to this . . . I have gained my point in putting off my marriage for three months, by which I have gratified the independent spirit of my character in avoiding any addition of obligation to those on whom we are already

too dependent. I have satisfied the feelings of my heart by fulfilling the tender duties they dictate to my father and my family. I have obtained a more thorough knowledge of your character from the development of your feelings in your letters; I have satisfied my woman's delicacy and the bienséance of the world, by avoiding the appearance of rashness in uniting myself for life to one whom I knew but a month.

She convinced herself of the reasonable nature of her argument, and stayed in Dublin. She reported dire things about her father, and the medical man responded, recommending that Robert shouldn't drink so much whiskey. Robert himself, taking on a new lease of life, wrote to his would-be son-in-law, and advised him on the best way to treat his daughter: 'You've had a great deal of patience with her lately; don't let her ride the bald filly too much, and if she won't go quietly in a snaffle, get a good bit and curb for her.' And still, Sydney wouldn't come back. She wrote again, excusing herself because she was collecting material for a new novel, and as it had an Irish theme, she had to stay in Dublin:

The reason is [she wrote, reasonably enough] that a good old Irishman has sent me twenty thousand volumes of old Irish books to make extracts from, and I am to return them directly, and here I am in poor Dad's room, just after binding up his blistered head, and I am just going to work pell-mell.

And so the letters went back and forth, his despairing because he was genuinely in love, her's exercises in evasion, as she was not yet cured of her habits of coquetry, playing these out in Dublin as well as in the correspondence to her betrothed. At last Lady Abercorn wrote to her:

I own I think if you are not here by Christmas you use Sir Charles very ill indeed; let me give you a piece of advice which I know from a long knowledge of the world that it is very unwise for a woman when she intends to marry a man to let him for a moment suppose he is not her first object. For after marriage people have more time to reflect and sometimes it might so happen that a man might recollect that though he was accepted for a husband, that past conduct proved it was more par convenance than from attachment; now I know you will say that as Sir Charles is not a very great match, he cannot ever imagine that you married him

for ought but himself; but that will not be so considered and
I recommend you to play no longer with his feelings.

The worldly advice was taken. Sydney was well aware of the
dangerous game she was playing with Morgan's affections. His
letters showed that he was not quite so starry eyed about her as
before. 'Love you certainly less than I did. It is more T.C.M.
and Miss O. and less Mortimer and Glorvina' said one.
Another told her 'Such as you are, you are necessary to my
happiness, so I must e'en marry you.'

The warning note was there, and she had flirted away her
chances with other men before. But then she hadn't wanted
marriage. Now she could be Lady Morgan, and that was
another card in the game. In January 1812 she returned to
Baron's Court. To begin with her reception was chilly.
Everybody was displeased with her, but she put her charm to
work, and soon she was back in her former favour. An eyewitness of this carry-on wrote to Olivia:

> The ceremony is to take place in a few hours. The coquette
> has behaved very well for these ten days past. She really
> seems now attached to him. He is in as great a frenzy as ever
> about her . . . However I must tell you Glorvina is minding
> her ps and qs.

And still she twisted and prevaricated. Morgan was certainly
not marrying her without a knowledge of her capricious nature,
and if she had wanted to test his devotion, she could not have
put any hero of her romances through as many trials of love. At
the end, she was taken by surprise. On a cold morning in
January she was sitting by the library fire in her morning
wrapper when Lady Abercorn opened the door and said
peremptorily: 'Glorvina, come upstairs and be married; there
must be no more trifling.' Sydney was led upstairs, willy-nilly,
to her ladyship's boudoir, where a table was laid for the
ceremony, the family chaplain in full canonicals, and Sir
Charles ready to receive her. None of the many visitors in the
house knew of what had happened until Lord Abercorn stood
up after dinner, filled his glass and drank to the health of Sir
Charles and Lady Morgan.

In the *Gentleman's Magazine* of the day others could read:
'January 20th, 1812, at Baron's Court, Tyrone, Sir T.C.
Morgan of London, to Sydney, eldest daughter of the veteran
Irish comedian, Owenson, and author of *The Wild Irish Girl*
and *Woman, or Ida of Athens*.'

CHAPTER 7

THE SWORD OF RED HUGH

In one of her prevaricating, procrastinating letters to Morgan, explaining why she couldn't come home to marry him, Sydney had written: 'You have met with a more formidable rival in O'Donnell of Tyrconnell than all your jealous brain ever fancied in generals, aides de camp, and Dublin lawyers.' He was duly warned, for with whatever items of trousseau she was bringing, she had packed old history books relating to the Elizabethan wars in Ireland, and the exploits of Hugh O'Donnell, the Red Earl. Fictional rivals for his wife's affections were not the only problem for Sir Charles. All her life she had had to be the strong one, making decisions for her father and sister, as well as for herself. She had earned a living for all of them; she was used to success and flattery. Her courage and independent spirit had been developed in a hard school, and what had been virtues in her single state could make for a stormy domestic life. Sir Charles had his own ideas about love and marriage: 'The woman who marries me must be identified with me', he had written to her during their difficult engagement:

> I must have a large bank of tenderness to draw upon. I must have frequent profession and frequent demonstration of it. Woman's love is all in all to me; it stands in place of honour and riches, and what is yet more, in place of tranquillity of mind and ease; without it there is a void in existence that deprives me of all control of myself and leads me to headlong dissipation, as a refuge from reflection . . . [and, reasonably enough] I set up no tyrannical pretensions to man's superiority, and have besides a personal respect for your intellect over other women's . . . but I never will submit to an assumed control of the woman's side; we must be equals.

On these terms she had accepted him, and in financial

settlements and whatever else they brought to the marriage they were equal. Nor did she come empty handed. She had saved five thousand pounds from her writing, and this sum and anything else she earned was to be hers, while the reversion of his fortune was to be settled upon the daughter of his first marriage. It was checks and balances all the way with them. He was unambitious, inclined to indolence; she encouraged him to be energetic and outward-going; he kept her steady and equable, and by his educated taste and integrity improved the standard of her work conspicuously. All through her life she repeatedly acknowledged 'the long and ennobling companion-ship of one who taught and prized truth above all human good, and proclaimed it at the expense of all worldly interests'.

All the same, the first year of their married life had its stormy passages, and part of the trouble was money. It was what she called 'the worst of all human evils – poverty' that kept them tied to the Abercorns, where it was easy to live on their patrons' fifty thousand pounds a year, but she longed for a home of her own – 'be it ever so tiny'. She wanted to get Morgan away from his comfortable dependency, and take his chances in the world where she knew his talents would prevail – and where he could show off his title. She wrote to Lady Stanley about her own projects:

> I am at work again, but with the sole view of making some
> money to furnish a bit of a house in London, which coûte
> qui coûte we must have. My book will be a genuine romance
> of Elizabeth's day founded on historical facts . . . I would not
> write another line to add the fame of Sappho to my own little
> quota of reputation did not necessity guide my worn out
> stump of a goose quill.

But *O'Donnel* was to be much more than a pot-boiler to make money. It was more ambitious than anything that she had written before and, in the course of its production, Sir Charles, who was already a liberal in politics, came to share his wife's nationalist sentiments. This was just as well, for with this book she managed to offend several of their influential patrons, by including unflattering and recognisable portraits of them among her characters.

But these were early days in its conception, and for months after her marriage she had been deep in correspondence with her old army of antiquarians and scholars, checking facts for the period. She was brought to a halt by the sudden death of her father. Owenson's death was announced in the Dublin newspapers of 28 May 1812, with many generous tributes. The *Freeman's Journal* said:

> The revival of Irish music within these last thirty years was entirely owing to his exertion, and his exquisite mode of singing his native airs both in public and in private. His conduct as a father . . . went far beyond the common line of parental duty and tenderness; his public life considered, it was unexampled.

In this one year Sydney had found a husband and lost the father who had been so dear to her; the father of whom she had written in her first book of poems:

> Come thou thrice dear shade, for ah, no more
> Thou true and loved resemblance, will we part,
> For till the last faint thrill of life is o'er,
> Dear shade, I'll wear thee next my beating heart.

The shade then had been his portrait; now his death broke the emotional bondage which had stopped her from making a really deep relationship with any other man. She wrote to her brother-in-law:

> It appeared to me impossible that my own dear father, who was my child as well as my father could die – nor I don't believe it yet! it is to me as if a curtain dropped before life. I can look neither to the past nor to the future without connecting everything with him, and the present is all, all him! The tie which existed between us was not the common tie of father and child. He was the object for which I laboured and wrote, and lived, and nothing can fill up to me the place he held in my heart.

Perhaps it was true that nothing ever did, but now her father was dead she was able to transfer to her husband without reserve that tenderness and whole hearted attention that his nature demanded, and he in his turn, in a full abandonment to her will, agreed to leave the Abercorns and live wherever she wanted. This, surprisingly enough, in view of all she had said about her dream of a 'baby house' in London, turned out to be Ireland. In spite of the death of her father she seemed, more than ever, drawn back to her own country:

> It is my intention to sacrifice the rest of my life to the

> HEART and to live in Ireland if those I love cannot live with
> me in England, where interest and ambition equally call
> Morgan and myself; he has no wish, scarcely any will but
> mine, and is ready to make my country his.

She was realistic enough to know that it would not be easy to
leave the Abercorns:

> They have not the remotest idea that we can or will leave
> them. If we (what they would call) desert them, we shall risk
> the loss of their friendship, which would indeed be a loss –
> but if we remain we lose time, and it is quite fit that Morgan
> should establish himself soon somewhere . . . we are dying to
> be in our own little shabby house, and we are tired of
> solitary splendours and of the eternal representation of high
> life.

It took them a year to extricate themselves from the Abercorns'
web. Sir Charles applied for a minor official appointment to the
Marshalsea Prison in Dublin. They stayed with the Clarkes on
the north side of the city until they found a house of their own
in Kildare Street, in an area developing fast as 'upper class
residential'. In the mid-eighteenth century this area had been
open land, until the young Earl of Kildare bought a site in 1743
and built his new town house there. When it was pointed out to
him that the site was rather remote, he replied with sublime
assurance: 'They will follow me wherever I go', and of course
they did.

Kildare Street was fast becoming one of the most fashionable
quarters of the city. Running between Trinity College at one
end, and Stephen's Green at the other, it housed the exclusive
Kildare Street Club, into which, it was said, all the sons of the
landed gentry would fall as if on to an oyster bed. The
fashionable St Anne's Church was round the corner, and in
1820 the Shelbourne Hotel was built out of three houses at the
Stephen's Green end. In fact, Sydney's modest 'nutshell' of a
house was right in the centre of high Ascendancy Dublin life,
and it was her supreme achievement to make it a centre of
artistic, social and literary activity. She had lived as a guest, a
boarder or an employee all her life; sometimes in great
splendour, sometimes in squalor; she had never owned a home
of her own, and now she plunged into housekeeping with all
the creative enthusiasm she had given to novel writing. She was
practical, and clever with her hands; she could make clothes

and curtains, and was a good cook, and before long, 35 Kildare Street was something to boast about, particularly to Lady Stanley who had given her many lessons in the art of being comfortable. She wrote:

> We have at last got into a home of our own; we found an old, dirty, dismantled house, and we have turned our piggery into a decent sort of hut enough; we have made it clean and comfortable, which is all our moderate circumstances will admit of, save one little bit of a room which is a real bijou and it is about four inches by three, and therefore we could afford to ornament it a little. It is fitted up in the Gothic, and I have collected into it the best part of a very good cabinet of natural history of Sir Charles, eight or nine thousand volumes of choice books, in French, English, Italian and German; some little miscellaneous curiosities and a few scraps of old china, so that with muslin draperies, etc, etc, I have made no contemptible set-out . . . I was thinking that maybe Suzette could enrich my store in the old china way, if she has any refuse of that sort which you may have thrown her in with your cast-off wardrobe – a broken cup, a bottomless bowl, a spoutless tea-pot – in a word anything old and shattered that is china and of no value to you, will be of use and ornament to me . . . With respect to authorship I fear it is over; I have been making chair covers instead of periods; hanging curtains instead of raising systems, and cheapening pots and pans instead of selling sentiment and philosophy.

Whether in housekeeping or in authorship she could make a little go a long way, and could produce a great effect with a piece of drapery here, and a broken teapot there, so long as they were bright and colourful enough. Her years with the Abercorns, however, had taught her the value of real comfort and good food, and she had a talent for both that became an asset to Dublin social life.

Unfortunately, the house was not ready to receive the one particular visitor whose political opinions combined with his social status would have made him a very welcome guest to her salon at any time. In January 1812 the young Shelley, with his even younger wife Harriet, came over to Dublin. He admired Sydney's last book, *The Missionary*, so much that he would have made serious efforts to meet her if she had not been caught up in the gilded prison of Baron's Court. There is no record of them meeting in Dublin, but Sydney, when she eventually came back later in that year, would no doubt have heard from friends like the United Irishman Hamilton Rowan, and the nationalist lawyer John Philpot Curran, of the wild young poet who sought them and other sympathetic friends out.

Shelley, just nineteen, lately expelled from Oxford for proclaiming atheism, had married the sixteen-year-old Harriet Westbrook, and had taken her and her sister off to Ireland, looking for a 'Cause' worthy of their endeavours. In Ireland he thought he had found one: there, he declared, more than anywhere else, the cosmic struggle for political independence and religious liberty was being fought out. Shelley knew very little of Irish parties or internal politics but he believed that the gospel of reason and charity, the thoughts of William Godwin and political justice, could restore order from chaos. He came, this idealistic innocent abroad, to tell the Irish people that he supported Catholic Emancipation, but only as a token of the victory of reason over all intolerance and all superstition, including Catholicism itself.

He had great plans to produce a pamphlet, 'An Appeal to the Irish People', proclaiming his sympathy as an Englishman with their aims, and suggesting a peaceful solution for their difficulties. Harriet and her sister Eliza were instructed to study the history and sorrows of Ireland, and after a storm-tossed journey lasting twelve days, the three of them landed in Dublin, and took lodgings in Sackville Street. Harriet, who had through her reading become an ardent Irish patriot, immediately bought a red cloak – à la Glorvina. If only Lady Morgan had been at home, how she would have loved to have taken them under her wing, for here were two romantic lovers, worthy of her own pen, daring all for Ireland and idealism.

Shelley's energy was almost as dynamic as her own. In no time at all he had engaged a printer, and had run off 1,500 copies of *The Address to the Irish People*. He sent copies to all the leading Irish patriots, to various liberals in England, to Harriet's father, to his own father, and to his father's lawyer. A man was engaged to place copies in Dublin's sixty taverns, and to sell them throughout the city, price sixpence. And with a pile of pamphlets Harriet and Shelley walked through the streets giving them away to anyone who would take one. Harriet was young enough to see the funny side of all this important work of influencing the Irish. 'I am sure', she wrote to a friend in

England, 'you would laugh were you to see us give the pamphlets. We throw them out of the window, and give them to men that we pass in the street. For myself I am ready to die of laughter when it is done, and Percy looks so grave. Yesterday he put one into a woman's hood of a cloak; she knew nothing of it and so we passed her.'

Shelley made enough impression upon the Dubliners, in spite of the rumour going round that he was only fifteen years old, to be invited to address the Aggregate meeting of the Catholics in Owenson's old theatre in Fishamble Street, now used for political meetings. Such meetings attended by Catholics and liberal Protestants were not forbidden but were carefully monitored, and government spies were thick in the audience. Shelley spoke for an hour, in his shrill, almost girlish voice, and his youth, his English accent, and his extreme views did not endear him to the audience of leading Catholic shopkeepers and rising middle-class, with their richly dressed wives, who occupied the boxes as thought this were the opening night of the opera. 'Riches' said Shelley 'have generally the effect of hardening and vitiating the heart'. He extolled the virtues of the 'Pythagorean' diet – earnest vegetarianism, and urged the working man to abjure violence and drink.

His audience listened to him politely enough, apart from a bit of hissing when he criticised the clergy, but they were not going to take seriously the opinions of someone who looked like a schoolboy and had been expelled from college for atheism; Shelley distributed the last of his pamphlets and left Ireland for ever. The Castle spies gathered up their notes, and sent them ahead of him to London. He was rather disappointed by his Irish experience. He wrote to a friend:

> Prejudices are so violent, in contradiction to my principles, that more hate me as a freethinker than love me as a votary of freedom . . . I have at least made a stir here, and set some men's minds afloat . . . I may succeed but I fear I shall not . . . . The spirit of bigotry is high.

Poor Shelley was neither the first, nor probably the last Englishman inspired by generous idealism who has hoped to solve what has always been known as 'the Irish problem', and left more puzzled than he started.

Had Sydney been in Dublin she would have advised Shelley better, but she was busy coming to terms herself with a

different strand in the twisted skein of Irish history. Her new
hero O'Donnell was proving to be a difficult subject. She had
declared herself ready to write an Irish romance founded on
historic facts, and set in the time of Elizabeth. The market for
historical novels had been stimulated by the publication of
Walter Scott's *Waverley* in 1814, and Sydney had a strong
instinct for judging the market. The name O'Donnell was of
great prominence in Ireland, especially from the thirteenth to the
sixteenth century. They were the chiefs of Tyrconnel, that part
of Ulster which is now Donegal, and shared the overlordship of
Ulster with the O'Neills, the lords of Tyrone. Sometimes these
two great families united with each other against the English in
a policy of national resistance, and sometimes they murdered
each other in tribal conflict.

In 1592, Hugh Roe O'Donnell, who has been described as
the last of the old Gaelic kings, was declared the chief of
Tyrconnel by his father. He was then only twenty years old, but
his previous experience of the English had made him their most
dangerous enemy. When he was only a boy of sixteen he had
been kidnapped by Sir John Perrott, the Lord Deputy, and kept
in chains for more than three years in a dungeon in Dublin
Castle. He escaped, and for the next few years went
permanently 'on the run'. For ten years he waged a bloody war
against Elizabeth's army. With O'Neill he conspired with Spain
– England's arch enemy – to fight a holy war and restore the
Catholic faith. In 1601 he brought his army of Ulstermen fröm
the north to the south of Ireland, and met up with the
Spaniards at Kinsale. Here, the Spanish and the Irish chieftains
were completely routed by Elizabeth's general, Lord Mountjoy.
Red Hugh escaped to Spain in order to consult further with
King Philip II, but there, poisoned by James Blake, a British
agent, he died. He was thirty years old, and with his death and
the subsequent flight of the rest of the Northern chieftains, the
Tudor conquest of Ireland was completed, and the old Gaelic
system was broken. The lands of the O'Neills and the
O'Donnells were confiscated and given over to planters and
colonists.

He was the perfect hero for Sydney, a bright-haired young
man who was a prince of Gaelic Ireland and champion of the
Catholic faith. Hunted, imprisoned and eventually killed as a
traitor by the English, the Spaniards had buried him with great
solemnity as a member of the Third Order of St Francis, and as
a great prince of Ireland, in the church of San Francisco in

Valladolid. The church and his grave has completely disappeared, but when they buried him there nearly four hundred years ago, 'Princes came walking behind it – and all Valladolid knew – and out to Simancas all knew – where they buried Red Hugh.'

Sydney began her task with great enthusiasm; she had collected a mass of source material when she was in Dublin making excuses to postpone her marriage. Sir William Betham, the Ulster King of Arms, had shown her O'Donnell family documents, including a mysterious Cathach, or reliquary, never opened in human memory on account of a traditional curse on anyone who should discover what it contained. But the more research she did, the more she realised that she could not write about the realities of the past, if she wished to succeed in her avowed intention to be a force for conciliation in the affairs of England and Ireland. The facts of sixteenth-century Irish history proved too terrible even for her powers of romantic interpretation. This was not the fairytale world of Glorvina and the Prince of Inishmore. There was no Mortimer to learn the lesson and promise to behave with 'civility' in the future; this struggle was to the death. The swords on both sides were dripping with real blood, and the religious implications were far too hot for her to handle. She herself could not really understand or entertain religious prejudice. In fact in *O'Donnel* (thus she spelt her hero's surname, although the real family name is 'O'Donnell'), she stated through the words of the Duchess of Belmont, her heroine, her own doctrine of scepticism: 'as to belief, I believe in nothing, and deny nothing . . . to doubt is my creed, and not to wonder is my motto'. Her liberal principles made her the champion of toleration everywhere. In her own country it was the Catholics who were oppressed, and so she was a committed advocate of Catholic Emancipation. It is difficult in this secular age to comprehend what a generous stance this was for her to take, for in Ireland at that time the Protestant church was the church of the Ascendancy upon which her popularity and favour depended. Furthermore, her mother's militant allegiance to Protestantism had influenced her enough in her youth for her to see the blackrobed priesthood as sinister intriguers of the Curia, linked with the Spain of the Counter-Reformation, and sharing the 'narrow and illiberal views of a crooked and illiberal power'. After the first volume of her novel 'based on historical truth' she found she could not proceed:

In touching those parts of Irish history which were connected
with my tale it would have been desirable to turn them into
purpose of conciliation . . . to leaven that heavy mass of
bitter prejudice which writers both grave and trifling have
delighted to raise against my country. But when I fondly
thought to send forth a dove bearing the olive of peace I
found I was on the point of flinging an arrow winged with
discord . . . I discovered, far beyond my expectations that
I had fallen upon 'evil men, and evil days' and that in
proceeding, I must raise a veil which ought never to be
drawn.

So Sydney abandoned the novel, drawn from 'genuine history',
and started again retaining some of the information about the
Elizabethan wars and the O'Donnell family, but taking as her
hero a contemporary soldier of fortune, one of the type that she
had met in Kilkenny in her schooldays. She made her hero
Roderick O'Donnel – rightful heir to the family name, but
forced by fate and his allegiance to the Catholic religion to try
his luck in the armies of foreign kings. She sets her fictional
hero against 'The flat realities of contemporary life', by which
she means the sort of high society she was then accustomed to.
She places him in a lonely house in the wilds of the Donegal
countryside, and brings him face to face with a wandering
party of English aristocrats, on their way as tourists to see the
Giant's Causeway. (She herself had become familiar with all
this part of Ireland when touring Ulster with her father's troop
of travelling players.) The story of his family and their downfall
comes out in the course of this enforced relationship. The house
where the party shelters is bare and impoverished, but the great
hound that accompanies the O'Donnel everywhere wears a
silver collar, engraved with the words: 'Tirconnel 1603'. The
pedigree of the O'Donnell family beginning with Niall of the
Nine Hostages hangs on the wall, next to a portrait of a man in
a religious habit – the Abbate O'Donnel – a Spanish Jesuit, and
Roderick's uncle. Over the fireplace hangs a sword. The basket
hilt is worked in gold, and the blade is thickly encrusted with
rust-red blood. This is the sword of the Red Earl – Hugh Roe
O'Donnell – and the blood that still stains it is the blood of the
English throats that he cut. But that is past history, and she is
not going to write about the past. The sword stays on the wall,
and Roderick O'Donnel tries to live in a world where liberal
opinion might one day be made more receptive to Irish

Catholic claims, particularly if one of those Catholics could be shown to be 'that almost unbelievable thing, an Irish gentleman who was of native race, and a Catholic', for in the ordinary acceptance of literature at that time the Irish gentleman was always a Protestant, and only the Irish retainer allowed to be a Catholic. Lady Morgan broke this stereotype with *O'Donnel* in her efforts to win religious freedom for Irish Catholics in their own country.

She did this, however, to the great disapproval of some of her former admirers and patrons. Lady Cahir, the Countess of Glengall, who had lent her some of the history books for her research wrote to her: 'I venture an opinion . . . not even your seducing pen can make it palatable to my old English prejudices . . . do not mix anything of religious or political opinions in a work intended only to amuse; it will lay you open to animadversion and party may influence opinion'. She replied to this criticism saying that she was very hurt by this attack, and that her Irish prejudices were just as strong as Lady Cahir's English ones could ever be.

> Let me assure you [she wrote, however] that my hero is a loyal man. If it was ever given out that I was writing a book which had politics for its subject and a traitor for its hero I might go sing about it in the streets like the Bards of old, for certain it is my public would not buy it, and of course the public could not read it.

But her critics were not satisfied. When the Lord Chancellor, Lord John Manners, who had once, at Baron's Court, been friendly enough to give her his favourite recipe for salad dressing, read far enough into the book to discover its emancipationist sympathies, he ordered it to be burnt in the servant's hall, and he never spoke to her again.

Like Sydney's own position, the sword of Red Hugh is a very equivocal symbol. Roderick O'Donnel – unwilling to give offence – is content to leave his ancestor's sword on the wall, while he broods over ancient wrongs and falls deeper into poverty and despair. He must behave in a negatively noble way to prove her point about the Catholic gentleman. But she creates another character who can fight valiantly against the unjust laws which deny him and all other Catholics their rights. This is the Duchess of Belmont, a sort of 'feminine Puss-in-Boots' who weaves in and out of the plot sorting it all out. She is manifestly modelled on the author, but a great change has come over Glorvina. She is no longer a princess of Celtic myth, but a woman of the world, clever, witty and sensible. In the beginning she appears as a much put upon governess, a Miss O'Halloran, working in the family of Lady Singleton, who is represented as opinionated and domineering, and a pen portrait to the life of Lady Cahir. Miss O'Halloran is the daughter of an eccentric Irish artist who was much celebrated during his lifetime but died very poor. She had all the talents and almost all the eccentricity of her father; 'living entirely among clever men and left to educate herself as it pleased God, she was at once the most naive and clever little creature in the world, a mere child, but amazingly droll and out of the way.' Obliged to become a governess, she adopts a protective mask of stupidity, but every now and then startles the self-important empty people of fashion with a penetrating comment, or sceptical laugh. By some sleight of novel writing she becomes the Duchess of Belmont, the wife of an old peer who had known her father. He conveniently dies before he can assail her virginity, and leaves her a rich and brilliant widow. Time passes. O'Donnel is invited to England to stay in the great country house of Lady Llanberis, easily recognisable as Lady Abercorn, who was always looking for interesting guests with which to amuse herself. The Duchess is a fellow guest, and for a while he does not recognise her as the little governess that he met in the wilds of Donegal. He, with only pride and gentlemanly reticence to his name, and not at all 'amusing' to the great ladies, slips deeper into disfavour and poverty, and is preparing to go away again to seek his fortune in a foreign army. The Duchess has other plans; she, lively and energetic, rescues him from all adversity, helps him to regain some of his ancestral property, and finally marries him.

Sydney's attitude to plots was rather like her attitude to dates; she did what she liked with them. One of the most interesting things about O'Donnel, conceived as it was during her time with the Abercorns, is the picture it gives of herself struggling for her own dignity in that atmosphere of patronage. The tone of the book is witty and goodnatured, but she is delighted to pay back any outstanding debt of insolence that 'Miss O' might have incurred. The set pieces are as sharp as any to be found in Sheridan. Mrs Sneerwell and Mrs Candour would have felt quite at home. Lady Llanberis is made to pay for all the times Lady Abercorn changed her mind, and sent Sydney on vain errands, or yawned dismally when things weren't diverting enough. But, of course, Lady Llanberis cannot help but admire the Duchess of Belmont, and makes everyone else admire her too. She says of her:

> There is certainly nobody like her. I have all my life preferred that sort of person who came from nobody knows where; they are so much more amusing than people of fashion, who are nothing else but people of fashion. Now the Duchess of Belmont is really a most extraordinary creature, and has all sorts of talents; she has the gift of 'raconter' in great perfection; makes a good story out of nothing at all, and mimics in a manner which is nothing short of miraculous!

Jane-Anne's reactions on reading the book are not recorded, neither are her opinions of the thumbnail sketch of her husband's character:

> To be legitimately bon-ton one should be high-born, apathetic, and reserved; constitutionally cold, and habitually silent; talked of by many, known to a few, devoted to none, and 'ennuyé' by all. In a word, you must be a thing absorbed by itself, and perpetually engaged in the contemplation of its own divinity.

Sydney, who in her social life had laid herself open to accusations of social climbing and snobbery, nevertheless in her novels cast a very cold eye on the owners of those high sounding titles.

O'Donnel is full of her own experience of life in the Big House and, written at a time when she was longing for a home of her own, it is not a flattering picture. This is Roderick O'Donnel's view, and her own at that time:

> The comfortless grandeur of a great house struck him in all its coldness – where the fireside niche, the central point of domestic sociality is always wanting; where there is solitude without privacy, and where the feelings, like the guests are dissipated and abroad for want of some attractive influence to fix and concentrate them at home.

Fortunately, the publication of *O'Donnel* saw her safely back at home, in Dublin. She was at last free, in her own circle of friends, her own family, her own town. She was back also with the sort of Irish politics that she could cope with – patriotic but not violent; liberal and conciliatory; relying on influencing decent English opinion to be receptive to reasonable claims.

This is the world she projects in *O'Donnel*. Her principal characters are high-minded and the peasants and servants who stand around and admire her proud, melancholy, dispossessed gentlemen are only the supporting cast. Never does she conceive that they might, one day, be the ones who will take up the bloodstained sword of Red Hugh.

The book came out in 1814, in three volumes, and once again she had the good fortune to find a publisher who suited her better than any other since Phillips. Henry Colburn was just coming to the forefront of the publishing scene in London. He had a remarkable flair for judging the taste of his age, and was 'the first of the gambling publishers', as Michael Sadlier called him in his bibliography of nineteenth-century fiction. According to Sadlier, Colburn had his own literary reviews in which he could puff his own books, 'he developed advertising to a degree hitherto undreamt of. He had his diners-out who talked of his books at dinner tables . . . he debauched the critics and put them on his pay sheet.' In the age of the Regency, with its passion for exclusivity and bon-ton, it was Colburn's genius to see that a literature written for the exclusives by the exclusives would also appeal to the growing class of post-war *nouveau riche* who aspired to join the elite. One of his axioms was the drawing power of a title, and it was probably Lady Morgan's newly minted one, as much as her literary reputation, which made him pay £500 for *O'Donnel*. The Irish element of this novel made it very different from his usual stock-in-trade of balls, gambling scenes, marriagebroking, and political gossip.

O'Donnel was worth every penny he paid. It went rapidly through an edition of two thousand copies, which made it a 'best-seller' for its time. Apart from the coldness with which it was received in Irish Ascendancy circles, who could not forgive the politics, no matter how high-minded they were, a great many people found it a vast improvement upon her earlier novels. Walter Scott liked it very much for 'having nature and reality for its foundation'; Mary Russell Mitford, expecting to laugh dismissively at it, found herself laughing with it; and Maria Edgeworth also found it very entertaining. Anne Plumptre, who wrote a popular guidebook to Ireland, took *O'Donnel* with her on the packet boat from Liverpool for reference, and found that most of her fellow passengers on the boat had already read it.

Henry Colburn's star was rising fast, and he was looking for new ventures. When he heard that Lady Morgan was contemplating writing a book about France, he quickly put his marker down, and made an offer. This promised to be exactly what he and the public wanted – an exclusive's travel book, with literary overtones.

CHAPTER 8

ALL THE WORLD'S IN PARIS

Like a cook with a heavy hand on the garlic, Sydney Morgan has often been criticised for using too many French phrases both in her writing and her conversation. It was, of course, very 'bon ton' in those days for 'ladies' to show off any knowledge of French they had, for this was proof positive of a cultivated education, but Sydney took the practice to extremes. Even her Irish novels are peppered with '*fermes orneés*' and '*illustre malheureux*'; before 1816 she had never crossed the Channel, even though her second novel, *The Novice of St. Dominick*, is set rather sketchily in sixteenth-century France.

Since 1789 France had become a country that could only be explored through its literature and despatches from the war, for after the French Revolution it had been cut off more or less completely by continual blockade or some other form of hostility. The Napoleonic War made travelling almost impossible, except for a short period during the abortive Peace of Amiens in 1802. Then thousands of English tourists, most of them from the 'idle rich', went to see for themselves what had happened to their once familiar playground now that it had exchanged its monarchy for a pagan republic with consuls, senators, a Temple to Mars, and a calendar that dated world history from the start of the new regime. That period of peace was very short, and those unfortunate enough to be on French soil when the war started again in 1803 had to stay for the next twelve years as hostages of Napoleon. Confined to the town of Verdun, the chief depôt for prisoners, the English colony nevertheless set about making an approximation of Regency London in miniature, with exclusive clubs, gambling, racing, cockfights and masked balls. Opera singers and ballet dancers were imported from Metz in Alsace Lorraine, along with everything else necessary to the life of an Englishman of rank and fashion. Even in revolutionary France, milord could, by virtue of his style and money establish his exclusivity.

All this was, of course, in the great 'tradition of the English abroad for in the eighteenth century the Grand Tour was a necessary part of an upper-class education: 'A man who hasn't been to Italy' said Dr Johnson, 'is always conscious of an inferiority.' To have studied the classics at school, and then to have visited the tomb of Virgil or the countryside of Pascal and Descartes made a man truly cultivated. The lessons in art and architecture acquired on those journeys shaped the look of country houses and estates everywhere. Palladian villas in England and Ireland had their parks landscaped after the scenery depicted in the paintings of Poussin and Claude, newly acquired for the ancestral halls of Britain. Crates of marble columns and pagan gods arrived at the docks to make a classical approach for the otherwise quite modest plain brick facades. And in the library the cultivated gentleman read his Horace and planned to plant myrtle trees. Then came the long drawn out war, and the young gentlemen put away their guides to the galleries, and now only visited the Continent under arms, and riding behind gun carriages.

When in 1815 the victory of Waterloo finally restored the peace, the old order itself had undergone a revolutionary change. Travel was no longer the prerogative of the gentry. Having been confined to their own small island for so long everyone wanted to go and see what had been happening for themselves. The roads of the Continent were thronged with middle-class Englishmen who had made their fortune during the war, and with adventurers and carpetbaggers who hadn't made it yet, but meant to, as quickly as possible.

In 1815 it seemed that everyone was on the move. Large numbers of French aristocrats who had fled the Revolution as emigrés returned to Paris. The victorious English descended upon the city in thousands, in uniform or as civilians. At the height of the tourist invasion it was estimated that the number of English in the capital was fourteen thousand. Others went, again in their thousands, to walk or ride across the battlefields of Waterloo. The unfortunate few who had to remain at home consoled themselves by singing a popular song: 'All the world's in Paris'.

The first cross-channel steamer was introduced in 1816; a regular service between Dover and Calais started in 1821, and in France, Germany, Italy and Switzerland hotels sprang up like mushrooms all along the main routes. Experienced travel writers were in great demand. One such commentator, John Scott, wrote in 1815:

> The British public regarded France during the season of their seclusion with sentiments of wonder, certainly not unmingled with awe; they knew it only in tremendous results, as a volcano is known; the interior process by which these were produced was hidden from their eyes and formed the subject of many an anxious but uncertain speculation. It was natural therefore that they should rush towards it at the first moment of admission.

There were Irish in Paris, too, but their situation was different from the triumphant English. The special relationship between Ireland and royalist France had fostered the Wild Geese, men who had fought in the French Army against the British. Many of their families had become French citizens. Later another wave of Irish exiles arrived. The United Irishmen had taken from revolutionary France their ideas of liberty and equality, and had hoped for French help in establishing their own republic; when that hope was defeated in 1798, many of them took refuge there. Now that France was defeated there was no place for them in the restoration of the monarchy. Ever since the Peace of Amiens, in 1803, their hopes in Napoleon had declined, and so did any French encouragement of Irish national aspirations. Some Irish political exiles had taken service in the French army; others lived clandestinely in discreet poverty, hoping for better times; many others slipped away to America. By 1815 the number of United Irishmen living in Paris was down to about half a dozen, and in September of that year the Irish Legion, a regiment originally composed of Republicans willing to fight under Napoleon was disbanded, and many of its officers left for the United States. Paradoxically, now when the French emigrés were returning home, the Irish had no country of their own to return to, and had to go further afield.

The English had no such burden of history on their back. They had won the war; their young sons could now once more make the Grand Tour, while their elders took the waters at German spas. Gamblers could avoid their creditors in Calais, as Beau Brummell did in 1816, and poets and novelists could again use romantic foreign settings for all they were worth. The Anglomania that raged in Paris during the summer of 1815 was feverish; it was social invasion more spectacular than the military one. The Duke and Duchess of Wellington were in residence like reigning monarchs supported by Lord and Lady Castlereagh, and other English grandees. The English gave dinners, balls and took boxes at the theatre, and the Opera, where the great success of the season was amazingly enough a ballet, danced by an all French cast called the 'Battle of Waterloo'.

So, when in April 1816 Sydney decided to go to France she was very much in the swim. She was well placed strategically. The French themselves were very curious about the outside world, and in particular foreign literature. She was well known in Paris as a novelist before she even set out. She had many ideas of her own to test against the new regime. Sympathetic to republicanism in her own country; anti-clerical, and a devoted pupil of the liberal teachings of Rousseau and Madame de Staël, she now had to contemplate the consequences of the restoration of the monarchy. Any regime was bound to come as an anti-climax after the genius of Napoleon and the brilliance of his court, but the restored royal house seems to have been singularly lacking in glamour. The new king, Louis XVIII, so fond of food that he was called Louis les Huitres, was now immensely fat and clumsy. He had been for many years in exile, and had never expected to reign. Though he believed in his hereditary divine right he remembered his brother's fate on the guillotine, and conceded to the new conditions of monarchy 'without faith and with very little hope'. So he returned as a constitutional ruler, giving France a Charter of Rights which was a compromise between the old divine right and the revolution. In 1816 there were three main political parties. On the right were the Ultras, the dominant party in the Chambre des Deputés, who were *'plus royalists que le roi'*. It was said that they had forgotten and learned nothing during their exile. They were in favour of the full restoration of the *ancien regime*, press censorship, the return of all lands confiscated and the restoration of political influence to the clergy. They disapproved of the Charter and supported the King's Absolutist brother, the Comte d'Artois, later to be Charles X. The centre party were the constitutionalists who accepted both the King and the Charter, though they held that the authority of the King was not dependent upon parliamentary majorities. On the left were the independents, still influenced by the principles of 1789; their chief theorist was Benjamin Constant, close companion of Madame de Staël, who saw the safeguard of liberal principles in a parliamentary monarchy in the English

manner. Their leader, or rather figure-head, was the old hero of
the War of American Independence, General La Fayette.
Although Sydney's circle of acquaintances and contacts was
wide, it is clear that her sympathies would lie with this group.

Madame de Staël had always been an inspiration to Sydney.
She had taken the theme of *Delphine* and *Corinne* – that
women must determine to live their own lives against the
conventional domination of men – for her own in her first two
novels. Now she was stirred by the publication of *De
L'Allemagne*, a book which was causing a sensation both in
England and in France. A comprehensive study of German art
and literature, it was also a political treatise hoping to inspire
the Germans as well as the French with that longing for the
rights of man and the principles of liberty to which Madame de
Staël had been faithful since the start of the French Revolution.
In 1813, Napoleon, who had twice before deported her from
France, considered the new work to be an oblique attack upon
him, and had the printer's plates and the entire edition of the
book destroyed and she was once again sent into exile. A
second manuscript of the book, however, had been saved and
smuggled to England, and so Madame de Staël went to
London.

She was received with enormous interest. The triumph of her
reception must have been reported in Dublin and lifted the level
of Kildare Street gossip. It was said that:

> In the immense crowd that collected to hear her at the
> Marquis of Lansdowne, and in the houses of the other
> principle nobility of London the eagerness of curiosity broke
> through all restraint; the first ladies of the kingdom stood on
> chairs and tables to catch a glimpse of her dark and brilliant
> physiognomy.

John Murray published *De L'Allemagne* in October 1813 and
paid 1,500 guineas. Sydney knew from her own experience
what it was like to be lionised by that exclusive set. In some
ways the comparison between the two writers was justified.
Both were devoted daughters; both were brilliant conversa-
tionalists and liberal in politics, and both had written novels
with strong women heroines; but there the resemblance ended
and Sydney would not presume to claim anything further. De
Staël's ardent feminism, her active participation in politics and
her stormy private life were on a far different level, and her
intellectual calibre was regarded internationally with awe. *De*

21 *Madame de Staël as Corinne* by Vigee-Lebrun

L'Allemagne is a landmark in European literature for it introduced to the French and to the English the great literary and philosophic movement that had inspired Germany during the previous half century. It discusses the work of Goethe, Schiller, Herder and Lessing, and launches the new school of Romanticism known as *Sturm und Drang* which dominated European literature for many years to come.

Lady Morgan's *France* had no such portentous message for Europe. It was a highly personal look a life and society at that particular time – a brilliant piece of journalism, reporting straight from the frontline. Although it caused great controversy, *France* was extremely readable, and very widely read. Lady Morgan's prefaces are always very much more serious in intent than the actual content of her books, and the preface to this one claimed very solemn intentions: 'I attempted to expose the evils of despotic governments, in opposition to the blessings and benefits of representative government, to display the fatal effects of a powerful and intolerant superstition as opposed to the enlightened doctrines of rational and revealed religion.' Strong words indeed, but the book was to be received more gently than *De L'Allemagne*; it started no great movement, nobody sent her into exile, or destroyed the first edition. Her real achievement was to give an impression of all aspects of French society which had come within her range of vision, with comments, in so far as they were relevant, on the recent history of France. It was her talent for going everywhere that made her such a lively commentator. Vivacious and sociable, at ease with all classes of society from her washerwoman to great statesmen, she never hesitated to ask questions or failed to draw information out of people. She was particularly interested in fashion and food, and gave the most vivid impressions of both: from the *salade de volailles* and champagne in the Paris restaurants to the savoury ragout simmering in a large marmite over a wood fire in the peasants' hut. The lavish display to the public of the trousseau of the Duchess de Berri, daughter-in-law of the king, made her criticise the 'boundless extravagance and idle vanity' of the court. She was at home in every aspect of French society. She wrote: 'It has frequently occurred to me to have witnessed the most opposited discussions and listened to the most contradictory opinions, in the course of the same evening; assisting at a royalist dinner, drinking ultra tea, and supping en republicaine.' She also acknowledged her almost obsessive occupation with French phrases with a disarming honesty:

> The frequent recurrence of French sentences and dialogues which break up and disfigure the text; a fault which arose from my anxiety to give impressions with all the warmth and vigour with which I received them; to preserve the form with the spirit; to repeat the jargon of the court, of the cottage, the well-turned point of the duchess or the patois of the peasant, as I caught and took them down 'de vive voix' in my tablets, or retained and recorded them in my journal.

Sir Charles and Lady Morgan were received in Paris as people who combined high rank with intellect, and were welcomed unreservedly everywhere. 'Like Charles Lever's Mrs Paul Rooney, and Thackeray's Mrs Rawdon Crawley, those parvenu ladies of fiction who shook off their doubtful antecedents in Paris after Waterloo and were received in circles which would have looked askance at them in England, Sydney found herself appreciated for her fame, her wit and her self-assurance, without any of the condescension that tinged the manner of her exalted friends in England and in Ireland. She, for the most part, avoided the fashionable English, who still found her title slightly absurd and raised their eyebrows at the pretensions of the little ex-governess. Instead, she concentrated on the French and whatever Irish exiles she could find who were still in residence. General Lawless, ex-United Irishman, and veteran of the Irish Legion wrote home to his cousin Lord Cloncurry: 'I like extremely this lady; she is agreeable, witty and with as little conceit as can be found in a woman of her merits.'

Sydney's reputation had gone before her, and she did not need all the letters of introduction that she had brought. She later remarked: 'I had nothing to do but sit quiet and to see and receive all that was best worth seeing and receiving in France.' In a few weeks, at their quarters in the old Hotel d'Orleans, Rue Petits Augustins, Faubourg St Germain, the Morgans were visited by such men of note as Baron von Humboldt, the celebrated explorer and scientist, Abbé Gregoire, the revolutionary Bishop of Blois, and Baron Denon, Napoleon's Director-General of museums, and companion of his Egyptian campaigns. Sydney, with her marked capacity for friendship with women, made lasting ones with the Marquise de Villette, Voltaire's adopted daughter, and Elizabeth Patterson, the American heiress who had married Napoleon's brother Jerome, and had been abandoned by him. The great bluestocking idols of her youth were now on her visiting list. She went to see Helen Maria Williams, friend of Johnson and Boswell, whose *Letters from France* written before the Revolution she had first read in a 'green arbour in Bracklin Castle'. In Miss Williams's 'sober and learned party', being served tea by a servant who 'looked as wise and literary as the rest of the party', they talked of Madame de Staël, far away in Italy who nevertheless had sent messages of friendship to Sydney. She was complimented on her dress, which was a bit showy for that sober circle as she was dressed in readiness for her next appointment – a ball at the residence of the ex-Lieutenant-General of Ireland. Having been told that she had made the dress herself, all the serious ladies in their black bonnets exclaimed their amazement that a 'femme savante' could sew! Sydney tried to tell them that she had no learning at all, except a little bog-Latin picked up in the wilds of Connemara from the mythical hedge schoolmaster who she always produced when she indulged in false naivety; she insisted that her authorship had originated in dire necessity, and that her real profession was not 'femme savante' but 'femme'. *The Wild Irish Girl* was treading the boards again.

Sydney could not be so irrepressibly roguish with another great mentor of her youth, the celebrated Madame de Genlis, whose name had filled her with such awe when she had noticed it, a few years before, in the Visitor's Book of the ladies of Llangollen. It was said of Madame de Genlis many years after her death: 'She was the object of admiration and adoration by some and the object of the most cruel jealousy by others, and early in life she became the butt of frightful malice. Yet she never ceased to triumph and to please'. This double-edged treatment by the world gave her and Lady Morgan something in common, but neither of them would have recognised it. Félicité de St Aubin, Comtesse de Genlis, had been born in 1743, into the higher ranks of the French aristocracy. Before the Revolution she and her husband held positions at the Palais Royal in the court of the Duc de Chartres, later to become the Duc d'Orleans, and better known as Philippe Egalité. Felicité became Philippe's mistress, influencing and directing his Girondist sympathies against the regime. In an attempt at discretion Philippe appointed her as governess to his children, one of whom was later to become Louis Philippe, King of France. Her pupils included two little girls of mysterious origin, one of whom was said to be her own daughter by her royal lover. This child grew up to become the beautiful and tragic Pamela, known to Sydney, and Irish history, as Lady Edward Fitzgerald.

During the Revolution both her husband and Philippe were guillotined and Felicité went into exile under a cloud of scandal, for Philippe had signed the death warrant of the king his brother, under her influence. But her resilience was as formidable as her intellect, and she came back to Paris, in Napoleon's favour. He offered her a pension if she would write him letters, and called her 'the inimitable'. French society applauded her as a charming and brilliant woman, and she was known throughout Europe as a prolific writer of educational

22 *Stéphanie Felicité de Saint Aubin, Comtesse de Genlis* by Antoine Vestier

books for children, the moral tone of which did not seem to be
affected by her own ambiguous reputation, 'the most amorous
of pedagogues' according to the writer St Beuve. This woman
who had lived with kings and princes, with philosophers and
artists, was yet the inspiration of a much later woman writer,
George Sand, who claimed that she derived her own first
socialist and democratic ideas from reading de Genlis. It was
inevitable that Sydney would seek her out for she was
everything she admired – aristocratic lineage, and radical
principles taken to the edge of the guillotine.

In 1816 Madame de Genlis was seventy years of age, and

living a life of seclusion and penance in the Convent of the Carmelites, in Paris. She replied to Lady Morgan's letter requesting permission to visit with exquisite formality:

> The name of the author of such charming works is as well known to Madame de Genlis as it ought to be; although she lives in great solitude she will be charmed to know personally her, the feeling of whose soul she already loves and adores. It is Madame de Genlis who would have been the first to solicit the favour of seeing Lady Morgan if she had known she was in Paris.

As a young governess in the wilds of Roscommon, Sydney had admired to idolatry those formidable learned women, de Staël and de Genlis. And now she was meeting them on equal terms, with books as well as a title to her name. But she still confessed to feeling a high beating throb of expectation when she presented herself at the convent door. She found Felicité's surroundings simple but characteristic. There was a gilded harp and white alabaster vases filled with fresh flowers; there was a piano covered with the newest music and a great crucifix of ivory. Sydney reported:

> I had despaired of seeing a person out of whose works I had been educated and whose name and writings were intimately connected with all my earliest associations of books and literature, when an invitation brought me at once to her retreat in the convent of the Carmelites. Madame de Genlis received me with a kindness, a cordiality, that had all the naiveté and freshness of youthful feeling. When I gave her her lute to play for me it did not require the drawing up of a single string. All was energy and occupation. She conversed with great earnestness, but with great simplicity.

Sydney also asked her several questions, more direct than stilted politeness usually allowed: 'Had teaching always been a passion with Madame?' 'Not at all' was the astounding answer, 'It has always bored me, but now that I am old it is the only way that I can do any good.' This was indeed a revelation. Did it mean that the enthusiasm shown in the schoolrooms of the children of the Duc de Chartres was only a way of disguising her relationship with Pamela? Lady Morgan was dazzled by the personality of the great celebrity she had just interviewed. Her admiration was not returned.

Felicité wrote in her memoirs that Lady Morgan was lively

and agreeable but not beautiful. 'It is a pity' she added, 'that for the sake of popularity she· should have the mania for meddling in politics.' She went on to regret Sydney's vivacity and springing way of walking, and that she had not learned that 'noisy manners and gesticulations are not in good taste'. Sydney had obviously not benefited enough from her early readings of the moral tales of Madame de Genlis.

Life for all these women who had lived through the danger and the drama of the past twenty-five years in France had been more eventful than any novelist could plot; Sydney's new friend Madame Patterson Bonaparte had had her full share of melodrama. She was an American heiress who had been married and deserted by Napoleon's youngest brother, Jerome. He had been an ordinary naval officer when, on leave in Baltimore, he met and married Elizabeth Patterson. In 1804, however, he found himself a member of the Imperial family of France. As Napoleon had no children by Josephine, the hereditary succession had to come through the brothers, and so Jerome agreed to have his marriage annulled in order to make an advantageous political match – which he subsequently did to the Princess of Wurtemberg, and became in time the King of Westphalia. Sydney formed a real friendship with the much wronged Madame Patterson, admiring her because she did not play· the victim or the martyr but held her place in French society with a kind of scornful gay courage – hating Napoleon for what he had done to her, but still admiring his genius. These two were still corresponding thirty years later, in mutual admiration of each other's character. But now Napoleon's day was over, and the Bourbons reinstated. Lady Morgan wrote frankly about her distaste for the 'ancien regime' and the mediocrity of the Restoration, but she attended all the balls. She and Morgan went to one given by the Duke of Wellington to celebrate the Duc de Berri's marriage, where she was presented to all the royal duchesses; in a single night they were at a great international reception at the English embassy and an exclusively French reunion of the Princesse de Tremouille. She wrote: 'After a month of bals-parés, soirées, reunions, and operas we were obliged to give in, and to stay one night at home.'

Sydney's and Morgan's days were filled with interest and importance. Artists showed them their work; theatre boxes were placed at their service; they were guests of the Académie française. The Baron Denon, who had campaigned in Egypt with Napoleon, presented Sydney with his great book of engravings of Egypt. For most of the time they stayed in Paris, but occasionally went down the country to Sevre et Maine to visit and pay homage to the Marquis de la Fayette, champion of liberty in both France and America, and one of Sydney's great heroes. He did not let her down. She wrote admiringly:

> We found General LaFayette surrounded by his patriarchal family; his excellent son and daughter-in-law; his two daughters (the sharers of his dungeon in Olmutz) and their husbands; eleven grandchildren and a venerable grand uncle. Such was the group that received us in the salon of La Grange; such was the close knit circle that made our breakfast and our dinner party, accompanied us in our delightful rambles through the grounds and woods of La Grange, and constantly presented the most earnest unity of family interests, habits, taste and affection. To have lived under the roof of La Fayette, to have conversed with him, and listened to him, was opening a splendid page in the history of man.

Sydney, with her eye for what was novel, did not just observe the French. The English in Paris were a source of much astonishment to the French, who had not seen the like of a London 'dandy' before. That creation of Beau Brummell and the Regency was now in full flower in society and in literature. They took Paris just as Wellington, very much in the 'dandy' style himself, had taken Waterloo, and the French admiration for these exquisitely dressed and eccentricly mannered youths made her remark:

> I have seen the sudden appearance of a London dandy make as great a sensation in a French assembly by its novelty and incomprehensibility as the arrival of a new species in the Jardin des Plantes . . . It was one evening in the apartment of the Princesse de Volkonski when one of these fashionmongering boys, newly arrived in Paris, appeared at the door of the salon, flushed with conscious pride of the toilette, and reconnoitring the company through his glass, I had the honour to be recognised by him; he approached and half yawned, half articulated some enquiries, which he did not wait to be answered, but drawled on to somebody else, whom he distinguished with his notice. A very pleasant little Frenchwoman . . . stared at him with unsated curiosity, and

evident amusement, and when he has passed on asked, 'Mais qu'est ce que cela veut dire?' I answered: 'C'est un dandi'. 'Un dandi!' she repeated 'un dandi! c'est donc un genre parmi vous, qu'un dandi?'

Realising that the book, if it was to be successful, must be as topical as 'le dandyism', the Morgans returned home to Dublin in the Autumn, and she set vigorously to work, encouraged by the letters that followed her. Madame Patterson wrote: 'The French admire you more than anyone who has appeared here since the Battle of Waterloo. Everyone talks of the work you are to publish, and great expectations are formed from it.' La Fayette also wrote in eulogistic terms: 'Your short sojourn here has left an impression upon us which makes us proud of corresponding with you, and we hope to receive another visit soon . . . already we are beginning to look about us to see what would please you when you come.'

Colburn was anticipating great things from the book, and offered her a thousand pounds. But she thought she could get more, and offered it to Constable. They considered it; Walter Scott advised in an editorial capacity: 'her last novel was excellent and her book will be clever, but it depends a great deal on how long she was in Paris.' In the end Constable's partner turned it down: 'I shrewdly suspect that Lady Morgan's subject is far beyond her powers. I will act upon this supposition, and say nay. So much for Paddy Morgan!'

Colburn jumped in again; 'No other bookseller, I am certain, takes the tenth part of the pains I do in advertising, and in other respects I do not think any one will in future cope with me, since from January next I shall have under my control two journals.' These were the *New Monthly Magazine* and the *Literary Gazette*, a weekly devoted entirely to book reviews. He repeated his offer of a thousand pounds plus an extra fifty pound royalties for the third edition of *O'Donnel*. This was accepted, and by March 1817 the book was finished. Sir Charles, who had given up all medical practice except for the position at the Marshalsea, in order to support and travel with his wife, contributed four long and weighty chapters, well documented with statistics on French law, medicine, finance and politics; rather heavy ballast to his wife's airy impression-istic style. There were several hitches in the publishing operation, chief of which seems to have been Lady Morgan's difficult handwriting, which Colburn plaintively mentions more than once. But on 17 June 1817, Colburn announced that *France*, in two volumes, quarto, had been launched on the 'swelling tide of his best puffs and preliminary paragraphs', and that he was sure he would sell out the first edition before the end of the month.

CHAPTER 9

LADY MORGAN
CROSSES THE ALPS

That very superior person Lady Abercorn once said that in her opinion 'little Owenson' would much rather be abused than not noticed at all, 'as her great talents did not prevent her from being as vain as possible!' There was no danger of *France* being ignored – Colburn's publicity had seen to that, and now that the Morgans were back in Dublin, they waited anxiously for the reviews to come in from both sides of the Channel. In his life of Lady Morgan, W.J. Fitzpatrick sums up the general tone of criticism: 'Lady Morgan's work, while it afforded the friends of liberty a high and valued treat, stung corruption to madness and revenge'. In short, the lady had been completely on course. Her opinions pleased those who shared them and enraged these same critics who had previously attacked her for her partisan support of Ireland. In France, Madame de Staël, who had suffered a devastating stroke at the age of fifty-one, had the book read to her on her death bed, and was reported to have been pleased with it. La Fayette said that it was the best contemporary work that had been produced on France, but that the little errors that slipped into it would give an opening to her enemies.

These enemies, both French and English, didn't need much prompting, and seized at every chance to attack her. She was accused, in both languages, of irreligion, Jacobinism, indecency, vanity and ignorance. The French Royalist press were outraged at her open distaste for the restored Bourbons and their pretensions, and at her undisguised approval of the original idealism of the French Revolution and the administration of Napoleon. The bright and breezy way in which she discussed sexual relationships and upheld women's right to behave in a free and open manner was also regarded as shocking, not to mention her criticism of the old religious domination, with its political priests and lavish ceremonies.

In her letters to Olivia she reported enthusiastically several visits she had made to the Comte de Segur, friend of La Fayette. He was an ardent feminist who had paid homage to the courage, ability and perseverance of French women during the Terror, publishing openly his gratitude, respect and admiration for them. He told her that men were always 'least oppressive to women at periods when the tide of their own political liberties were at the lowest'. Olivia responded by writing one of her satirical verses celebrating her sister's forthright libertarian opinions by calling her: 'an elegant artist, a radical slut, and a right Bonapartist.'

The feeling against her was strong enough for the French government to issue an injunction against her coming back to France. Benjamin Constant, the ardent colleague of Madame de Staël, refuted in detail the objections of her foes:

> If she had represented the French as a debased and depraved
> nation; if she had lamented over the corruption of manners
> and the absence of morality and religion . . . her work would
> have been vaunted as a chef d'oeuvre . . . she does not make
> it a crime in the patriots of 1789 that they failed to foresee
> the future; she absolves Philosophy from the errors of
> ignorance and from the excesses of faction.

More importantly, her much admired Lady Charleville, who had lived in France approved:

> Your work charms me; it breathes a fair spirit of
> philanthropic inquiry and observation of facts and effects,
> most interesting to every friend of humanity. The style is
> clear and nervous, and at the same time playful, and suited in
> its tone to the lighter matter, though the graver observations
> are given 'en philosophe'. I think the writing is excellent as
> the materials are interesting and well digested.

Some of her French critics attacked her for not appreciating the plays of Corneille and Racine and, from her vantage point as an actor's daughter, for criticising the style of traditional French acting. One such critic nevertheless praised her for her 'equitable and generous attitude' towards France. 'You have had the courage' he told her, 'to admit that there are still virtues, talents and worth on the banks of the Seine, the Rhone and the Loire. By this dereliction you have earned the animadversion of the loyal presses in Great Britain.'

The 'loyal' presses had already had their beady eye on her for sometime, but now they were outraged. For years the British press had represented the French as fiends and Napoleon as the devil himself, and now here was this Irish writer of trumpery novels, this woman, with the audacity to praise many features of French life, both in the time of the Revolution and under Napoleon, at the expense of England. She dared to argue that the overthrow of the king and his court had been for the general good of the nation, and stigmatised the restoration of the monarchy by England and the Allies as a great mistake. The book created an amazingly widespread controversy; not only did newspapers of all shades of political opinion join in, but books were written about the book in France and in England. How Colburn must have rubbed his hands; any publicity was always good for trade, and the third edition quickly followed the second.

From past experience, Sydney was prepared for some heavy personal abuse. In fact in her preface to the first edition, she invited it:

> There is one review at least which must necessarily place me under the ban of its condemnation . . . as being foreign to its own exclusive creed. I mean the *Quarterly Review* . . . it may look like presumption to hope or even to fear its notice, but I know by experience that in the omniscience of its judgement it can stoop to break a butterfly upon a wheel.

Her challenge was quickly taken up. In July 1817 the *Quarterly* published a twenty-five page review that exceeded even its own usual level of ferocity. It is difficult in this age of multi-media to appreciate how influential these periodicals were. There was among the reading public 'an irrepressible passion for discussion which succeeded the fall of old systems' (Cockburn). At their lowest level, the periodicals were thinly disguised publishers' catalogues, but at their powerful best they distilled a heady mix of politics and literature; reviewers became as important as authors, and reflected the growing weight of public opinion. Since they sold at the generally prohibitive price of five or six shillings, the 'public' in question was a limited but influential one, and the demand was growing. The *Edinburgh Review* and the *Quarterly*, the two leading reviews at the time of Waterloo had a circulation between them of well over 20,000 and, of course, there were several readers for every copy bought. This hunger for authoritative opinion on the state of things reflected the uncertainties of the time.

In 1815 England was beginning to suffer the reaction that seems to be inevitable after a prolonged war. Promises made in the time of danger were not kept. The millennium of brotherly love was obviously not at hand. In fact the transition from 'a state of war to a state of peace', to quote Castlereagh, one of the men most responsible for the reshaping of Europe, was productive of great domestic misery. Thousands of people were out of work, and all over Europe the dreadful weather of 1816 and 1817 caused a disastrous failure of crops. The mood of disillusionment and revolt was reflected in the literature of the time. Mary Wollstonecraft had already made her brave statement. The young men who had grown up during the Napoleonic Wars were in natural opposition to the rulers who doggedly guarded the politics and the religious attitudes of the conservative past. Poets such as Byron, sceptical and irreverent in works like *Don Juan* and *Childe Harold*, brought joy to the young and deep offence to others on the opposite side of the political divide. Hazlitt, Keats, Shelley, Leigh Hunt, 'exploding like bombs', in the way of the young left-wing poets of the 1930s, had to be contained and cut down to size by the mandarins of the Establishment; as the liberal and sceptical tone of some of the most gifted writers of the day grew stronger, the supporters of the government hardened their line of inflexible conservatism.

The great reviews were a powerful tool on either side. The reading public went to them as if to the Delphic Oracle, for signs and portents. Their editors were generally powerful public men, and the question of their appointments was discussed with as much seriousness as if they were to be ministers of government. Not all the periodicals were reactionary. The *Edinburgh Review* the first to be really influential, began in 1802. Intended to be a high Tory vehicle, it became a much needed outlet for liberal opinion in the hands of such editors as Francis Jeffrey and Sidney Smith. Smith later wrote of the state of England when the journal began:

> The Catholics were not emancipated; the Corporation and
> Test Acts were not repealed; the game laws were horribly
> repressive – steel traps and spring guns were set all over the
> country; prisoners tried for their lives could have no counsel;
> a thousand evils were in evidence which the talents of good
> and able men have since lessened or removed.

The *Edinburgh Review* flourished because its literary and

intellectual content was outstanding. But it was not loved by
the government for its politics: 'it's disgusting and deleterious
doctrines' as Walter Scott put it, and there was a powerful
lobby to promote a rival review, as lively and as well edited,
but one that would get its politics 'right'; that meant being
opposed to parliamentary reform, Catholic emancipation, and
any easy line with foreigners, or the Irish. In 1809 the
Quarterly Review was started. Its policy, like that of the
Edinburgh Review, was to use the best talents available, to pay
well, and also to libel, blackguard, blackmail and bully any
writer who did not further the cause of Tory government and
the High Church of England. One of their chief contributors
from the start was J.W. Croker, Lady Morgan's dedicated
enemy, who had promised years ago in Dublin that one day he
would call her out: 'The Wild Irish Girl is not forgotten. Some
circumstances have hitherto prevented a continuation of my
former critical observations upon that subject, which will be
immediately resumed.' This was the enemy she was anticipating
when she threw down her challenge to the *Quarterly*; she
didn't have long to wait.

John Wilson Croker, born in Galway in 1780, was one of
those Irishmen who early on in his career had decided that the
best way to succeed would be to turn the old tag on its head,
and become more English than the English. With him that
meant giving unswerving loyalty to the high Tory position, no
matter how hostile this might be to his native land. His slashing
attacks on Sydney were always dictated by fear of the damage
her novels might do to his chosen party. Croker was well
rewarded for his services and rose fast. As a young lawyer he
had written anonymous pamphlets on Irish society, including
the Irish theatre, always belittling the native character and
applauding the authorities. In 1807 he was elected MP for
Downpatrick, and now in England was made Secretary to the
Admiralty. His official career began with a spectacular
exposure of a colleague's misappropriation of funds; he
opposed the Reform Bill; helped to purchase the Elgin Marbles;
helped to start the Athenaeum Club, and appropriately enough
introduced the word 'conservative' into party labelling.

But it is his role as contributor to the *Quarterly* that brings
him back into our story. Implacable enemy of any shade of
liberal opinion, Croker was the natural star of the periodical
when it was founded and went on to write two hundred and
seventy articles for it, making enemies of Macaulay, Disraeli

and Thackeray among others, on his way. Macaulay, while saying that he hated him 'more than cold boiled veal', also said that he was 'a man who would go a hundred miles through snow and sleet on the top of a coach to search a parish register and prove a man illegitimate or a woman older than she says she is.' But of course the *Quarterly* was a high class production for gentlemen. An article on the French novel, published in 1836, showed how his political bias affected his literary judgment. About Rousseau he tells us a 'baser, meaner, filthier, scoundrel never polluted society', and he finds the same pollution in the works of Dumas, Hugo, Balzac, and George Sand. Shelley was described by him as a man with a 'disgraceful and flagitious history', and he was in the habit of asking the publisher Murray to send him 'fools' to review so that he could 'roast' them. Of course he was a terrific snob, and his attitude to Byron, whose politics he detested, but who was nevertheless 'a gentleman', was always more respectful than his line on a 'Cockney' like Keats, whose *Endymion* he notoriously demolished and according to legend, broke the poet's heart. With such a declared enemy, Sydney needed all the friends she could muster.

The anonymous but inimitable review of *France* in the *Quarterly* began by reminding the readers of the lady's track record: 'Those tomes of absurdity, those puzzles in three volumes called *Ida of Athens*, *The Missionary*, *The Wild Irish Girl*, and that still wilder rhapsody of nonsense *O'Donnel*.' Then the main charges were laid: 'Bad Taste – Bombast and Nonsense – Blunders – Ignorance of the French language and manners – General Ignorance – Jacobinism – Falsehood – Licentiousness and Impiety.' Sydney was accused, with all the emotive words in a classical scholar's locker, of every crime from bad spelling to 'comforting the enemies of France, her own country and of the civilised world'. Perfectly innocent comments, such as the fact that a statue of the Virgin could only be found with great difficulty to carry in a village procession, were twisted into the claim that an actual living virgin was impossible to find in that particular part of rural France. On this point, the reviewer requests his readers 'to consider what manner of a woman she must be who displays such detestable grossness of which even a jest book would be ashamed'. From accusations of licentiousness, the reviewer rises to a climax of indignation against 'the profanation of which this audacious worm prides itself'. This over-heated language, the length of the review, and the puzzle of the anonymous reviewer's real identity were the sensation of the Season. Of course the sales went up; four editions in England, two in France and four in America were quickly exhausted.

Other Tory journals such as *Blackwood's* denounced *France* but the virulence of the *Quarterly* was on its own. Rumour first assigned authorship to Robert Southey, the Poet Laureate, who though he was a dedicated Tory, denied this vehemently: 'her opinions are bad enough, but I would rather have cut off my right hand than have written anything so unmanly and disagreable as that criticism'. On the basis of gentlemanly conduct, Lord Byron protested to John Murray as publisher of the *Quarterly*:

> What cruel work on Lady Morgan! You should recollect that
> she is a woman; though to be sure they are now and then
> very provoking; still as authoresses they can do no great
> harm, and I think it is a pity so much good invective should
> have laid out upon her when there is such a fine field of us
> Jacobin gentlemen for you to work upon. It is perhaps as
> bitter a critique as ever was written!

Croker sometimes admitted and sometimes denied that he had written the review, depending upon who his audience was, but Sydney recognised his unique style, and made it known that in her next novel she would take her revenge. For her next novel was very much on the way. Her travels in France had led her to make comparisons with her own country that were highly critical of the state of things as they were in Ireland. She wrote:

> The French peasant has not to encounter any one of the many
> evils that press upon the neck of the Irish peasantry, and the
> imposts which rendered unavailing the industry of his father
> . . . now scare him no longer even in his dreams. His time, his
> labour are his own, and the spot to which he devotes them is
> a land of promise to which the light of liberty first directed
> him.

Sydney's republicanism, and her sense of Ireland's wrongs had been sharpened. The editor of the *Athenaeum*, H.C. Chorley, wrote about her development at that time: 'The strong national enthusiasm, at once somewhat indiscriminate in its warmth and limited in its scope, will be seen to have ended in fearless and decided political partisanship, in the espousing of ultra liberal doctrines, abroad as well as at home.' The Wild Irish Girl was growing up. Her third specifically Irish novel *Florence*

Macarthy stepped out of 'the mists that do be on the bog' into her own experiences of Ireland as it was in her time. The social problems, the environment, and most of the history are contemporary, but it has to be admitted that being a novel about Ireland, and by Sydney Morgan there will be plenty of ivy growing around tombstones, and plenty of nostalgia for lost glory. Here is her description of the ancestral home of her hero; it could be an allegory for her lost, ideal Ireland:

> The massive stone pillars on either side, overgrown with lichens, still exhibited some vestiges of handsome sculpture: the capital of one was surmounted by a headless eagle, the other showed the claw and part of the body of a goshawk – both natives of the surrounding mountains, and well imitated in black marble, drawn from their onceworked quarries. Two lodges mouldered on either side into absolute ruin, and the intended improvement of a Grecian portico to one, never finished, was still obvious in the scattered fragments of friezes and entablatures, which lay choked amidst heaps of nettles, furze-bushes and long rye-grass. . . . . The precipitous declivities which swept down from the rocky foundations of the house to the over had been cut into terrace gardens, a fashion still observable at the seats of the ancient nobility of Munster; and it was melancholy to observe the stunted rose-tree and once cultivated but now degenerate shrubs and flowers, raising their heads amongst nettles and briars and long grass, and withered potatoe stalks.

The new sense of political reality, and her brave championship of themes which must be unpopular to her Ascendancy patrons, was helped by the support which she got from her marriage. Morgan – 'my ultra-liberal husband' as she called him – was her most zealous and stalwart ally. He matched her in his sceptical attitude to organised religion and hatred of bigotry, and he championed civil and religious liberty with such ardour that he became one of the founders of the campaign for Catholic emancipation. When they had first met he had been the captive of the Abercorns, fond of good living, and indolent, in a mood of inertia caused by the death of his first wife in childbirth after one year of marriage. He had seemed content to drift along in this sinecure, filling his day with little duties and his dilettante hobbies of music and reading, although in his early manhood he had been a keen scientist and a friend of Edward Jenner, the pioneer of vaccination. Sydney had shaken him out of this cosy, but aimless passivity, and persuaded him to develop his talents. He responded to her active mind, got himself an appointment in the Marshalsea Prison and at the same time built up a private practice in Dublin. He was a free-thinking sceptical humanist and, before Darwin, he rejected theological orthodoxy and published two books, *The Philosophy of Life* and *The Philosophy of Morals* which raised such a storm of opposition and censure from conventional belief – he was accused of 'diabolically undermining religion' – that he retired from general practice and devoted himself to his wife, and their joint efforts to extend the world's knowledge of the condition of Ireland.

Sydney, with all her love of society that had made her sing for her supper so many times, no longer needed to play the charming little colleen in order to be invited out. Now she had her own salon, and a husband who supported and encouraged her. And by the time the second edition of *France* came out, she had finished three quarters of *Florence Macarthy*, which she offered to Colburn, along with a science piece by Sir Charles, for one thousand, two hundred pounds for the two.

Florence Macarthy was her bid for serious consideration as a novelist of contemporary Irish life and manners. In a brief introduction to the first edition, Sir Charles pointed out that its theme was 'the reaction of the execrable system of "divide and govern", the demoralisation and insecurity which the system inflicts upon the agents no less than on the victims of oppression', in short it is an indictment of the bureaucracy which sprang up in Ireland after the Union.

But *Florence Macarthy* is also about genealogy – false identities and clouded birthrights. It is about land, and the deceptions and intrigues which a hunger for land fosters – the most Irish of themes. It is above all about national identity and a love of country. At the same time, surprisingly enough, it is a good romantic read. At the heart of it is the heroine, as wild, fascinating and will-o'-the-wispish in her capacity to be in two places at once as any of Sydney's other heroines; this is Florence Macarthy, Countess of Clancare. Of all the self portraits in her novels, *Florence Macarthy* contains the most literal autobiographic details, and her own *raison d'être*. It was also her way of getting her own back on Croker, as the villain of the book is a full-length caricature of her old enemy in the shape of Counsellor Conway Townsend Crawley, ambitious son of a landgrabbing agent.

Others had taken Croker on – Macauley and Disraeli being particularly firm with him, but Sydney's portrayal gave him his Irish dimension, and was instantly recognised on both sides of the water:

> If ever there was a man formed alike by nature and education to betray the land that gave him birth and to act openly as the pander of political corruption or secretly as the agent of defamation, who would stoop to seek his fortune by effecting the fall of a frail woman, or would strive to advance it by stabbing the character of an honest one – who would crush aspiring merit behind the ambuscade of anonymous security while he came forward openly in the defence of that vileness which rank sanctified and influence protected – that man was Conway Crawley. He was yet young, but belonging to the day and the country where he first raised his hiss, and shed his venom, success already beckoned him towards her, with a smile of encouragement, and a leer of contempt.

Many of her readers shared Sydney's obvious enjoyment in this settling of an old score.

The novel concerns the decay of an ancient and eccentric family of Irish aristocrats who have become absentee, with the consequent rise of their unscrupulous land agent, Darby Crawley, who now controls their estates. The final stage in his rise to glory is to be the election of his son as MP for the constituency. As in *O'Donnel*, a house party of bored and supercilious English appear on the scene, including some recognisable portraits from the Abercorn *ménage*. The hero, Fitzadelm, is an Irish exile who has won military fame abroad. His father is mad, obsessed with the past; his brother is unable to cope with the wiles of the Crawleys, and all the family are cursed with what the local peasants call 'the black drop'. That is until Florence Macarthy comes to the rescue. She is descended from the true Irish – kings of Munster – the ancient owners of the estate. Being very poor she makes a living as a novelist and is a lion of London society, but she spends most of her time doing good works on her small Irish property, providing schools and cottage industries for her adoring tenants. With theatrical sleight of hand she slips in and out of the story in numerous disguises, confounding the wicked Darby Crawley and his revolting son Counsellor Con Crawley, Castle hack, service toady, and lightly disguised dead ringer for John Wilson Croker. When he speaks of the Countess there spews out of his mouth a flood of abuse like 'tomes of absurdity and vagueness, of daring blasphemy, of affection, of bad taste, bombast and nonsense'. We have heard it all before, and when he denounces the lady novelist as 'this mad woman, this audacious worm', there is no doubt that it is the chief contributor to the *Quarterly Review* who is speaking.

But as in all Sydney's national tales, the real value of *Florence Macarthy* is not the romantic plot, the lively picture of fashionable life in Dublin, nor the character studies of the native Irish, but the key it gives to the puzzle that is still vexing our own times – the nature and dichotomy of Irish nationalism. Who are the Irish? Who are the Anglo-Irish? 'What is my nation?', as Shakespeare's Captain MacMorris once asked. For into *Florence Macarthy* come crowding in all the tribes; the native Irish, the old English, the Normans, the Catholics who left, the Catholics who stayed, those who collaborated and those who went up in the hills on their keeping. We meet Terence oge O'Leary the spoilt priest turned hedge school-master; we met Hyacinth Daly, of Daly's Court, a character based upon Henry Grattan, once the leader of the Protestant parliament that ended with the Act of Union. We also meet with the Whiteboys up in the hills – outlawed men who have taken whatever law there is into their own hands. In *Florence Macarthy* all things are solved by the marriage of the Countess, daughter of the old Gaelic order, and Fitzadelm, last of the old Norman aristocracy. Between them, ancient enemies though they once were, they will confound the upstart Crawleys, carpetbaggers, conmen, and creatures of the corrupt adminis-tration. The happy ending comes with the united couple pledging themselves to Ireland's good:

> For convinced by a close and attentive observation that the land of their birth was hourly sinking in the scale of nations, under the oppression of delegated authority, and the neglect and absence of its natural protectors, they acted with their energy and perseverance upon the dictates of experience, and illustrated by their example the truth of a maxim now more generally felt and admitted, that IRELAND CAN BEST BE SERVED IN IRELAND.

This is her own manifesto and her hope. It is also the end of the book.

But the very first page of *Florence Macarthy* is strangely potent, and more prophetic than Sydney could possibly have known. For the ship that brings the exiled Fitzadelm back to his native land at the start of the story, is called *Il Librador*. Sydney wrote this book in 1818, and could not know, for the name had not yet been coined, that Daniel O'Connell her uneasy partner in the struggle for Catholic emancipation, would be called and known all over Europe as 'The Liberator'.

That which made her a good reporter in her travel books, gets in the way – as always – with her romantic plots. The sketchy stage effects and melodramatic expedients contrast oddly with the political discussions and statistical details of the state of affairs then existing in Ireland. In a modern world, she might have been a writer with the analytical style of Rebecca West or Mary Macarthy, but circumscribed by the conventions of novel writing at that time, and the demand for a picture of Ireland that conformed to the stereotype, the exigencies of plot get in the way of shrewd observations of political reality, and sharp pen portraits of contemporary protagonists. The plot might be wildly improbable but the background and the details are meticulously accurate. Of these, Jonah Barrington, himself a shrewd observer of the Irish social scene wrote:

> Nothing is exaggerated as to them, and Crawley himself is the perfect and plain model of the combined agent, attorney and magistrate, a sort of mongrel functionary whose existence I have repeatedly repudiated, and whom I pronounce to be at this moment the greatest nuisance and mischief experienced by my unfortunate country.

English critics were not so kind. The *Quarterly* did not review *Florence Macarthy* but took occasion to mention it in discussing another book: 'We have reason to know from *Ida of Athens* the first, we believe of her monstrous progeny to that sooterkin of dullness and immorality *Florence Macarthy*, English ladies view them all with equal disgust.' This reference was probably to the novelist Mary Russell Mitford, who put forward a typically English lady's point of view:

> A vast deal of incredible antiquarianism, and 'Ireland, Ireland, Ireland' as the one single sauce of all these viands forms the principal ingredients of this puffed-off novel. After all, Lady Morgan, if she would vigorously abstain from all French, bad or good, keep at a safe distance from that eternal Ireland (I would not trust her so near as Holyhead), and make up her mind not to allude to Napoleon . . . might well write books worth reading and worth praising.

But Colburn was delighted with the success of *Florence Macarthy* and even more with that of *France*, and he was shrewd enough to know where Sydney's real money-making talents lay. He put it to her that she should write a companion volume to *France* on a country still more torn with discord – Italy. She was longing for another trip abroad to visit her French friends, who had never ceased to write to her, but there were two obstacles. One was lack of money, and the other was the injunction issued by the French government. To her joy Colburn offered two thousand pounds for the book on Italy, and La Fayette wrote, assuring her that the ban was only a political gesture and would not be put into effect. In her diary for August 1818 she wrote of the invitation:

> This morning as I was on my knees, all dust and dowdyism, comes the English post . . . old Colburn – no!, not old at all, but young, enthusiastic Colburn, in love with *Florence Macarthy* and a little 'epris' with the author – 'ITALY – by Lady Morgan' – and makes a dashing offer of two thousand pounds; to be printed in quarto like *France*. We are to start off immediately, Morgan, of course, consenting. He is, in fact, charmed. How he will come out with his Dante and Tasso! Alas, that money should have so much influence over our noble intentions! Knowledge? Power? not a bit of it! Money is power! And so we start on our expensive pilgrimage . . . looking out for a comfortable travelling carriage for I hear that travelling in Italy is beyond everything desolate and unaccomodated, worse even than a journey to Connemara, where people still travel by the stars.

She had to keep her preparations to leave Dublin a secret from her sister Olivia, who was just going to have her third child. Sydney, who loved her 'dear little toddles' wrote in her journal how sad she was to leave them all:

> I am sure that nepotism is an organic affection in single and childless women. It is a maternal instinct gone astray. Aunts and uncles never love wisely but too well. Besides it brings with it responsibilities without authority, and imposes duties without giving rights. And so – bye bye babies!

Eventually she wrote to her darling Olivia, still awaiting her '*mauvais quart d'heure*', long letters describing the dreadful journey by sea and by land to London and their reception there. Among all the excitable name-dropping there was mention of a friend she had made on her first triumphant visit in the wake of *The Wild Irish Girl*'s publication: 'My note and card to Melbourne House was answered by a note and basket of fruit from Lady Caroline, who is at Brockett. What a true heart and what a fanciful head. She is to be in town immediately.'

The true heart and fanciful head belonged to Caroline Ponsonby, daughter of the Earl of Bessborough and cousin of that Sarah who had eloped to Llangollen so long ago. She was about the same age as Sydney now claimed to be, and came from that closed circle of Whig families that ruled society in Regency England. Her mother's sister was Georgina, Duchess of Devonshire, and she was brought up as one of the 'Devonshire House girls', in an atmosphere of great wealth and extra-ordinary permissiveness. The women gambled, sometimes as heavily as the men, and took as many lovers. As political hostesses they influenced the affairs of the state. The children, legitimate and illegitimate alike – 'children of the Mist', as they were called – were brought up to be amused, and be amusing; to be tolerant to everything that would bring pleasure, and hate only injustice. They were taught that there need be no restraint on behaviour so long as some outward semblance of propriety was maintained. Caroline was alternatively spoilt and neglec-ted; a witness to her mother and aunt's hectic love affairs and gambling crises, she was taken on triumphal jaunts abroad, or left at home in the charge of servants. She was always feverishly excitable and wilful, and it was a great relief to her family when in 1805 she married William Lamb, heir to the other great Whig grandee, Lord Melbourne. In 1812 Byron, another '*enfant terrible*', published *Childe Harold*, and after the day of publication wrote: 'I awoke one morning and found myself famous.' He also found himself the current passion of promiscuous ladies in high society, including Caroline Lamb. The account of her pursuit of him, and their short, but very public love affair was given in full autobiographical detail in *Glenarvon, or the Fatal Passion*, Caroline's novel published in 1816, which was a scandalous success both in London and Paris. Sydney must have read it with interest, knowing most of the characters it portrayed. In fact one of these, a rare sympathetic character, an amalgam of the Duchess of Devon-shire and Caroline's own mother, bears the name of Lady Morganet, too close for coincidence!

Glenarvon was the ultimate in public exposure. Published

anonymously but in the full glare of easy recognition, it ran into three editions in as many weeks. The middle classes bought it to read about the permissive way of life of their betters; the upper classes bought it to read about each other. Sydney perhaps did not admire it much as a novel, with its Gothic absurdities and its ramshackle plot. However, it was no more melodramatic than Caroline's own behaviour when, dressed up as a page, she burst into Byron's rooms, or than her scandalous gift to him of a lock of her pubic hair, and her very public attempts to stab herself for love of him. Byron, extricating himself as well as he could from the affair, responded brutally to her passionate demand that he should remember her:

> Remember thee; remember thee!
> Till Lethe quench life's burning streams
> Remorse and shame shall cling to thee
> And haunt thee like a feverish dream.
> Remember thee! Ay doubt it not,
> Thy husband too shall think of thee,
> By neither shall thou be forgot,
> Thou false to him – thou fiend to me.

Her marriage nearly foundered on the book, rather than on the affair, and most of society ostracised her. Her real crime was that she did everything in public. By Sydney remained loyal to her, and found sweetness in her, as well as the wanton streak. She wrote in her diary about this trip to London and Lady Caroline's position:

> If she does not always act wisely for herself, she generally
> acts only too well towards others. On hearing of our arrival
> in town, her first self-indulgence was to send us a basket of
> fruit and flowers; the next was to invite us to Brockett Hall,
> and finding that we could not go she overlooked all
> inconvenience of her London house at this season – carpets
> up and curtains down – she had her couchette put up in one
> of the sitting rooms at Melbourne House, and there she is
> stopping whilst we remain, with no other motive than to be
> of use to us. Since I made her acquaintance before my
> marriage this has been invariably her conduct towards me.

Caroline, isolated because her own set were cutting her, consoled herself with her new role of lady novelist and cultivated Sydney as representing the literary life. She came to value Sydney's friendship greatly, and after her mother died, she confided in her more than anyone else; Sydney's diary is full of descriptions of Caroline and her stories of her childhood and upbringing. She went often to Melbourne House where the heroine of her own scenario would drape herself on a couch and act the part of famous novelist and mistress of the man she described as 'bad, mad, and dangerous to know' – her fatal passion.

There were many other people to see in London, the redoubtable Lady Cork and Orrery, more aged and rouged than ever, saw to that. The social round was so demanding that in a letter to Olivia she had to confess: 'Morgan and I always have a little tiff going home ... I always wanting to stay longer; he wanting to come home sooner.' Olivia, as she had been all her life, was her dearest confidante. She told her everything, from the triumphs to the disappointments. Among all the talk of duchesses and their goings-on, there is some homely stuff about dressmaking:

> To rig myself out in Paris I have had to set myself up with an evening dress, and though materials are extraordinarily cheap here, work is wonderfully dear, so dear that I cannot get a plain dress made up under a guinea and a half. However I have made myself a very pretty dress with my own two hands – white satin with a deep lace flounce. With the skirt I got on beautifully, but as to the corsage, fortunately there is scarcely any, what there is being covered with falls, frills and lace, so it does not signify how the body is made.

Having got her wardrobe together, and dealt with Lady Caroline, in August she was ready to go to Paris, and start the whole extravaganza all over again. The political situation in France had changed considerably since her first visit. The Allies' occupation was coming to an end, and the moderates now held the balance of power. A constitutional majority had passed a new electoral law in 1817 which widened the franchise; even now only some hundred thousand men out of a total population of twenty-nine million had the right to vote. The new law favoured the liberals, and annual elections from then onwards showed a continual swing to the left. Sydney, who had so openly showed her affiliations in *France*, followed these developments with intense interest and her diary and letters give a good deal of space to the elections of 1818 in which her hero – the now rather aged La Fayette, was a successful candidate, and to the subsequent ministerial crisis. In her capacity as a good reporter she was present at the swearing in of the new deputies; and she wrote to Olivia:

> We seldom go to the theatres, but I was at a spectacle the other day worth all the theatres together, the Seance Royale des Chambres, or opening of Parliament. The hero of the day was La Fayette. I never saw such a sensation as he excited when he arose to take his oath to the king. His calm, emphatic way of saying 'Je jure' was quite affecting. I never saw him so grand, so noble. He stood silent and conspicuous by his superior height while the peers were throwing up their hats and white feathers and screaming with the Royalist ladies – 'Vive le roi!', as if the senate was a playhouse, which in fact it was.

During this opening session of the Assembly she caught a glimpse of the 'fine head and pale impassive countenance of Lord Castlereagh, bearing forward from the diplomatic tribune'. It was to be her last sight of the 'perpetrator of the Union in Ireland' as he died by his own hand in 1821.

The Morgans had taken apartments for the winter months in the fashionable Faubourg St Honoré, and Sydney having received so much hospitality, felt ready to reciprocate. Sometimes she was just 'at home' to the ladies, and reports to her sister:

> This being at home is by no means an expensive concern. In some houses they give nothing at all; I give simply tea. The other night a lady called for a lump of sugar; she had no sooner began to eat it than almost everyone called for a lump of sugar, and there was my whole party, each with a bit of sugar in their hands. Now you will allow this is entertaining your friends at a cheap rate, as you can provide a whole party at the expense of a pound of sugar!

Growing more ambitious she started to hold a 'Wednesday evening', a weekly event which grew so popular with all the fashionables in Paris that guests had to stay in the corridors and perch on the tables. One evening twelve nationalities were represented, but on the whole she tried to 'keep as clear of the British as possible, as they are neither profitable nor amusing'. The English, who were not invited, naturally felt aggrieved, and one lady reported to her family:

Lady Morgan is quite the sight of Paris; people flock to her house as they would to a wild beast show. She has Talma, Madame Georges, and all the other lions, foreign and home-bred. She and the Rochefoucaults are very thick – a great proof of their want of tact, for she is the most impudent pretender to literature I ever met with.

But the French, apart from the 'ultras' and royalists continued to love her. Denon arranged for the painter Berthon to paint her portrait, the one that hangs today in the National Gallery of Ireland. She was also initiated into a lodge of female freemasons, the grand mistress being her friend the Marquise de Villette, adopted daughter of Voltaire.

How Olivia, stuck at home in Dublin, with her cheerful middle-class husband, with old Molly, and her many preg-nancies, received these high-flying letters from her sister we do not know; there are no letters of hers extant, and in any case she does not seem to have written many, as Sydney is often forced to complain: 'No letter yet arrived from you!' But wherever she went, no matter how much work she had to put in on her books, or on letters to other people, Sydney always wrote long and detailed letters to Olivia. In some ways she was still continuing the role she had played when she was the protective elder sister, minding the motherless Olivia in some anonymous theatrical boarding house. Now, instead of fairy stories, it was a glittering non-stop soap opera of real life duchesses, princesses, princes, all the illustrious names of Europe; sharing with her sister the amazing experiences of her own life as though it was still a bed-time story. Sydney had moved so far away from those early days, and yet through Olivia she clung tenaciously to the past; the smaller triumphs of Dublin society, the confident exchanges of wit and malice, and the continuity of family life in the house in North Great George's Street, where there were now three little girls, and a new baby in the cradle. That is where the memories of her father were stored.

His sister Olivia had always been Sydney's responsibility. She was pretty, with long golden hair, and had always been a little delicate. She had married young, in order to provide a home for her father, as well as herself, and had become well settled, before Sydney, with a house and a carriage, and a husband who was knighted for his medical skill. Sir Arthur Clarke, if not the most romantic of suitors was a good provider, and both prosperous and popular. As his wife, Olivia had a place in Dublin society. He had strong ideas about the medicinal value of baths, and in that city of nicknames was inevitably called 'The Knight of the Bath', and Olivia was known as the Lady of the Lake. She herself had a real talent for comic verse, and had her own circle of admirers. Her sister's triumph had encouraged her to write a comedy, *The Irishwoman*, which was produced and published without, however, setting the Liffey on fire. Sydney was proud of Olivia as well as protective towards her, but at the same time always a little possessive. She sent her presents from France and sweets for the children, but never seemed to get enough in return. In one letter from Paris she makes an open complaint:

> Your letters have at last arrived . . . From all these I learn that 'Florence' is disliked, abused and cried down; but whether you or Clarke ever saw or had it, or liked it, I cannot discover, as you never think it worth your while to say so. I thought it deserved a little more attention than this from my own people, whatever the world might think; but alas! I never was a prophet in my own family.

But for the most part Sydney showed love and concern for Olivia, and confided to her an intention of giving up writing after this trip:

> If I live to accomplish the work I have now in view, I have done with authorship for the rest of my life, for I am quite worn out. Do not say to any one I am going to write on Italy, but to travel for amusement.

Gradually the round of entertainment, with three or four invitations every night, had started to exhaust even her inexhaustible energy. At the end of March she wrote:

> I never know the enjoyment of one day, one hour to myself. Strangers of all countries not only write to me to receive them, but actually force the door, dispute the point with my servant, and then think they excuse this intrusion by talking to me of my 'reputation européan'. You have no idea how I pant for silence, solitude, and a long journey, which thank heaven, we are now about to begin.

The practical Sir Charles, who was not only a most devoted husband but his wife's doctor as well, helped her to withstand the demands of the coming journey to Italy. He had hired a

23   *Wild Italian Landscape* by Salvator Rosa, National Gallery of Ireland

German built travelling carriage – a Berline – complete with a cupboard full of 'eatables and drinkables', and on 4 April 1819 they set out. Every stage of the journey was described fully in letters to Olivia; five days getting to Lyons through eternal plains which reminded her of Tipperary – 'and dreary villages and bad inns render the scene truly Irish'. Arriving in Lyons she was pleased to be told by the innkeeper that her room was the one once occupied not only by Madame Recamier, but by Madame de Staël as well during their different terms of exile – 'so I was on classic ground'. Two days' journey brought them to Geneva, and the joy of seeing Mont Blanc at sunset was equalled by the thrill of breathing for the first time 'the free air of a Republic'. In Geneva they were given a civic reception and offered a house and garden on the lake for as long as they wished to stay, but they regretfully declined. After pausing at Chambery – 'which is not much larger than Drogheda' – for two or three days, they crossed the Alps in a snowstorm:

> It snowed all night, and we began our ascent in a shower of snow, with four stout horses pulling our light carriage. My imagination became completely seized as we proceeded, and I sat silent for nearly seven hours, my teeth clenched, my hands closed, and my whole existence absorbed in the sublime horror that surrounded me. As we descended a slow spring gradually opened on us, the snows were melting, the trees budding, and once arrived in the lovely plains of Lombardy, the same glowing summer presented itself. We passed a day at the first Italian town we reached, Susa, at the foot of Mount Cenis.

With this description of the magical Italian spring, she also confided a little uncertainty:

> I am in very low spirits, and rather nervous and wakeful; but from this moment I am all Italy's. I feel as though we had a grand vocation; of our earnest truthfulness I have no doubt, but in our power for aiding the great cause, the regeneration of Italy, we feel little confidence.

CHAPTER 10

LORD BYRON APPROVES

The romantic image of Italy, like that of Ireland, was one of picturesque ruins and sublime scenery. Sydney had made this analogy for herself when she had visited the art galleries of Kilkenny Castle many years before, comparing the paintings of Salvator Rosa with the savage grandeur of Galway and Sligo. Italy's history seemed equally tragic. Foreign rule and economic and political decline had turned the glories of the Renaissance, and the proud Venetian Republic into mere sources of loot for the rest of Europe; Italy was now just a repository of the classical past, a necessary part of the Grand Tour. But in spite of centuries of decline it was still considered the fountain head of European civilisation, and travellers from all over the continent came south to learn the language in which so much great literature had been written, to see the ruins of the Forum and the Campagna, and to take back some piece of art or antiquity, albeit as cheaply as possible.

The Italians themselves, broken up into ineffective regions, under foreign rule and crushed by taxation and censorship, consoled themselves as best they could with music, masquerades and banditry – that is, until the French Revolution burst upon Europe. Napoleon, who was of Italian stock, spoke the language and acknowledged kinship, came into Italy to drive out the Austrians and curtail the power of the Pope, and at the same time bring the benefits of the French version of the rights of man to one and all. He crowned himself King of Italy with the ancient Iron Crown of Lombardy, and started to reform and vitalise the whole country.

But the Congress of Vienna which followed Waterloo, restored the status quo and brought back the minor *principes* and *principessas*. Italy, with eighteen million inhabitants, was fragmented once again into seven states, five of them ruled by the Austrian royal family. Feudal rights were restored, and in

24   *Enniskerry* (Co. Wicklow), from drawing by Francis Wheatley

Rome the Index and the Inquisition were reinstated. The
Austrian Chancellor Metternich defined the term 'Italy' as
merely a geographical expression, and for the next thirty years
did his best to keep it that way.

But some of Napoleon's work could not so easily be
eradicated. He had given the Italians a new concept of
nationality and self-government; he had started to reform the
legal system with the Code Napoleon; he had built roads,
bridges and canals and brought people together. Many Italians
were unwilling to give up this newly acquired taste for national
independence. Books were written; secret societies formed, like
the Carbonari, with which Byron had been associated. It was
all very unstructured and tentative, but it was exactly what
Sydney and her freethinking husband were looking for.

During their recent stay in Paris, in spite of all the social
demands, they had spent several hours a day getting ready for
the visit by reading up Italian history. Charles spoke the
language, and was well read in the classics. Sydney's knowledge
was only sketchy but at the same time adventurous. She might
well be able to quote tags of Tasso or Petrarch, but for the
most part it was unknown territory. Some aspects, of course,
were all too familiar; she could recognise suppression of liberty
by tyranny wherever she saw it, whether in Italy, Greece or Ireland, and she made sure that she had the right credentials and
introductions to people who would guide her in this direction.

The authorities knew this, and had her under surveillance.
While she was being given civic receptions in Bologna and
Milan, the Italian secret police reported:

> In re espionage over Lady Morgan and her husband, the
> nature of the political views which your Excellence agrees
> with me have been expressed by the Morgans, husband and
> wife, who have recently arrived in that city demands the
> most rigorous and careful supervision over them personally.
> I doubt not that your Excellence will have already directed
> that this should be done, and therefore I await the expected
> result.

But no surveillance could curb her intentions to see what she
wanted to see. The Italian tour was characteristically thorough
and successful. If her Italian was sketchy, her energy was
wholehearted, and she never spared herself, in spite of attacks
of rheumatism and mosquitoes alike. Milan, Bologna, Florence,
Rome and Naples – wherever they went the Morgans saw

everything, and as in France they met with generous hospitality. The Italians could not compete with the rich English and other foreign visitors who crowded the cities; other travellers at that time have noted that the palaces of the nobility were furnished with pictures and little else, and that they saved on meals also. At receptions for example, all the Venetians offered was chocolate and iced water, in order to spend heavily on the carriages and ornate clothes which raised their prestige. Sydney wrote to Olivia: 'All the English say we are the only strangers for whom the Italians make dinners.' In her flow of letters to Olivia, she is always the brilliant travel writer, giving the impression of a huge carnival. Her own triumphs are never played down; as she had been in her letters from country houses in Ireland when she was only a humble governess, she is always the centre of attention. There were firework parties for her on Lake Como; balls were given in her honour; in Milan, all the professors of the University in full regalia were put on parade to greet her. Morgan fished on Lake Como; they met Volta, inventor of the voltaic battery; they practised the Spanish guitar; Sydney was given boxes at the opera, and carriages were put at their disposal.

In her letters home to Dublin the scenario takes on the aspect of Grand Opera. In Florence, the Countess of Albany, widow of Bonny Prince Charlie and 'the legitimate queen of England' in Sydney's book, put out all her gold plate when entertaining them to dinner. In Rome it was the same.

They visited Pauline Borghese, sister of Napoleon, and soon met the rest of that family. Olivia was told:

> Madame Mere, Napoleon's mother sent to say she would be glad to see me; we were received in quite an imperial style. I never saw so fine an old lady – still quite handsome. She was dressed in a rich crimson velvet, trimmed with sable with a point lace ruff, and head-dress.

The letter to Olivia described how the pictures of her sons, daughters, and grandchildren, all in royal robes, hung on the walls, dominated by the head of them all, old M. Bonaparte, no doubt in decent bourgeois black. Sydney could not fail to marvel how far one family could rise. 'You see', said Madame Mere when she showed Sydney her miniatures of her four royal sons, 'when my son Buonaparte sat for me, I made him lay aside his crown.' How Sydney's father would have loved the high theatrical camp of her stories.

The new Duchess of Devonshire, queening it in Rome, arranged an audience with the Papal Secretary of State, Cardinal Gonsalvi. Sydney's interest in this prince of the church had been roused by the reports of his liberal views – he was nicknamed '*Il Giacobino*', the Jacobin, and it was said that he had approved of Napoleon's proposal to abolish the celibacy of the clergy. She wrote it all out like a play. The scene – the Quirinal chapel of the Vatican. The cast – the wealth and prowess of Europe, and as in her novels, herself, always upstage:

> As we stood in the partial shadow of one of the grand
> columns, with some streaks of bright light falling from a high
> window on the rich robes and diamond buckles of his
> eminence, I was struck by the oddity of the group. The fine
> figure and countenance, and the magnificent costume of the
> Cardinal – the sibyl air and look of the British peeress,
> whose tall slight form was rapt in a black, velvet mantle,
> surmounted by a black hat and one sweeping feather, and my
> own little 'Red riding hood' appearance, as Irish as if I had
> never left the banks of the Liffey. It was the picture to fill the
> canvas of a Callot or a Caravaggio.

Olivia, back home on the north side of the Liffey, in all the small ordinariness of Dublin life, must have felt a bit out of her depth, but among all the gossip about people she didn't know, and would probably never have the chance to meet, there was news of an old friend, the Thomas Moore whose singing had so enchanted her when she was a child.

He had become a great celebrity since those days, and was now a friend of Byron, and accounted Ireland's greatest poet. In 1803, as a way of giving Moore an income he had been made a Registrar of the Admiralty Prize Court in Bermuda, but the seclusion of the islands was not to his taste, and he soon appointed a deputy and returned to London. But in 1818 the deputy had absconded from the island, leaving Moore responsible for about three thousand pounds of debt, and the poet was in deep trouble, obliged to live abroad for three years to avoid the debtor's prison. He was now in Italy on his enforced continental tour and had met up with Lady Morgan in Florence. He brought messages from Byron – himself in enforced exile because of behaviour too scandalous even for Regency society. Sydney writes:

Moore said we were expected at Venice, and that he had
heard of us everywhere. Lord Byron bid Moore tell Morgan
he would be happy to make his acquaintance, but not a word
of encouragement to his 'lady intellectual'. I never saw
Moore gayer, better or pleasanter. We have begged him to
come and breakfast with us every day, and he goes with me
the day after tomorrow to the comic opera.

Moore's diary shows that he visited the Morgans or met them
in society every day; that they had fifty Irish names alone on
their visitor's book, along with as many as twelve other
nationalities, and that Dr Morgan was useful to him profes-
sionally as well as socially for he cured him from an attack of
inflammation of the leg.

Sydney's letters to Olivia were as full of information and
entertainment as she could make them, but she still had the
book to write. It was time to go home, and in May of 1820
they returned to Dublin. She had been away for nearly two
years, and when she got home she found that the house which
had been let for that period had been wrecked by the tenant,
who had absconded with furniture, leaving rent unpaid and
damage that needed more than three hundred pounds to put it
right. She needed to earn some money. She wrote to her old
employer Mrs Featherstone:

I am now writing eight hours a day to get ready for
publication by December, and endeavour to keep out of the
world as well as I can, but invitations pour in. People are
curious, I suppose to hear some news from Rome, and I
want to keep it for my book.

The book had been heavily publicised by Colburn and eagerly
anticipated. She was now at the height of her literary fame.
France had gone in to several editions in England, France and
America; *Florence Macarthy* was in its fifth English edition and
had been dramatised, like most of the successful novels of the
time, for the Surrey Theatre. This was an enterprise of
fluctuating fortunes in the Blackfriars Road, dating from the
latter half of the eighteenth century. Sometimes it was an arena
for circuses, and sometimes it was a theatre, and now under a
new, hopeful management it was trying out adaptations of
best-selling novels. She was kept very much in the public eye by
the attention of her old enemies also, for the *Quarterly* had a
jibe at her in almost every issue, and had now, in 1817, been

joined by a new Tory journal. *Blackwood's*, lighthearted, but
equally malevolent, ridiculed 'Miladi' regularly. They, too,
were waiting like mischievous vultures for the publication of
Italy.

Italy was advertised to appear simultaneously in London and
Paris on 15 June 1821, and produced an even greater sensation
than the work on France. Published in two quarto volumes,
and owing a great deal to Beckford's *Italy* and other
contemporary accounts, it is certainly too long, and over-
weighted with guide-book descriptions and historical sum-
maries. But Sydney succeeds in communicating her own intense
enjoyment and mixes in – with all the descriptions of art,
architecture and scenery – her own moral and political stance.
For as in *France*, she observed and passed judgment. Her
commonsense and egalitarian philosophy overwhelms her sense
of awe. In her opinion the numerous petty states of Italy,
puppets of the Austrian emperor, were destroying the rapid
modernisation and enlightenment brought about by Napoleon.
She ridiculed the pretensions of regal ceremonial, calling the
King of Sardinia 'king of the anchovies'. She attacked the
supremacy of the Roman Catholic church, accusing it of 'power
supported by violence fearing and feared; religion disfigured by
imposition, degrading and degraded' and she made fun of the
'Images of culinary martyrdom' which she found in the
paintings of tortured saints and martyrs everywhere. She
deplored the end of the reforms that the French had brought to
the status of women with 'the new and liberal system of female
education, raised upon the ruins of that demoralising bigotry,
which was calculated to make women concubines and devotees,
but which could not produce good wives and mothers.' She
found similarities with the wrongs of Ireland, and made a
daring attack on the English government for their breach of
faith with the Italian patriots. She did not mince her words:

> It is humiliating to find England upon all occasions the
> political scavenger of Europe, performing all that dirty work
> with which more crafty cabinets contrive not to sully their
> character; but far beyond the folly and wickedness of such
> acts is the hypocrisy with which they are accompanied.

The book inevitably produced the usual violent reaction of
praise and abuse. Byron, a more or less paid up member of the
Carbonari himself, wrote to Moore from Italy:

> Her work is fearless and excellent on the subject of Italy;
> pray tell her so. I know the country. I wish she had fallen in
> with me; I could have told her a thing or two that would
> have confirmed her position.

But his recommendation did not stop her from being proscribed by the King of Sardinia, the Emperor of Austria and the Pope. All this made her feel a satisfactory sisterhood with Madame de Staël. And after that, the English press was unleashed.

By the first of July the book had been mauled by every ministerial print, newspaper and magazine in England. The same old insults were trotted out; she was called 'an ambulatory scribbler of bad novels' who indulged in nonsense, ignorance, indecency, irreligion, Jacobinism, and premeditated perversion of facts; she was a 'petticoated ultra radical author' and her book a 'monstrous literary abortion'. As always, Sydney was ready for a fight and had anticipated her critics by writing *A letter to the Reviewers of Italy*. This was printed by Colburn and bound up with remaining copies of the book, as well as being sent to all subscribers. He also had it reprinted as a supplement to the October issue of his own journal, the *New Monthly Magazine*. Her main thesis was that the campaign against her was inspired by 'hired agents of the authorities' in the hope of preventing her books from being read: 'They have attacked me at every point where the woman was most susceptible, the author most sensitive. They have attacked my public profession, and private character, my person, my principles, my country, my friends, my kindred, and even my dress.' And then she went on the attack herself with undisguised enjoyment. She dubbed the editor of the *Quarterly* 'the boss of Billingsgate', and cited the 'blood stained pages of *Blackwood's*, referring to a recent duel in which the editor of a rival journal had lost his life. Those were brutal times, when reviewers of books used both pen and pistol. She took on, too, the editor of the *Edinburgh Review* – 'this lord of literary misrule, this ignoramus, the pseudo reviewer, this Captain O'Blunder'.

But she had by no means silenced her critics. Coming on to the battleground, the *British Critic*, a journal edited by a clergyman primarily for clergymen, first went for Sir Charles, for being married to such a woman, and accused him of being in a state of 'intellectual hermaphroditism', and then the clerical review summed up his wife's character:

Herewith she spew'd out of her FILTHY MAW
A flood of poison, horrible and black:
Her vomit full of books and papers was . . .

So much for the opinion of the reverend gentlemen.

The *Edinburgh Review* was less poetic. In its next number it devoted twelve pages to the 'letter' more abusive than ever, calling her 'an Irish she-wolf', a 'blustering virago' and, after alluding to the 'mad aspersions of a wholesale blunderer and reviler', and 'the strollers' barn where she was bred', the reviewer thought that she must have become 'maudlin from an extra tumbler of negus in the forenoon'. The gentlemen of the press, no doubt pillars of propriety and churchgoers to a man, thus added snobbery, racism and anti-feminism to their strong political prejudice. But the malign jokes did not stop there. In the more ribald Tory papers, Croker got up a mock 'Royal Commission' to inquire into her age, which ended its proceedings by declaring her a 'female Methusaleh'! Then, in January 1822, he and his cronies solemnly took the opinion of the Attorney General and the Solicitor General as to whether the Lord Lieutenant of Ireland had the right to confer the honour of knighthood. Both gave their considered opinion that since the Act of Union no such right existed, and that accordingly the titles of Sir Arthur Clarke, and Sir Charles Morgan were null and void.

The time wasting, frivolous case dragged on for eighteen months before it was thrown out. But the journals did not let it drop. It was too good a joke to lose. The comic newspaper *Blackwood's* immediately started to call her 'Mrs Morgan' and the 'ci-devant Miladi'. During that year there were twenty-seven separate jibes in that one magazine alone, ranging from full page attacks to passing jeers at her squint, and her childlessness. There's no doubt that the spite and malice, and particularly the attempt to deprive her of her title, hurt her, but they only served to strengthen her consciousness as a liberal, a nationalist and a woman. She took the insults for what they were — attacks not only upon her talents as a writer, but on her country, her politics and her sex, and she knew why she was pursued with such public virulence. She was no Tom Paine in petticoats; she only wanted a just reconciliation of all the talents in Ireland; she had even romanticised the aristocracy to a degree that made people call her a social climber, and yet these powerful men who shaped public opinion hated and feared her. Was it because she was popular and easily accessible, and therefore much more dangerous in her way than an open partisan polemicist? She used her lively and romantic fiction like a minefield wherein she planted her subversive opinions. Her footnotes, the constant comparisons, the criticism of English government are as packed with politics as her observations on the restoration of the *ancien regime* in France and Italy. She was different from other women writers of the time in this respect: brought up as her enemies said 'in a strollers' barn', she had been saved from mediocrity and squalor in those days by the striking of heroic attitudes and her love of heroic words. She was in love with the ideas and the philosophy that had led directly to the French Revolution and, like her father, had hoped that great changes would come from this event to Ireland. The disaster of 1798 had killed that hope, and she had had to come to terms with things as they were, both in France and in Ireland; but she still had almost a missionary vocation to make the world acknowledge her country's claims. And so her Tory critics feared her and in spite of their jeers and ribaldry, they really took her very seriously indeed, thus paradoxically acknowledging her potency. They were not going to have this impudent woman forever stirring up trouble. So they tried to denigrate her and belittle her work in the eyes of the public.

The public however bought *Italy* in such quantitites that Colburn wrote a letter to *The Times* stating his entire satisfaction at the result of his investment, and that he would 'be most happy to receive from the author another work of equal interest on the same terms'. On the continent the book was eagerly read, but because of the official ban it could not be discussed openly. Before it was completed there had been an unsuccessful rising in Naples, and another was brewing in Piedmont. Some of the Morgan's contacts were implicated and imprisoned. Lady Morgan was held partly responsible by some people for the misfortune of her friends. When Lord Holland's son visited Italy a year or two later he noted in his diary: 'Lady Morgan's book has done incalculable harm here, especially to those she praises for having liberal opinions, and for that many have been banished, imprisoned or watched.' But the Italians who knew who their real enemies were did not see it that way. For many years afterwards many of the political exiles wrote to her in Dublin to ask for help in some form or other – and as she had responded to Barnaby Fitzpatrick in Dublin, she now worked unstintingly on behalf of the refugees.

She was glad to have stopped travelling and to be back in

25   *Salvator Rosa*, self-portrait, National Gallery of England

Dublin. In all the glamorous accounts of high society in France and Italy there had been in her letters home a latent nostalgia for the small social pleasures of her own town. She had lived too long in the houses of the great to be impressed with the social aspirations of the rising Dublin bourgeoisie or, as she put it: 'its Miss McGuffins, and the rest of your twopenny Misses and Masters', but she thought she could do better. She had begun to dream of having a salon of her own, enthroning herself like the Countess of Albany in Florence, among a circle of guests, or like Lady Cork in London, inviting people of all tastes and talents so long as they were distinguished or amusing. She had a real flair for society, and more important – she had a great talent for food. On her travels she had kept a notebook of all the good recipes she had enjoyed and now, in Dublin, a city not particularly noted for its cuisine, nobody refused invitations to her dinner parties prepared for the most part by herself with whatever domestic help she had available. But for all this entertaining and refurbishing of her house she needed money, and so she contracted with Colburn to produce another book as quickly as possible. In the art galleries of Italy she had conceived an idea for a romance based on the life of Salvator Rosa, the Neapolitan painter of baroque 'sublime' scenery. Now she had seen the wild mountain landscapes of Italy she became interested in the character of the man himself. After writing one chapter of the novel of which he was to be the hero, she decided to write a biography instead, to 'raise the veil of calumny from the splendid image of a slandered genius'. She had found another noble cause for which to battle.

Salvator Rosa was born in 1615 in Naples, and died in 1673. He was a great painter of picturesque landscape and one of the founding fathers of Romanticism. His self-portrait in the National Gallery in London tells a great deal about him. A handsome melancholy man, dressed in black, holds up a placard which says in Latin: 'Be silent, unless you have something to say which is better than silence.' But he was never silent himself, and wrote a number of controversial satires on art and government which endeared him to nineteenth-century liberals like Lady Morgan when she read about them. His paintings underline his legend, which was summed up by Horace Walpole, when he crossed the Alps in 1738: 'Precipices, mountains, torrent, wolves, rumblings, Salvator Rosa!' Sydney, looking for material, found that all references to this painter had been obscured by prejudice and politics. The *Parnasso Italiano*, art history approved by the Church and authorities, described Salvator in highly unfavourable terms. 'Low birth; an unregulated mind – one whose life had been disorderly.' She found something suspiciously familiar in all this, and went back to first sources. She wrote in her introduction that he was 'in fact the precise reverse in life and character of all that had been represented by the hired literary hacks, which he had so boldly and so ably attacked both by his pencil and his pen.' She concluded that it was 'not the vice of the man' that called up this obloquy 'but the moral independence and political principles of the patriot'. She identified wholeheartedly with this image of a patriot attacked by hired literary hacks, and her ensuing book was always her own favourite among her works.

Originally research was impossible, and information from Italy was increasingly hard to come by. She wrote in her 'Preface': 'Of the number of distinguished friends I made and left in that country, few now reside there; many have been condemned to death; the greatest number have saved their life by perilous evasion, and exile.' She made use, therefore, of the friends she had among the English upper classes; Salvator Rosa had become very fashionable with wealthy patrons of art ever since Edmund Burke's *Treatise on the Origins of our ideas of the Sublime and the Beautiful* was published in 1767. Here 'sublime' defined nature as awe-inspiring and untamed, producing emotions of 'delightful horror and terrible joy'; emotions which were considered necessary for a fully civilised life, if one lived in a quiet country mansion in pastoral England; this taste for the 'sublime' explains a great deal of the popularity of the Gothic novel and, by the same token, of *The Wild Irish Girl* when it first appeared. So there were a lot of wildly romantic Italian landscapes, with bandits and outlaws sheltering in caves hanging on the walls of English country houses. Every patron of art who owned a Salvator Rosa was canvassed. Caroline Lamb obtained copious notes from her brother William Ponsonby, and the Duchess of Devonshire sent a list of all the Salvators she could find in Roman art galleries. The biography shows its origins as a novel with Salvator, who spent some time in his early youth living rough with the banditti of the Abruzzi, being depicted as romantic and dangerous a hero as Red Hugh O'Donnell, hiding out in the Wicklow mountains through an Irish winter. It is lively, fictionalised biography, reporting incidents and dialogue with the assurance of an eyewitness. Her hero, like her heroines, took on many of her own traits of character, and he paid the same price for his boldness as she herself had recently paid:

> Calumny met him at the gates of Rome, defamation was at its dirty work again, and professional envy sheltering itself under party feeling attacked the principles and opinions of a man whose genius and successes were the true causes of the persecutions he endured.

Sydney's traditional enemies more or less ignored *Salvator Rosa* but she was so bruised and persecuted by the Tories, that when the leading Whig publication the *Edinburgh Review* gave her book to William Hazlitt to review she expected better treatment. He too had suffered mauling at the hands of her revilers for the same reasons – he was a radical. But he was also full of male superiority and wrote a patronising piece, damning her with faint praise, and criticising her for 'playing the diplomatist in petticoats', and 'strutting the little Gibbon of her age'. In short, he objected to her poaching on the male preserves of scholarship and art.

It was fortunate that in this period of persecution from her reviewers she was safe in the warm admiration of her Dublin circle. Her evenings at 35 Kildare Street were the brightest event in the social calendar, and for fifteen years she conducted Dublin's only salon. For there had been a great change in that city's social climate. In 1800 the Register showed 269 peers and 300 MPs with houses in the city, but by 1821 only 34 peers, 13 baronets and 5 MPs lived there. In her novel *The Absentee* published in 1812, Maria Edgeworth had already described very succinctly the consequences of this change:

> From the removal of both Houses of Parliament, most of the nobility and many of the principal families among the Irish commoners either hurried in high hopes to London, or retired disgusted and in despair to their houses in the country. Immediately, in Dublin, commerce rose into the vacated seats of rank; wealth rose into the place of birth. New faces and new equipages appeared. People who had never been heard of before started into notice, pushed themselves forward not scrupling to elbow their way even at the Castle; and they were presented to my Lord-Lieutenant and to my Lady Lieutenant; for their Excellencies might have played their vice-regal parts to empty benches had they not admitted such persons for the moment to fill their Court.

The Misses McGuffins and their like had at last arrived. But although much of the fashionable and political distinction had disappeared, Dublin was nevertheless the second city in the British Isles, and remained an important legal, administrative and ecclesiastical centre, a big garrison and a university city. It was always a patchwork place of extreme extravagance and poverty in close proximity. And its intellectual life was also very uneven. Mathematics, the law and medicine were justly famous, but it was impossible to keep a literary journal going, and the theatre had still to depend completely upon importations from London. The learned societies which had been started in the eighteenth century were still hanging on, but in a report made on the affairs of the Royal Dublin Society – once the pride of the enlightened members of the Ascendancy – the writer deplored the fact that so many of the annual subscriptions were in arrears. So it was no wonder that Lady Morgan was a popular hostess and that everyone from the Lord Lieutenant down wanted to be on her guest list. It was seldom that a visitor to Ireland, if he had any claim to celebrity, escaped an invitation. Though when George IV – the first English king to come to Ireland on a peaceful mission – visited Dublin in 1821, just after his Coronation, the Morgans deliberately left town in order to escape the wildly hysterical celebrations. This was a very controversial visit, with the Catholics still denied emancipation and the country in a state of resentful apathy. Many nationalists continued to boycott the Castle and the court on principle. The Lord Lieutenant and his party worked themselves up into a patriotic frenzy, and the Protestant tradesmen and professionals were very gratified at all these proceedings. But so were the rising Catholic shop-keepers, who under the leadership of Daniel O'Connell, by now the most prominent figure in the Catholic campaign, hoped that at this time, and with this king, they might gain some advantages. The gombeen men and the shoneens, derogatory terms for shopkeepers too much occupied 'with their greasy till', were very prominent in the arrangements for the celebrations.

So the city was decorated with triumphal arches; a new Round Room was constructed at the Mansion House in order to entertain the king in style; a portable latrine was measured for the king's capacious rotundities, and Dan O'Connell waited to meet him at the harbour of Dunleary. To the shame and embarrassment of the old style patriots, O'Connell knelt in homage to receive the king. The king was said to be speechlessly drunk on arrival, and stayed that way for most of his visit. Dan O'Connell, though he was to become the most important leader of the Catholic masses, in early nineteenth-century Ireland, was never forgiven for that obeisance to 'the gluttonous despot' as Byron called his king. An Irish witness described the scene with scorn: 'And Ireland like a bastinadoed elephant kneeling to receive the paltry rider'; and again Byron, from his exile in Italy raged at the way in which this occasion had betrayed the Irish nationalist cause:

My contempt for a nation so servile though sore
Which though trod like the worm will not turn upon power.

In the meantime, the Morgans distanced themselves from the distasteful jamboree, communicating instead with old gentle-manly patriots like Hamilton Rowan who had once been secretary of the Dublin Society of the United Irishmen, and as such had served his time in the prisons of His English Majesty. He wrote to the Morgans: 'Until I saw George the Fourth, I never met a person who in features, contour and general mien outdid their caricature!' George IV left Ireland, drunk as he had arrived. Dunleary was renamed Kingstown, and Dublin went back to normal. Nothing was changed – the Catholics were still denied the franchise. The Morgans returned to Kildare Street, and Sydney proceeded to embellish her house with all the trophies of her travels. She created for herself a background worthy of any of her adored French savantes – a temple of learning and culture. Like a stage designer, she placed herself in her little red boudoir, writing at a rosewood secretaire. Gloating in self congratulation, she wrote:

There she sits surrounded by the inspiring semblances of deathless wits and immortal beauties . . . by bookcases that glitter in gilt vellum and rosy russian, with Dante illustrated on Sevres vases, and the loves of Petrarch and Laura told on teacups. This literary petite maitresse – this collector of French toys and collator of Irish chronicles – this trifler by taste, and author by necessity . . . c'est moi!

Her own appearance was equally flamboyant at this time, and aroused comment wherever she went. Someone who met her first at a vice-regal reception in Dublin wrote:

Here it was that I saw Lady Morgan for the first time, and as I had long pictured her to my imagination as a sylphlike person nothing could equal my astonishment when the celebrated authoress stood before me. She certainly formed a strange figure in the midst of that dazzling scene of beauty and splendour. Every female present wore feathers and trains, but Lady Morgan scorned both appendages. Hardly more than four feet high, with a spine not quite straight, slightly uneven shoulders and eyes, Lady Morgan glided about in a close cropped wig, bound by a fillet or solid band of gold, her large face all animation and a witty word for everybody. I afterwards saw her at the dress circle in the theatre – she was cheered enthusiastically. Her dress was different from the former occasion but not less original. A red Celtic cloak, formed exactly on the plan of Granuaille's fastened by a rich gold fibula or Irish Tara brooch, imparted to her little ladyship a gorgeous and withal a picturesque appearance which antecedent associations considerably strengthened.

Her ladyship had every reason to feel pleased with herself at this point in her career. One more dream had become reality; one more hastily conceived sketch turned into a long running successful theatrical piece even though it was set in her own drawing room. Madame de Genlis might have her alabaster lamps, and de Staël her autographed works of the great French *philosophes*, but she, little Sydney Owenson, looked around a room also filled with tributes from the great. Now she gave herself over fully to this new lifestyle. For a while all serious writing was abandoned. Dinner parties and musical evenings took up all her creative energy. She played her harp, and danced set jigs; her sister sang and recited her comic verses, and all interspersed with operatic arias from visiting Italian divas – Madame Pasta, and Madame Catalini, no less. Her nieces, pretty and talented were growing up, and they also were called upon to perform. 'Kitty Kearney' followed the strains of 'Norma'. Irish folksiness with operatic flourishes became her speciality. The carriages that drew up to number 35 brought the most comprehensive cast, worthy of any O'Keefe extravaganza, with his cast list of football players and kings of Ireland . . . Singers, dancers, Italian and Spanish refugees, Irish and English radical politicians, and above all the literary set. She was unfailingly kind to aspiring young writers. Samuel

Carter Hall, the journalist, who with his wife Mrs C.M. Hall wrote many sketches of Irish life later wrote of her:

> She was entirely free of literary jealousy – she would aid and not depress young authorship; she was often generous with her purse as well as her pen and tongue; there was nothing mean about her; she never put the young aspirant for celebrity aside to pay more attention to a titled visitor.

One such aspirant whom she might have resented for poaching on her preserves seldom missed her evenings, though he was a difficult guest. This was the Reverend Charles Robert Maturin whose personality was outstandingly eccentric even for Dublin. His first two novels were in fact a direct attempt to cash in on her success, being called *The Wild Irish Boy*, and *The Milesian Chief* using her formula of romantic nationalism, but injecting it with his own distillation of bombastic extravagance of language, tangled plots and impossible incidents.

Dublin has always loved 'characters', and Maturin was one of the favourite sights at that time, more famous for his mincing walk, his love of dancing and his tightly corseted figure than for his writing. He was born in 1782, and took orders after graduating from Trinity, but gave more time to his lurid Gothic novels than to his clerical duties. He was a playwright as well as novelist, and had a success with a drama called *Bertram* which Lady Morgan persuaded Kean the actor to perform at Drury Lane, but Maturin soon spent all the money this earned him on wild extravagance. Sir Charles constantly raised money to help, but nothing could remedy his absent-mindedness. He occasionally arrived at Kildare Street in his dressing gown and slippers, and often went to parties a day too late. If he felt the 'estro of composition' come upon him while he was writing, he placed a wafer on his forehead, so as not to be disturbed. His most famous novel *Melmoth the Wanderer*, with its vampires and souls sold to the devil, influenced the work of Baudelaire and Balzac, and is still in print, but everything else he wrote has been forgotten or ignored, as it was in his own lifetime. He died in 1824, at the age of forty-two. The street theatre of Dublin missed him, more than did his parishioners, and Lady Morgan, practical as ever, tried to get help for his wife and children, after his life of wild and eccentric extravagance ended in their abject poverty.

Sydney, who in her youth had seen so much of the misery of financial irregularity, prided herself on her hard work and its rewards. She took nothing for granted and wrote about this characteristic of her nature:

> I have so little confidence in the certainty of this life that I always live as if I were going to die. I never stir from home for more than a month, without settling my little affairs, and altering or adding to my will as circumstances direct. I am never in debt one shilling. Poor people ought always to pay ready money, by which means they live as if they were rich. By not doing so the rich often live as if they were poor, and die insolvent.

This thrift allowed her to write in her account book: 'May 9, 1824. . . . By my earnings since April 3, 1822 I have added to our joint stock account such sums as make the whole £5,109,7s 0d . . . from £2,678.11.6 as it stood at that date.' Not a despicable sum, comments her literary executor, to have made by her own industry and saved by her own thrift.

CHAPTER 11

REAL LIFE IN IRELAND

As soon as *Italy* was published, Colburn suggested that Sydney write a companion volume on Germany. He offered her the tempting sum of two thousand pounds but she turned it down. Dublin was still the place where she wanted to be; she basked in the affection of her sister and her family; her young nieces doted on her, and called her 'little Mamma', and old Molly reminded her of her youth when she was 'Miss Syd'. Sir Charles, too, was happy in Dublin. Indolent by nature, he had all the activity he wanted there with his music and his own bits of philosophical writing, and the admiration of like-minded friends. They continued to contribute occasional pieces to Colburn's magazine the *New Monthly* and in this journal Sydney published a long essay on absenteeism, which was a highly charged combination of historical survey and economic argument, proving that the English by their 'treachery and tyranny' first made Ireland uninhabitable, and then punished its inhabitants for trying to leave. With characteristically stiff upper lip the English bought this scolding piece in such quantities that it was republished in book form in 1824.

The reluctance to travel did not extend to London, and in 1824 they crossed the Irish sea once more. Sir Charles had his scientific cronies to visit, and Sydney divided her time between the many Italians now in exile in England and her old high society friends like Lady Cork and Lady Charleville. She also gave a great deal of time to Caroline Lamb on this visit. By sad coincidence Byron's funeral took place while the Morgans were in London. The poet had died of fever in Greece, and his body, parcelled into a wooden chest, and then packed in a cask full of spirits was brought to England to be buried. Morgan went to the funeral, and Sydney noted in her diary:

The public wish was that he should be buried in the Abbey,

but his sister would have him buried in the family vault and insisted on his funeral being a Peer's funeral, from which the vulgar public, the nation, was to be excluded. There would not have been a single literary person there but Rogers and Moore, his personal friends, had not Morgan and Campbell at the last moment suggested others. All was mean and pompous yet confusion; hundreds of persons on foot, in deep mourning, who came to pay this respect to one of the greatest geniuses of the age.

And so she said goodbye to Byron. Lady Caroline, who by some awful freak of fate accidentally met the cortége on its way to Newstead Abbey, collapsed with grief and fell into a nervous illness from which she never really recovered. When she died in 1828 she left to Lady Morgan – as she had always promised she would – Byron's portrait and some letters, and these became prize exhibits in the little red boudoir in Kildare Street.

On this visit to London there was an encounter with a very different 'great' poet. That ubiquitous recorder of the sayings of poets, Crabb Robinson, has reported:

Wordsworth and Lady Morgan were invited to dine at I forget whose, house. The poet would on no account take her downstairs, and he disturbed the table arrangements by placing himself at the bottom while her ladyship was at the top. She was either unobserving of his conduct or resolved to show him she did not care for it, for she sent the servants to beg him to drink a glass of wine with her. His look was as solemn as if it had been a death summons. I was told that she asked her neighbour – 'Has not Mr. Wordsworth written some poems!'

Amusing as London always was – whether for sparring with Wordsworth, meeting Moore for tea at Lady Cork's, or haggling with publishers, they were anxious to get back to Dublin, where the really interesting things were happening. There she was not only the undisputed queen of the literary set, but also an important political hostess. The cause of Catholic emancipation, which she had supported ardently for more than twenty years was no longer a political heresy. Sir Charles was also very prominent; he had been charged with the collection of the signatures for a great Protestant petition for the repeal of Catholic disabilities, and for a while Kildare Street was the scene of great events. Sydney gave dinners for the 'elite of the

26 *Daniel O'Connor* by George Mulvany, National Gallery of Ireland

elite' as she called the men behind the scenes, and she was herself admitted to the most secret negotiations. An entry in her diary for 1826 reads: 'I was last night at a private party at the Castle. I was (as of late I have constantly been) the centre of a circle.' Her host, the Lord Lieutenant Lord Anglesey became so well disposed towards her mission that rumours of her influence reached the king who was opposed to emancipation, but was now having to swallow the fact of its inevitability. These meetings were charged with drama for the 'circle' of Castle officials, with representatives of the handpicked Catholic groups, and the spokesmen for the Orange opposition, had now to include the controversial and flamboyant figure of Daniel O'Connell, head of the Catholic Association, and undisputed leader of the unenfranchised Irish Catholics. 'Thirty years ago', she wrote with relish, 'the roof would not have been deemed safe which afforded O'Connell and such as he shelter.' It was O'Connell who in 1821 had so obsequiously welcomed George IV to Ireland, but now he was on a very different road. As the king had not fulfilled any of the promises made on that visit, Dan had shaped his Catholic Association into a mass movement, vociferous and potentially dangerous. His persuasive oratory and physical presence gave the downtrodden and poverty stricken people new heart. He was a hero in the old style and he belonged to them. His 'army of beggars' loved him; they called him 'King Dan', 'The Liberator', and 'Tribune of the People'. There was no title affectionate or extravagant enough for him.

But Lady Morgan had growing reservations. He was taking the cause of nationality in a direction she could not follow. She found his mob oratory and excessive use of 'green' hyperbole offensive. She wrote mockingly:

> That first flower of the earth, first gem of the sea O'Connell, wants back the days of Brian Boru, himself to be the king, with a crown of emerald shamrocks, a train of yellow velvet and mantle of Irish tabinet, a sceptre in one hand, and a cross in the other, and the people crying 'Long live O'Connell'. This is the object of his views and ambitions. O'Connell is not a man of genius; he has a sort of talent applicable to his purpose as it exists in the land – a 'nisi prius' talent which has won much popularity.

She grossly underestimated him; he, however, saw her usefulness to the cause for which they both worked, and paid fulsome tribute to her in his most blarneying manner:

> To Irish female talents and patriotism we owe much. There is one name consecrated by a generous devotion to the best interests of Ireland – a name sacred to the cause of liberty, and of everything great, virtuous and patriotic – the name of an illustrious female who has suffered unmanly persecution for her talented and chivalrous adherences to her native land. Need I say that I allude to Lady Morgan? Her name is received with enthusiasm by the people of the country where her writings create and perpetuate among the young of both sexes a patriotic ardour in the cause of everything that is noble and dignified.

Honey-tongued Dan probably meant what he said at the time, but Lady Morgan knew that he was not really on her side. Although O'Connell came from that class of old Catholic gentry that she had romanticised in her novels; from a family that had survived the Penal Laws by educating its sons abroad, and by serving in foreign armies with the Wild Geese; he nevertheless was no Prince of Inishmore. For her he was a vulgar showman who covered everything with shamrocks and sentiment, and used the Catholic church as his own personal polling booth.

O'Connell was born in Kerry in 1775. He spoke Irish fluently from childhood, and knew the peasant mind and the strong traditions of oral culture. Educated abroad, he was in France at the time of the Revolution, and in spite of his sympathy with its aims, he hated the violence that went with it. He was no republican – with the Irish passion for genealogy, he claimed descent from the ancient kings of Kerry. To the Catholic masses he seemed a leader beyond compare who would lead them out of the mists of their defeated past, and show them a way to gratify their hunger for land, and yet keep the faith. Sometimes in the rose-coloured rooms of Kildare Street, where Sydney would be entertaining her literary guests, and discussing their latest work on the folklore and quaintness of the peasantry, there might be heard coming from the direction of the Liberties voices shouting 'O'Connell abu!', like an old Irish war-cry. And up in the hills and the lonely glens the country boys were putting new words to songs that had nothing to do with Handy Andy, or harum scarum Paddy.

But for the moment Sydney's name was linked with

O'Connell in the affection of the common people. And one of the greatest compliments that Dublin could pay her was to put her alongside Dan in a song. In the streets the ballad-mongers sang:

> Och, Dublin city, there's no doubtin'
> Bates every city upon the say;
> Tis there you'll hear O'Connell spoutin'
> And Lady Morgan making tay;
> For 'tis the capital of the finest nation,
> Wid charming pisantry on a fruitful sod,
> Fighting like divils for conciliation
> And hating each other for the love of God.

She was by no means the only one 'making tay' in Dublin at that time. Select committees in both Houses of Parliament were constantly inquiring into the 'state of Ireland', and the scandal of O'Connell standing for election in Clare and being returned by huge majorities, but not being able to take his seat because he was a Catholic, was dominating British politics. Ireland – this country so close and yet so foreign, was a constant source of wonder and terror. These peasants, previously as remote as tribes in Outer Mongolia, now wanted to send MPs to Westminster. Books on the Irish peasant 'As they really are' were eagerly sought. They ranged from the wild comicalities of Pierce Egan's *Real Life in Ireland* where the title page well describes the contents: 'Rovings, ramblings and sprees, bulls, blunders, bodderation and blarney', to serious anthropological studies of folklore and peasant life. Until this time Maria Edgeworth and Sydney had been the only serious novelists to take on Irish life. Now a whole new school of writers appeared, all claiming to be experts on the subject. In London there was, as there still is, a number of Irish literary freebooters, unable to make much of a living at home, but ready to put their unique culinary skills together to serve up a savoury Irish stew for the English. They knew that there was a ready market for the doings and sayings of poor Paddy if they were ridiculous enough, for if someone was irredeemably comical, he couldn't really be dangerous. The chief agent for this kind of promotion was a brilliant young man from Cork, William Maginn, who became the period's most vivid example of the gifted but destructive Irish journalist, with an excessive taste for drink. He was born in 1794, and was a child prodigy, going up to Trinity College, Dublin at the age of ten. He was a classical scholar of immense erudition, and from an early age sent poems and parodies under pseudonyms from Cork to the satirical magazine *Blackwood's*. In 1823 he came over to London to form a sort of round table of Irish talent. He was absolutely full of 'Hibernian' charm and cynical wit, and described himself as: 'A randy, bandy, brandy, no Dandy, Rollicking jig of an Irishman.'

The other Irishmen who gathered around him were usually Tory in politics, because they needed to please the paymasters in power, but were really alienated in every way from either party. Maginn found Ireland, as he found everything else, ridiculous but excellent copy. He was sponsored in London by John Wilson Croker, who picked him out to write anonymous political leaders for his own papers. Like Croker, he had an almost paranoiac hatred of nationalist Ireland, but unlike Croker he had a highly developed sense of surrealist humour which found his own affiliations equally ridiculous, and probably contributed to his fall into 'that pit abysmal' of drink and debt, which killed him off at the age of forty-eight. But he could be a convivial companion if he so wished; in his undergraduate days he had caroused in the Dublin taverns with Robert Owenson, and Thackeray in London learnt his journalism from Maginn, and how to hold his drink. With the power to commission, he urged Irishmen of every persuasion to 'write up' their native land, and his pages were always open to such work.

It was in this way that while Lady Morgan had been taking time off travelling in Italy and socialising in Dublin, books of Irish interest were coming on to the market from other hands. Many of these were cynical pot-boilers to catch the passing trade, but there were four books published in the year 1826, the writers all having been sponsored by Maginn, which were serious attempts to shape the English attitude to Ireland. One was by a member of Maginn's own Cork 'mafia' – he particularly liked to have men from his own town around him – Thomas Crofton Croker, a cousin of J.W. Croker. He was an amateur folklorist and antiquarian who for years had been collecting bits of local history, odd superstitions and remembered legends of the people of southern Ireland, which he published as *Fairy Legends and Traditions of the South of Ireland*. Maginn dubbed him 'the honourable member for fairyland', and he certainly brought into focus a new aspect of this troublesome peasantry who were making such unfairylike noises under O'Connell's banner. This book won the admiration of Walter Scott and the Brothers Grimm, and with it the banshee, the pooka, the leprechaun and the magical land of Tir-na-nogue entered Irish and English literature for better or worse. In the same year another of Maginn's protégés, Eyre Crowe, brought out three volumes of stories called *Today in Ireland*, showing a darker side of Irish rural life – the secret societies and the violence – and the opposing unbending landlord class. Though written from sincere and serious motives, these were both the works of Anglo–Irish Protestant writers, with inborn Tory and Orange sympathies. As Yeats wrote many years later in his own collection of *Folk Tales of the Irish Peasantry*, they did not 'take the people seriously, and imagined the country as a humourist's Arcadia . . . it's passion, it's gloom, it's tragedy they knew nothing of'. It was left to three Catholic novelists to penetrate the passion and the tragedy. *Tales of the O'Hara family* came out in 1826. John Banim, the chief partner of two brothers was the first Catholic novelist to write about recent events in Ireland from a native Irish point of view. It was like receiving despatches from the front, but from the other side. This is not the Ireland that Lady Morgan and Maria Edgeworth prepared the English readership for, but an interior Ireland, illuminated by the light of a turf fire in a peasant's cabin. The other book to be published in that year, *Tales of the Munster Festivals* by Gerald Griffin, was also different from the stories of droll, reckless peasants and rakish, dashing landlords. He wrote about an Ireland of small gentry, small farmers, small shopkeepers, with no political or social influence, who nevertheless lived lives of intense and primitive passion, serving the land, surviving the laws, and sustaining their proscribed religion.

Lady Morgan read the works of Banim and Griffin with great interest, and pondered at the changes that were coming to Ireland. She approved of their intentions, which were more or less the same as her own – 'the formation of a good affectionate feeling between England and Ireland', but she thought she could pitch higher. She had been collecting material for another 'national tale', and now started seriously to work on an historical novel, going back to the period of her own girlhood and the events leading up to the Union. *The O'Briens and the O'Flaherties*, or the great 'O' novel, as it was called, is today – if it is ever considered at all – regarded as her best work; it is a very brave attempt to explain the state of

Ireland, not only to the world, but to herself, as it examines honestly the frustrations and final defeat of her own kind of romantic patriotism. As such it is a touchstone for our own time, still confronted with the problems of a divided nation. The patriotic note is as strong as ever, but now there is no happy ending, and the prevailing note of pessimism is underlined when the heroine says to the hero: 'To be born an Irishman is a dark destiny at best; the last that the wise could contend with, or the proud encounter. Here genius is the object of suspicion to dull rulers, and of insult to petty underlings . . . and all that bends not – falls.'

As always, her depth of research and grasp of historical detail is very impressive. The first part of the novel is a long and demanding collage of historical documents, letters, bits of diaries, topography and reports to governments. It all adds up to a discursive history of settlement and conquest. After the lengthy prologue, narrative takes over and the story begins.

The plot centres around Dublin, and moves to a wild part of Connemara. Two old families of Gaelic stock, whose fortunes have followed the fluctuating course of events in Ireland, provide the crowded stage with exiles, some of whom have prospered abroad and returned to Ireland as counts of the Holy Roman Empire, or as Jesuit prelates. They meet with impoverished peasants bearing the same family name, some of whom have become outlaws and taken to the hills. There are planter upstarts, and Catholic lords who have changed their religion to keep their land. To the front of the stage comes the attractive young Murrough O'Brien, son of a man who has gained political and social power by serving the Ascendancy, but is now secretly returning to the Catholic faith, and plotting the restoration of 'old' Ireland. He hopes his son will carry out his plans, but his obsessions have driven him mad. Young Murrough is an uncomplicated, noble character untouched by his father's fanaticism. His patriotic feelings attach him to the liberalism of Grattan's policies as they were at the time, but when these are defeated he turns to the romantic and generous idealism of the United Irishman, Lord Walter Fitzwalter, a portrait of the real Lord Edward Fitzgerald. These two men, of noble birth, but of radical sentiments, represent everything Sydney wanted for Ireland. Murrough is also fantastically handsome, and the ladies of the vice-regal court – the 'fair oligarchs', bold and bored, pursue him with amorous intent. Her heroine, Beavoin O'Flaherty, is very different from these

27 *The Dublin Volunteers in College Green* by Francis Wheatley, National Gallery of Ireland

ladies of fashion. She is the archetypal Morgan heroine – a free, independent woman who comes and goes as she pleases. It pleases her for most of the book to be a nun, a powerful Abbess who, within the church, works against 'vulgar bigotry'; but when she wants to change her way of life, and incidentally the plot, she abandons her vows, inherits a lot of money from a Jesuit uncle, the Abbate O'Flaherty – and marries Murrough O'Brien. Apart from the lurching vagaries of plot, and the ease with which both heroine and hero change their locale and situation, the 'O' novel is full of marvellous things; there are brilliant set pieces of reporting from Sydney's own sharp observations – life in Dublin in the 1790s with the young gentlemen of Trinity College stirring things up; the Volunteers, dressed in green and gold rallying in the Phoenix Park; and the secret taking of the oath by the United Irishmen in the discreet gloom of some safe house. The descriptions of life with the old Irish gentry in Iar Connaught – 'half papist, half Jacobite', though nominally Protestant are as good as anything Somerville and Ross later came to write, and the chapter called 'Jug-Day', in which she describes how half the county – with their feather beds piled on to their jaunting cars – came to the Miss McTaafs' party to help them drink a pipe of Bordeaux wine, which has arrived from Wild Geese cousins in France, is a piece of genre writing worthy to stand with the party given by the Miss Morkans in Joyce's short story, *The Dead*.

It is a very political novel; for her portrait of Lord Edward, one of the noblest and most attractive of all Irish martyr-heroes, she had the authentic impressions of his old comrades, Lord Cloncurry and Archibald Hamilton Rowan to draw upon. She portrays him with a new sense of reality – impulsive and generous, but like his follower Murrough O'Brien 'knowing nothing of modern Ireland but her sufferings and wrongs; knowing little of ancient Ireland but her fables and her dramas, his mind had been stored with popular and poetic fallacies relative to all that concerned her.' Is she relating this condition to her own journey through patriotism? She accepts now that their cause must fail. Romanticism is not enough. Lord Walter, like his prototype Lord Edward, dies. The fictional Murrough O'Brien bends to fate, escapes to France, and becomes a general in Bonaparte's army. The last we see of him is in 1802, at the opera in Paris, listening to Haydn's *Creation*. The Abbess Beavoin O'Flaherty is now Madame O'Brien, with her own salon in Paris, and their flight from Ireland in order to survive

28 *Lord Edward Fitzgerald, Soldier and Revolutionary* by Hugh Douglas
Hamilton, National Gallery of Ireland

is a foretaste of what was growing in Sydney's own mind.

The 'O' novel was published in 1827 and in 1829 the bill for Catholic emancipation became law. The cause for which she had worked so hard was won, but the Ireland she had dreamed of was not in sight; it was as remote as the fairy tales of the new folklorists. Dan O'Connell was Ireland's master now, with his million peasants and the priests of Maynooth behind him. The paradoxes of Irish history and the ambiguities of Sydney's own nature did not diminish her courage, but weakened her certainties. This was to be her last national tale.

For once the critics did not concentrate their attack on the politics of the novel – she had already won that battle – but now they went for her in the name of womanly virtue. They did not like the free manners and witty speech of the fashionable women she portrayed – most of them taken from life from the Abercorn *ménage*. The *Literary Gazette* claimed that:

> we have painfully done our censorial duty . . . we grieve that such a picture should come from the pen of a woman; there is not only not a virtuous but there is hardly a decent female throughout the book. Ladies of rank are *rank*; abbesses and nuns are intriguing courtesans in this saturnalia of Irish life.

Sydney herself had been afraid that her book might shock the prudes, for the time that she was writing about was a more outspoken age. She wrote:

> I suppressed many droll things that had been related to me . . . I was murmuring my fears to Lady Cloncurry – a model of propriety. She set my mind at rest by saying that I had kept clear of extremes and dwelt more in the decencies than was at all characteristic of the time I described . . . There were in the Castle circle a posse of titled women of bold reputation who had the uncontrolled sway in everything. In short, the Dublin court of that period was like the manners described in *Grammont's Memoirs*.

But in spite of Lady Cloncurry's reassurances and Lady Charleville's verdict that there was nothing blasphemous or indecent in the book, most of the reviews adopted a tone of masculine outrage at woman's immodesty. Colburn was furious at this reception, for he knew that his women readers would be turned away from the novel if it was described as indecent, and he had invested a lot of money in it. As a consequence he started a new magazine, the *Athenaeum*, in opposition to the

Literary Review, and this became one of the most prominent of all the reviews of the nineteenth century. Sydney's answer to the attack was cheerful and positive. She immediately presented Colburn with yet another book – this time a collection of random essays. These were pieces from different experiences in her life. There were anecdotes of the important people she had met; stories of her travels; a bit of art criticism; derivations of words – anything that had taken her interest. Some were squibs a few lines long; others ran into many pages. But, of course, the real theme of this mixed bag is herself. It is a defence of her philosophy, her conflicting love of society and flattery, and her pleasure in just being Sydney Morgan. The chapter headings give the tone – 'My Book', 'My first rout in London', 'My reviewers', 'My visitors'. She is frank and witty about authorship and her own sex, and cheerfully admits for the first time that she is no longer young, and has looked upon her first wrinkle.

Before the book was published she describes in a diary entry a discussion she has had with one of her many foreign visitors to find a suitable title for this glittering miscellany. This visitor was Prince Pückler Muskau, one of the new breed of travel writers who had come to 'remote' Ireland to write about its interesting natives. Her international fame brought such travellers to her door and she, anxious to pay back some of the hospitality she had received in France and Italy, was usually welcoming. But this was not one of her sympathetic emigrés, exiled for his radical opinions. This was a German princeling, stiff with self-importance. She found him 'a creature fine and foppish, a sort of tartar turned dandy'. He arrived at an awkward time, when she was spring-cleaning, and was announced by her servant as 'Prince Pickling Mustard'; by which name he remained for ever in the Morgan chronicles. The Prince was not put off by dustcovers and pots of paint, but called several times. On one occasion he found everything much better regulated:

> Lady Morgan received me today in her authoress-boudoir, where I found her writing, not without some view to effect, elegantly dressed, and with a mother-of-gold pen in her hand. She was employed on a new book for which she had invented a very good title – *Memoirs of Myself and for Myself*. She read me some passages, which I thought very good. This woman who appears so superficial is quite another being when she takes her pen in her hand.

When the book came out in 1829, in two volumes, the title was not quite so self-obsessed. *The Book of the Boudoir*, as this collection of essays was finally called, makes her new position in relation to Ireland clear. In her introduction she states:

> I have written from my youth up under the influence of one great and all pervading cause – Ireland and its wrongs. But the day is now approaching when all that is Irish will fall into its natural position; when fair play will be given to national tendencies, and when the sarcastic author of *O'Donnel* and *The O'Briens*, having nothing to find fault with, will be reduced to write books for boudoirs, or albums in ladies' dressing rooms. Among the multitudinous effects of Catholic emancipation, I do not hesitate to predict a change in the character of Irish authorship.

She did not really expect that the victory of Catholic emancipation would solve everything, or anything. In fact the bill took away the right to vote from the very poor, and increased the power of the Catholic middle class. But the peasants who had been involved in the campaign realised that they had started to free their religion, and now they wanted to take their efforts further and free the land. All this she knew and sympathised with. She had written about the injustice of tithes – the system whereby Catholics had to pay a tax to maintain the Protestant clergy – in her *Patriotic Sketches*, and this was now the burning issue. But Sydney disliked and mistrusted O'Connell who was leading this particular campaign, and the increasingly clerical influence on Irish politics was not to her taste. She decided that she needed to get out of Ireland for a while, and make a second visit to France. But there too she found that the promise of 1818, when she had witnessed the election of her brave La Fayette to the General Assembly was not fulfilled. The country as a whole had been growing steadily more liberal, but the government had been moving to the right. The result was a dangerous tension which in a matter of months brought about the revolutions of July 1830.

But it was not so much the political climate that caught her interest but the change in taste and opinions. The wave of Anglomania which had swept over Paris in particular both amused and annoyed her. Calais was her first surprise:

> How English! Not a sanded floor, nor a sullied parquet are

now visible. Nothing but English carpets, and English cleanliness. The garcon cries 'Coming up' and the tea and muffins are worthy of the 'Talbot' at Shrewsbury. Not a jackboot, not a powdered toupee left; nothing to ridicule, nothing to blame; the age of tourists and of chivalry is alike over. What luck to have written my *France* while France was still so French!

Paris was even worse. The shops seemed to cater only for the ever present English, and the increasingly English taste of the Parisians with money. She found that she could not buy French sweets or confectionary, but was offered 'de cracker, de bun, de plom-cake, de spice gingerbread, de mutton and de mince pye, de crompet, and de apple-dumplin'. She could not buy French scent, but only 'de lavaender-vatre' or 'de Vindsor soap'. So overwhelmed was she by all this, particularly when offered a bottle of 'genuine potteen' (illicit Irish whiskey), that she wrote 'was it for this we left the snugness and economic comfort of our Irish home, and encountered the expensive inconvenience of a foreign journey in the hope of seeing nothing British?' Anglomania also expressed itself in the way the French dressed. Ever since the Revolution they had been accustomed to express their political opinions or literary tastes through costume and pose. From the start, the republicans were the 'sansculottes', disdaining the furbelows of the aristocracy. Now there was a style for every position. Sydney herself had always dressed for the part she was playing, with her Granuaille cloak, and Glorvina's golden bodkins. Now she saw ladies in Paris dressed in shawls of tartan plaid, straight out of 'Valtre-Scott', feminists in men's clothes, *à la* George Sand, and followers of Byron with 'open short collar and wild and melancholy look'. The romantics had their counterpoint in the dandies. On her first visit to France she had jeered at the French attempt to imitate the Regency cult of dandyism then at its height, now the French dandy had his own style. The *'merveilleux'* as they were called had very strict rules for what was fashionable. Lady Morgan's own wardrobe was taken to task, and she was told that she would never succeed in French society if she did not dress *á la mode*. 'You literary ladies are so hard to manage in all that respects the outward form of life' she was told. She describes the effects of this conformity: 'All the women seem to have stepped out of one mould like so many shapes of jelly for a ball supper. All the nether drapes seemed mathematically

29   French dandies of the Directoire, from a contemporary painting

measured to the same length and circumference – waist, hips and shoulders were all formed to the same type and proportion.' Needless to say, she resisted all attempts to mould her like a jelly, and rushed around Paris in her own role-playing clothes.

The French ideas of English life and style were taken not only from the visitors, but from novels popular in England in the late 1820s. Lady Morgan's own books had been translated into French, but now there was a passion for what were known as the 'dandy' novels, a new genre encouraged by the egregious Colborn, who was still adding to his fortune by brilliantly judging the taste of his age. The novels that he commissioned from people in high society were bought by aspiring exclusives who wanted a quick handbook to the fashion, wit and elegance of the *beau monde*. The French fell for this as avidly as the English. Many a neophyte dandy learnt the rules of the game in the reading rooms and public libraries of Paris where the fashionable novels could be read almost immediately after publication in London. Lady Morgan's fame was overtaken by such new bestselling authors as Theodore Hook, Lister, Edward Bulwer, and the young Disraeli, but she was still admired by a new generation of French writers whose other idols were Scott and Byron. Young writers like Stendhal, Lamartine, Balzac and Dumas recognised in her the tradition they prized in themselves – the wit and irony of the dandy, the political opinions of a radical, with the taste of melodrama and melancholy of the romantic. She 'flourished in their admiration and boldly ranged with them over aspects of literature, music, ethics and politics with a confidence worthy of Germaine de Staël herself. Her denunciations of Corneille and Racine continued to offend the classicists, and in politics she was as indiscreet as ever, maintaining her opposition to the Bourbon regime. Once again her portrait was painted by several artists, and she was also sketched in words. The royalist Chevalier de Cussy, who did not like her politics, also objected to her clothes:

> Her pretension appeared in her costume which was always eccentric; an immense beret of red velvet garnished with big white pearls; a bodice cut very low showing her neck, shoulders and back; a scarf draped with conscious picturesqueness, or allowed to flutter as she hurried through the room. Small, and ever restless, Lady Morgan is, with her bizarre costume very amusing to look at.

In a postscript to this second book on France, Lady Morgan admits how light and even frivolous are its records of a society on the brink of revolution. But she illustrates the dangerous divisions in that society by juxtaposing the sharp contrasts in her own experiences; one day she was the guest of honour with the Baron de Rothschild whose cook, the great Carême, made a cake marked 'Lady Morgan' in spun sugar, while the next day saw her visiting the poet Beranger, incarcerated in the La Force prison for writing political satires. She clearly rejoiced in the revolution of 1830 when it came, for it seemed to end for ever all chance of despotic rule under an absolute monarchy; the middle class had effectively asserted its power. She commented complacently 'Without a landed aristocracy, a king must be but the first citizen of a state – a crowned president.'

The Morgans left France just before the storm broke, and came home through Belgium and Holland. They stayed for a while in London where they bought the supreme status symbol – a carriage of their own. Lady Morgan had ridden in many carriages in her time – some with ducal crests painted on the side, but this one was her's, paid for by herself and, as she always declared, 'it came from the first carriage builder in London!' It resembled nothing so much as a green grasshopper both in shape and colour. Very high, and very springy, with enormous wheels, it was very hard to get in to, and dangerous to get out of. Sir Charles, who was short sighted, wore large green spectacles to match when out of doors. The joy of Dubliners at the sight of them driving out was only marred by the alarm caused by his erratic driving, and Lady Morgan incessantly springing up to warn him to take care – to which he replied 'with warmth, after the manner of husbands' as is reported in her *Memoirs*.

Meanwhile, she was busy turning her notes into a book; she had not made any firm contract with Colburn, so sure was she that anything she wrote would be welcome. He was slow in suggesting terms, so she offered the book to a rival firm, Saunders and Otley. She was rather glad of an excuse to cross Colburn whose methods of publicity had become embarrassing. Except for the great reviews which were governed by party politics, the literary papers were entirely in the hands of those publishers who advertised conspicuously, and Colburn boasted to Sydney that several journals had abstained from criticising *Italy*, adding 'I am intimately acquainted with the editors; and advertising with them a great deal, keeps them in check.' Sydney was not impressed with these methods, deploring 'the abeyance of moral courage and independent judgment on the part of those who were presumed to guide public opinion in literary matters'.

The news of the revolution in Paris and the banishment of Charles X in 1830 made her book very topical, as she had analysed the political situation and praised the Duc d'Orleans, the new king designate. Saunders and Otley gave her one thousand pounds for it, and it came out with an attached postscript bringing it up to date in 1830. But Colburn was furious with her, and wanted revenge. He put all his efficient machinery for publicity into reverse, and when the book was advertised by the new publishers he countered with more blatant advertising, offering LADY MORGAN AT HALF PRICE, saying that in view of the great losses which he had sustained by her former works, he would let his whole stock of her writing go at a discount of 50 per cent. She was horrified by the viciousness of his attack, for he had always treated her as his favourite author, his goddess of good fortune; he had given her presents, and begged her always to write on a table covered with green baize to protect her poor eyesight. Even the most vicious of her critics had never been able to stop the sale of her books – in fact their hostile notices had stimulated trade, but now the man who had promoted her so successfully was damaging her in the public eye. The damage was considerable. The booksellers didn't order; the journals ignored her, and the book, though in many ways superior to her first book on France didn't sell. Saunders and Otley entreated to have their contract modified. She wouldn't release them, and eventually the whole sorry business came to court. When cross-examined Colburn admitted that he had acted out of wounded feelings, and retracted all that he had said. He wanted to make amends, but Lady Morgan was finished with him. She promised to give her next book to Saunders and Otley and broke off all connections with Colburn's magazines. She was not the only one to find his methods distasteful, and some of her friends who had dealings with him withdrew their books. Maginn, now established in London as editor of the new magazine *Fraser's*, though no friend to her, was also at war with Colburn because of what he called his 'puffery'. In 1833 Maginn wrote:

> The puffers had poisoned the whole blood of our literature extending their infection over author, bookseller, reader, critic. All was either corruption or mystification, quackery or deceit. Three years ago it appeared to be so deeply rooted, and so decidedly triumphant that any opposition to it seemed hopeless, yet like all systems of deception it crumbled at a touch.

She was glad of all the support she could get. There were new magazines to write for and the *Athenaeum* had a new, sympathetic editor. She had one of her most amusing sketches published in the *Metropolitan* – 'The Memoirs of a Macaw of a Lady of Quality'. The lady in question was her old patroness, the Countess of Cork, and the macaw was a pet bird, an important part of that eccentric household, and famous for the number of eminent people it had bitten. With all her lawsuits, her 'evenings' and her journalism, she still was deeply interested in Irish politics. But it was with growing distaste that she viewed the Ireland that she had helped to bring about. Dublin ceased to be 'dear, dirty Dublin', but was now 'dull dusty Dublin'. She had written to Thomas Moore: 'Ireland is no more the country you left behind than it is Cochin China.' Whenever Moore came to Dublin he visited her; she gave parties for him, and they sang together around the piano as in the old days when they had both admonished Erin to 'remember the days of old, ere her faithless sons betrayed her.' But after one such visit she wrote: 'He sang as well as ever, but it made us all sad;

all his songs had reference to the past. I felt when I went to bed as if I had been at the funeral of old friends.' And, of course, there were many funerals, and more to come. Hamilton Rowan was dying; the last of the gallant old United Irishmen, who had once run a foot race in the presence of Marie Antoinette and the whole French court, and in spite of being in his riding boots, he had won with ease. Sydney wrote of him: 'He kept up his strength and remarkable appearance to the last. He might be seen in the streets of Dublin, a gigantic old man in an old fashioned dress, followed by two noble dogs, the last of the Irish race of wolfhounds.'

Old Molly, guardian of her childhood, was also fading fast, in a haze of whiskey and piety; there was melancholy sweetness in talking of 'the light of other days' with Moore. She was full of the sentiment that he evoked when he sang:

> You may break, you may ruin the vase if you will
> But the scent of the roses will hang round it still.

But she could spare only a limited time for that sort of indulgence. There was still work to be done and contracts to be signed. She was still that Sydney Morgan who had written in praise of female perseverance. She tried to push Moore into some activity, and suggested him as editor of the *Metropolitan* but he resisted; she wanted him to persuade John Murray, Byron's publisher, to take her on. Moore put this to Murray on his return to London, and reported the result:

Called at Murray's. Mentioned to him Lady Morgan's wish to contribute something to his family library, and that she has material ready for lives of five or six Dutch painters which she thinks would serve his purpose. The great John said, without minding the painters, 'Pray, isn't Lady Morgan a very good cook?' 'Why, you don't mean,' exclaimed I 'that she should write a cookery for you?' 'No,' said John coolly, 'not do as much as that; but that she should re-edit one of mine!' (Mrs. Rundall's by which he has made mints of money). Here ended my negotiations for her ladyship.

Chauvinistic as Murray's comments were – it is a pity that she wasn't asked for she could have written a splendid cookery book. All her life she kept recipes and knew how to intervene in an emergency when:

Poor old Mrs. Casey broke down from nervousness (or

whiskey) in the kitchen, and I had to dress half the dinner myself, which everybody allowed was supreme, particularly my matelotte d'anguille, and my dinde farci a la daube! It matters little how great dinners are dressed, but small ones should be exquisite or not given at all.

She also records a dinner she gave in honour of Paganini, the world famous violinist, when on a visit to Dublin; basing her menu on Florentine dishes, she made the great virtuoso exclaim after each dish 'Bravissisimo! Excellentissimo!'

In dire contrast to all this comfortable social life, there was at the same time a cholera epidemic raging in the slums of Dublin. Lady Morgan, for fear of contagion in such a small city, wanted to move out to the surrounding countryside. But Morgan, who was still consultant to the Marshalsea Prison, refused to go, saying that where there was most danger, there was his post. So she stayed in Dublin, by his side, her spirits made even lower by the publication at last of Prince Pückler Muskau's book which she considered grossly misrepresented and belittled her. 'I am properly trotted out in it' she wrote indignantly, 'I never ought to receive a foreigner into my house; this is the fourth time I have been the subject of attacks written by such guests.' She complained so much at this time about her life and her inability to work; she said that she was 'sick and weary of it all' – the attacks of the critics, the treachery of 'the Prince of Darkness' – that Sir Charles who was quite content to stay at home, playing his guitar, grew impatient with her. For a period, as well as being tired of her work and of life in Dublin, she was out of sorts with her marriage, and she wrote it all down in her diary:

May 28 1832. I am suffering beyond all conception from want of air and exercise. My house is small and confined; there is no through air, and I am never allowed to open a window to obtain it. When summer comes, Dublin is a dreary desert inhabited only by loathsome beggars, and I feel suffocated; I complain and say 'this is a hard fate'. My complaints are met with ridicule and vehement argument – sometimes with harshness; they are not borne with, because their cause is not felt, and all that makes my misery, makes the happiness of one who, by law and custom is the master of my actions, while books and easy chairs make up his whole wise scheme of happiness! All he says may be true, and I may be wrong; it may be weakness, caprice, an appetite for excitement, but still it is misery, and there is no reasoning with sensation. Men feel this and plead it for the indulgence of their own whims; poor woman is commanded to suffer and be silent, if she is so weak or wicked to have no control over her sensations!

Eventually she made her need of change evident to Sir Charles, and in July they made a flying visit to London where her *amour propre* was completely restored. 'My visitors began at ten o'clock this morning – authors, publishers, booksellers, and artists; afterwards some new and old cronies' she wrote, giving long lists of the famous and the fashionable who called. Back in Dublin after the break, she considered her previous low spirits, and said: 'I can hardly believe I am the person who wrote it; for now I am in high health and spirits and in great vigour of body and health. My trip to England, and air and exercise have restored the balance of affection between us.'

CHAPTER 12

THE PENSIONED
SCRIBBLER

The visit to London, enjoyable as it was, made Sydney aware that she was no longer the centre of attraction. When she had first appeared on the scene in 1810, a woman writing novels was as rare as a woman preaching, or as Dr Johnson put it, a dog walking on its hind legs. But now it was quite the occupation for fashionable ladies. As early as 1818 Lady Charlotte Bury, author of many – indeed some might think too many – novels of high society, wrote in her diary: 'People of "ton" have taken to writing novels. It is excellent amusement for them, and also for the public.' When the war with France ended, surprisingly enough there were no novelists of any note in London. In Hampshire Jane Austen was writing the last of her works commemorating the English country gentry. Walter Scott was celebrating the history of Scotland; Ireland had Maria Edgeworth, herself, and the new 'peasant' novelists like the Banim brothers, and Gerald Griffin. But in London they were still waiting for the school of 'silver fork' novelists to reflect the wit and scandal of the dandy Regency world. By 1830, however, such writers were in their heyday; men as well as women turning out upper-class stereotypes of manners and morals. The name 'silver fork' came out of the constant descriptions of dinner parties in these novels where, according to Hazlitt, in his essay on 'The Dandy School', the 'haut ton' could be immediately identified by their habit of eating their fish with two silver forks.

The ubiquitous Colburn published most of these fashionable novels. In fact, out of necessity he had extended the genre. In the middle of the 1820s there had been a severe economic crisis which had also hit publishing. About two thirds of the old established houses went down in the crash. It was the bankruptcy of Constable in Edinburgh, for example, which brought about the financial ruin of such a best-selling phenomenon as Sir Walter Scott. Even Henry Colburn talked of closing his business, but he quickly bounced back, for with his commercial flair he sensed that the reckless post-war mood was not yet spent. There was still plenty of high, and low, living. Gambling, racing, even dinner parties in debtor's prisons; these were favourite pursuits of contemporary society, and they were also the ingredients that sold books. Colburn knew that there was still plenty of money about, though not necessarily in the old places. The *nouveau riche* wanted to be titillated and also taught how to eat their fish 'properly', now that they were moving from Bloomsbury to Mayfair, and marrying their daughters into noble but impoverished families. Colburn soon found the ladies and gentlemen of the 'haut ton' who were prepared to write such books. At the literary parties Sydney met the new lions – Edward Bulwer Lytton, later Lord Lytton; Benjamin Disraeli, later Lord Beaconsfield, and the lionesses – Lady Charlotte Bury, the Hon. Caroline Norton, Mrs Charles Gore, and Mrs Rosina Bulwer Lytton. She got the measure of the Lytton lady very quickly, probably because she was Irish too:

> Mrs. Bulwer Lytton, handsome, insolent, and unamiable, to judge by her style and manners; she and all the demi-esprits looked daggers at me; not one has called on me, and in society they get out of my way. How differently I should behave to them if they came to Ireland.

Rosina Bulwer Lytton was not likely to call upon her in Ireland as she was very anxious to shake off any association with the land of her birth. Samuel Carter Hall, the journalist, records his experience of her:

> During his editorship of *The New Monthly* Bulwer gave a dinner party to O'Connell, and several Irish members. I was not present, but the next day I saw Mrs. Bulwer making some arrangements in the dining room, which she told me she was fumigating in order to get rid of the brogue!

Others were equally unfriendly. Disraeli, who seemed to skip out of any room that Sydney entered, made enough impression for her to record 'that egregious coxcomb Disraeli was there, outraging the privilege a young man has of being absurd.' She was provoked enough to write off her new rivals as 'flum-flamree novel writers of the present day'.

Back home again in Dublin she was treated with much more

respect by the young gentlemen of the Ascendancy, who in spite of their high Tory background still looked to her for their liberal education. She loved to lecture them on their duties as landowners and Irishmen. It was considered quite daring for these young members of the establishment to visit Kildare Street, and talk sedition. She boasted of 'Lady Morgan's School of young men – all the young liberals of the highest rank', and wrote rather smugly, 'It is thus we women, the secret tribunal of society, can mine and countermine.'

She was still trying to redeem Ireland with her own version of patriotism, in spite of her disillusion with O'Connell and the growth of his influence. In 1833 she published *Dramatic Sketches from Real Life*, which she gave to Saunders and Otley, as compensation for the relative failure of the second *France*. In an attempt to be different and meet the changing taste of the time, she threw 'the heavy ballast of narrative overboard', and presented her stories in a dramatised form. The longest sketch of three, *Manor Sackville*, was entirely devoted to Ireland, and carried on the theme of her national novels – the sufferings of the peasants through the negligence of absentee landlords, and the wickedness of agents; the other two dealt with English fashionable life, as lived with the Abercorn set, with the inevitable portrait of herself as Mrs O'Neill, the Irish novelist, observing satirically in the corner. But the book wasn't a success. She had worked over this theme too often for it to be either new or controversial, and without Colburn to 'puff' it, it went almost unnoticed among the reviews. The only magazine to give it an important, if unfavourable notice was *Fraser's* whose founder William Maginn was also interested in projecting an image of the Emerald Isle.

Maginn, who had started *Fraser's* in 1830 in rivalry to *Blackwood's*, was now in full effrontery. Like its editor, *Fraser's* was the *enfant terrible* of the literary world, a slashing, impudent and witty journal, a sort of *Private Eye* of its day. Its aim was to prick pomposity and pretentiousness everywhere, but at the same time it supported the government and the established church and was very selective in its targets for satire. Its weapons were ridicule, lampoons and burlesque. It was the manner of *Fraser's* to fix upon a particular victim and then attack with nicknames and parody; it had recently declared war upon the new group of fashionable novelists, with all their literary and social affectation of exclusivity. Deriding these as the 'Silver fork polishers', and the 'footman' school of novelists, Maginn unfairly included Lady Morgan in this group. Sydney had also committed the crime of being a 'she-novelist', a species for which *Fraser's* had only ridicule:

> A genuine she-novel trickles over and suffuses your passive being without occasioning you with the least annoyance. You have no trouble, past or present or to come. You will never be stimulated to recall by an effort of will that of which you possess an habitual knowledge . . . you never have to pause an instant without meaning, be it which it may, it lies upon the surface.

Fraser's found most women writers ludicrous, but reserved special ridicule for 'Miladi', and as well as parodying her dramatic sketches with an imaginary conversation between the Morgans and the Clarkes, attacked her on that old chestnut of her age calling her a 'relic of antiquity'.

Maginn capitalised on his Irishness as much as Sydney Morgan did on hers, but he was selling goods of a different kind. He revelled in the 'broth of a boy' image, whiskey drinking, aggressively stage Irish, and gathered around him a collection of similar 'Hibernians' who he recruited under his pseudonym of 'Sir Morgan O'Doherty', either from Ireland or Scotland. He wrote of this coterie:

> Scores of Paddies have started from the sod, like devils incarnate at the touch of O'Doherty's wand . . . look at their effusions . . . they all smack of the brogue, broad, pure and unadulterated, as on the green hills of Connaught; while the blarney that runs through them out-flavours the eloquence of Cicero.

In this way Maginn and his band of 'Paddies' contributed to that curious phenomenon of English culture, the anti-Irish joke, which has persisted since the twelfth century, when the two countries first got to grips with each other. The essence of the 'Paddy' joke is that it confirms the Englishman's sense of superiority over the native Irish. In this respect Maginn and Lady Morgan were in direct opposition to each other, he using his undoubted brilliance to belittle his own countrymen, and she applying all her gifts to raise them up.

Not only was Maginn a brilliant journalist, he was also a learned scholar; so confident a classicist that his best parodies were written in Greek and Latin. But he threw it all away, in a rake's progress from tavern to tavern. Nothing that he wrote

30 *Gossip, gossip, bore and bore*, drawing of Lady Morgan by Daniel
Maclise, *Fraser's Magazine*

has lasted, and he is remembered now for probably being the original of Captain Shandon, the Irish journalist in Thackeray's *Pendennis*. When he died in 1842, shortly after his release from a debtor's prison, one of his old friends wrote a humorous but affectionate epitaph to him which ended:

> Barring drink and the girls, I ne'er heard of a sin
> Many worse, better few, than bright, broken Maginn.

Some of the girls who knew him might not have been so forgiving. He ruined the reputation and the life of the poetess Laetitia Landon, and he left his wife and children destitute. But in spite of all he was no cold opportunist like Croker, and though a hard and sometimes dirty fighter, he was truly his own worst enemy. In spite of his many jibes at Sydney's expense, he had loved her father Robert Owenson, when he was a student in Dublin and they had had 'convivial' evenings together, and he was enough of an Irishman to respect her defence of her country, though it was beyond him to do the same. In *Maclise's Gallery of Literary Characters*, a collection of sketches and pen portraits taken from *Fraser's*, he included Lady Morgan in a collective drawing of *Regina's Maids of Honour*, Regina being the pet nickname of *Fraser's* and the maids being the few women of whom they approved. And in cheerful doggerel, Maginn tried to make amends:

> Miladi dear – glad are we to see you here.
> Naughty fellows, we must plead that with voice of angry
>   organ
> Once or twice we did, indeed, speak not civilly of MORGAN
> But we must retract, repent, promise better to behave
> She, we're certain, will consent all our former feuds to waive;
> And as we know she hates O'Connell, who calls her now a
>   blockhead old,
> We will say that in *O'Donnel* and in other tales she told,
> There is many a page of fun – many a bit for hearty
>   laughing,
> Some to shed a tear upon – some to relish while we're
>   quaffing.
> And that she can use the mawleys – she has shown upon the
>   Crawleys.
>
> Prate away then good Miladi – gossip, gossip, bore and bore
>   . . .
> All for him who to the shady grove has gone for years a score –

For the sake of old MacOwen, and his song of Modereen
    Roo –
For your father's sake we're going, never more to bother you

The 'gossip and bore' reputation tagged on to Lady Morgan
came mostly from men like Maginn, who held different
political opinions, and resented the force and liveliness of her
arguments. Other English writers, like Wordsworth and
Disraeli, who had publicly snubbed her, probably resented her
popularity, finding her a garrulous little woman from a
provincial city who gave herself literary pretensions. Of course,
she was extremely talkative, and restless and no doubt
trespassed into their Olympian heights of masculine superiority
where her brogue and her eccentric clothes made her an easy
target.

However, if Maginn's 'promise better to behave' sounds like a
Goethe was disappointed by Sydney's frenchified manners,
plenty of life in her yet, and a few more books. There was also
more travelling to do. Over the years, she had collected
material about Flemish artists hoping that Murray might
publish a book, but now she resolved to use this in a study of
Belgium, as a country which had recently undergone a
revolution and established a constitutional monarchy. Perhaps
she could repeat the success of France and Italy. In any event it
was an excuse to go abroad and have an interesting time. She
took Morgan and two of her nieces with her, and set off on a
tour up the Rhine, visiting Antwerp, Liege and Cologne.
Among other celebrities she met Goethe's sister. Ottolie von
Goethe was disappointed by Sydney's frenchified manners,
expecting no doubt that the Wild Irish Girl would still be a
roguish colleen. 'Ach, mein Gott', she is reported to have said,
'If she would have sold to me "Cushla machree" I would have
embraced her!'

The Morgans spent a month in Brussels, enjoying a more
sedate version of their former triumphs in France and Italy.
Sydney was delighted with the lack of pomp and display at the
royal court, and enthusiastically declared that at last she had
found a 'perfect example of the beneficial change in the
character of a people effected by the removal of oppression and
anti-nationalistist institutions'. Perhaps it was too perfect an
example – too simple and bourgeois anyway to make an
interesting book, or perhaps it was because Mrs Fanny
Trollope, who had just had a great success with her malicious

Domestic Manners of the Americans had decided to take on Belgium as well. On her return to Ireland, Sydney wrote to a friend: 'Lo! I find by the papers Mrs. Trollope has got the start of me; had bivouacked on my ground, and made the field her own.' But she was not going to waste good material; she turned her notes into a novel, and called it *The Princess, or The Beguine*. The editor of her *Memoirs* summed it all up most succinctly: 'Those desiring a picturesque guide to Brussels should read the 'Beguine', and it is a novel as entertaining as though it had been written for no other purpose than to adorn the idleness and beguile the ennui of 'des gens peu amusables.' So here we have a useful guide book and a bit of escapist fiction rolled into one. Reading it strictly as a novel, we find the heroine very familiar – being one who has risen to a high position in the world by the skilful exercise of common sense. She turns up in London as a vivacious Belgian princess who captivates an unhappily married English statesman. He does not recognise her as the beautiful half-Polish governess he had loved in his youth. In Belgium he becomes converted to democratic principles, and the princess is always at hand, sometimes disguised as a portrait painter, sometimes as an old nun, to guide and instruct him. Along the way Sydney manages to pay back an old score against 'Prince Pickling-Mustard' in her portrayal of a German travel writer, of ineffable conceit, Count Katzenellenbogen. She had a new publisher, Bentley, who paid her £350 for the book, and furthermore it was appreciated by Maria Edgeworth, who found it amusing:

> exceeding amusing, both in its merits and its absurdities –
> that harlequin princess in her blouse, wonderfully clever and
> preposterous – a Belgian Corinne. The hero is like one of the
> seven sleepers not quite awakened, or how could he avoid
> finding out who this woman is, who pursues him in so many
> forms? But we must grant a romantic writer a few
> impossibilities!

But even a writer of Sydney Morgan's romantic energy could not solve all problems, particularly those of Ireland. Her entry in her diary for Christmas Eve, 1833 reads: 'I must register an odd thought – the Irish destiny is between Bedlam and a jail – but I won't pursue it.' It was in this mood that the New Year opened for her. Her love affair with Ireland, the strongest and most selfless passion of her life, was over.

Her disapproval of the English administration was now

overtaken by her extreme dislike for the measures advocated by O'Connell. His combination of imaginative personality and compelling rhetoric had proved irresistible, and he was now known as 'The King of the Beggars' on account of the money that came pouring in, mostly the pennies of the poor. The 'O'Connell tribute' as it was called, enabled him to give up his lucrative law practice in order to devote his whole time to politics. He now had 39 MPs attending the English House of Commons, pledged to his support, and they were holding up all other business, vociferously demanding the Repeal of the Union. The country was becoming even more unsettled; there was violent agitation against the payment of tithes; landlordism was under threat, and the British government had recently brought in a strong Coercion Act. The Morgans could not support either side, and more or less withdrew from political activity.

Dublin was changing socially as well. Sydney, who temperamentally still belonged to the free-speaking liberated women of the eighteenth century – those ladies who had offended her non-conformist mother with their bawdy talk – could not endure the mealy-mouthed atmosphere that had come in with the upsurge of evangelical religion, now spilling over from England into Ireland. Ladies of rank now went in for prudery and 'good works'. What she called 'tea and tract parties' did not suit her style. In some quarters of Dublin she sometimes felt 'the very air breathes Methodism – every tree looks like a preacher'. Money was not so plentiful either. Her last books had not sold at all well, and now the post of physician to the Marshalsea, which had provided Sir Charles with most of his income, was to be abolished. At the beginning of 1835 they went to Cheltenham, then a fashionable spa. Sydney was looking for stimulating company and a health cure. She took her niece Olivia with her, and the younger girl, Josephine, joined them later. Her relationship with her nieces had become very important to her. She had always loved them and indulged them when they were children. They were very much influenced by her, and as they were pretty girls, and good musicians, she pushed them forward in Dublin society, where they were very much admired.

But now they were growing up and going their own way. Sydney, the eldest of the girls, and named for her, was going to be married in England, and the pattern was changing. Nanny, Sir Charles's daughter by his first wife, also lived in England, where she had been brought up by grandparents. Increasingly there seemed nothing to keep her in Ireland. The fact that Lady Morgan had no children of her own might have contributed to her restlessness, and dissatisfaction with the old familiar life. Sydney had always compensated for her own childlessness by her affection for her nieces; in fact she once wrote of her sister's daughters as 'her beloved children and mine'.

However, there was always a slight friction with their mother, who seemed to resist Sydney's influence over her daughters; perhaps Olivia was a little afraid that her rich and successful sister might take too much from the girls to compensate for her own childlessness. Lady Morgan's diary is full of hints of trouble: 'I had the pleasure of taking my two girls with me after a long dispute and struggle, and a little intrigue with their mother, as usual . . . I know there will be a storm in Great George Street . . . as their mother does not like to let them from her side.' But she carried her point, as she usually did, and her nieces danced and sang their way to social success as she had done. They were always at hand to entertain when she gave her parties. In fact, many of Sydney's visitors found the nieces more to their taste than the aunt. Prince Pückler Muskau wrote of his visit: 'I did not know then one of her most charming qualities –; that of possessing two such pretty relatives', and Tom Moore made similar remarks in his diary.

The eldest niece, Sydney, was already married in England when the Morgans went to Cheltenham with the other two girls. They moved on to London, and the visit ran into several months, but nearly ended in disaster. On the return journey to Dublin Sir Charles was taken ill, and had to be put to bed in a little wayside inn. The local doctor came quickly, and 'covering him with hot tile, mustard, blisters, bleeding him profusely, in a word saving his life – and mine!' She got him back to Dublin, but only just, and realised that she had been 'on the point of losing all that was most dear to me, and necessary to the future remnant of my life'. In 'wretched Dublin, the capital of wretched Ireland' she had to nurse him back to health in very difficult circumstances. They had left the house in Kildare Street to be redecorated while they were away, but on their return found it still unfinished and half painted. But she threw it open to visitors, first to Tom Moore, who arrived very old and bald, but still retaining his 'cock-sparrow air'. Although she was still miserable about Morgan's general condition, she could not

resist inviting the whole congregation of the British Association, who were holding a conference in Dublin at the time. She
wrote 'My soirée very learned, scientific and tiresome! Fifty
philosophers passed through my little salon last night'. She saw
a lot of Moore on his visit to Ireland, and found him egotistical
and shallow. He fulminated against the general spread of
knowledge, and the diffusion of cheap literature. In full
reactionary spate, he declaimed bitterly against women who
wrote: ' "In short", he said, "a writing woman is one unsexed;"
but suddenly he recollected himself, and pointing at me said
"except her".'

Dubliners who even to this day dearly love 'a character', saw
Lady Morgan as one to be cherished, and the more bizarre and
outlandish her clothes and her behaviour were, the better they
liked her. But the English visitors, even though they were
amused and entertained, found her, with her rouge, her vanity
and her voluble anecdotes a joke in slightly bad taste. The
diarist Creevey, visiting Dublin at this time met her at a dinner
party, and recorded his maliciously amused reaction:

> The Morgan was of course the lioness. She was dying for a
> display . . . In person she resembles a teetotum. Her face and
> neck were painted a bright red; her bonnet was of the same
> colour in silk, and circular in shape, turned up all round at
> the edge, with four red feathers at equal distance from each
> other, drooping or rather flowing from the bonnet like water
> . . . Her attachment to the colour was shown in her gown,
> and descended even to her shoes.

Her appearance might be cheerful enough, but the real
situation was gloomy. She no longer had a cause to campaign
for, nor stimulating work to absorb her. It was having a very
debilitating effect upon both of them. Sydney began a novel
about the Irish pirate queen, Grace O'Malley, a theme which
should have suited her admirably, but she laid it aside. She was
toying with an idea for a book about the status of women, but
it wouldn't take. She longed to go visiting and to be visited, but
Morgan, who had never really recovered from his last illness,
would not go out nor take exercise. He only wanted to sit
reading a book by a hot fire all day, and she had to accept his
lethargy:

> A more blameless life was never led; some great occasion
> would soon rouse him; he is always ready to meet an event

with energy, he has no external world; his world is within, and were it not for his fidgety wife he would never look out of it.

Both of them were sinking down into poor health, and her eyes, always weak, were getting worse. She records frequently the death of old friends; even the pet macaw of Lady Cork departed this life. On April 3, 1836 Lady Cork wrote to her:

Your old friend and mine departed this life a few days ago. He is buried in my garden, and his merits well deserve an epitaph from your pen. He commited but one crime, and only made a bit of an assault on George the Fourth's stocking. That was an offence merely, the *crime* was running away with a piece out of Lady Darlington's leg. . . . I have been ill with the tic, but am better now, and just going out of town for the holidays. . . . Don't forget I am ninety years old, and was, and am, and shall be to the end, your ever affectionate M. Cork and Orrery.

And then, one morning in May, 1837, there came a letter addressed to her which she read carefully and slowly. Sir Charles, seeing her so preoccupied, and thinking it was from one of her troupe of young men, said: 'Sydney, I wish you would eat your breakfast, and never mind your damned dandies.' She handed the letter to him triumphantly. It was from the Prime Minister, Lord Melbourne, and she had been granted the very first literary pension ever offered to a woman. It was for the very considerable sum of £300 a year. The fact that Lord Melbourne had once been Sir William Lamb, long suffering husband of Lady Caroline, might have influenced the giving of this reward for 'services to literature and to patriotism', but this was not in question. There was a job too, for Sir Charles. He was made one of the Commissioners of Irish Fisheries, and became lively enough again to write several papers on this subject.

Above all, the Morgans could now afford to go and live in England. Here was a paradoxical situation indeed. The English government, against whose administration she had campaigned all her life, was now giving her a pension for 'services rendered'. And Sydney, the great opponent of 'absenteeism', she who had written books and tracts showing it for the great evil it was, was now ready to leave Ireland herself. She had to face a lot of criticism on this matter, but she had her case prepared. She was no landowner, she maintained; all the soil she had ever owned was contained in a window box. And besides, her husband was an Englishman who had lived in Ireland simply to please her; now she must allow him to end his days in his own native land. In fact Sir Charles, who only wanted to be allowed to read his books, play his flute, and sit by the fire, would have been perfectly happy to do all this in Dublin, but because Sydney wanted to go, of course he agreed. Finally she convinced herself and her critics that she was coming to England to keep a closer eye on affairs there, and look after Ireland's cause.

Sydney had always loved London, and now came to it as a well-known writer with a pension awarded for literary excellence. The literary scene was not altogether pleased. The pension had caused a lot of resentment, for it was bigger than most given to other writers in much more straitened circumstances. By the standards of her day, Lady Morgan was very well off. She was reported to have £1,000 a year of her own money coming in, as well as her husband's income. In the fashionable world too there was plenty of malice. Lady Cork, though now over ninety, was still sufficiently lively to say that Lady M. was 'amusing enough as an Irish blackguard, but not to be endured in her attempt to play the fine lady'. She could put up with the eccentric Lady Cork, and Lady Charleville, the other influential hostess in London was still well disposed towards her. But there was no welcome from the third hostess of the literary set – Marguerite, Countess of Blessington.

The 'most gorgeous Lady Blessington' as she was called, had come through experiences that some commentators find, even now, too scandalous to relate, but in 1835 she had established the most brilliant salon in London, to which men, but not women, of fame and fashion came. She was born in Tipperary in 1789, and was then called Sally Power. In order to pay off his gambling debts her dissolute squireen father, one of Jonah Barrington's category of 'half mounted gentlemen', had more or less sold her, at the age of fifteen, to a captain in the British army stationed in Ireland. Her husband was also brutal and drunken, and after three months of marriage she fled from him to the protection of yet another army officer. She emerged from this mysterious retreat three years later, beautiful and, wherever she picked up her education, extremely well read in literature and the arts. For the rest of her life, however, it seems that she was incapable of any normal sexual responses. After many vicissitudes she married, or was married to, the rather simple-minded but extremely rich Charles Gardiner, Earl of Blessington, a man that Lady Morgan had met in her own youth, had disapproved of intensely, as one of the squandering absentee lords of Ireland, and had caricatured cruelly as 'Lord Rosbrin' in *Florence Macarthy* representing him as stage-struck to the point of lunacy.

But Sally Power had come to London with £30,000 a year and a coronet, which made her, if not respectable, at least very rich and fashionable. Blessington died, and his family repudiated her with lawsuits and injunctions which took away most of the fortune; but she was still beautiful and resourceful, and set out to make a handsome living by her own writing: a never ending stream of 'silver forks', and travel books, and the editing of 'Keepsake' annuals. These last were very copiously illustrated miscellanies of fashion, fiction and poetry, the forerunners of women's magazines, for which she commissioned artwork and articles. All in all, she was a very formidable rival to Sydney, and the fact that they were both Irish gave their relationship an edge. Lady Morgan professed to know more about Marguerite's past than was good for her, and her strictures were welcomed by all those who looked askance at that lady's high style. In his book *My Contemporaries* William Archer Shee notes that Lady Morgan had transferred her dislike of Blessington to his widow who had become 'her favourite aversion ... to allude to Lady Blessington is like shaking a red rag in front of a bull, and is sure to call forth some startling revelation in reference to her early career'. Lady Blessington responded in kind, making it known that in Ireland Sydney had been called 'Old eighteenpenny', because her eyes were different sizes, like a shilling and sixpence!

So much for the cut and thrust of literary life. But in spite of all this in-fighting London was welcoming enough. On Christmas Day 1837 Sydney wrote in her diary: 'I am really beginning my regeneration and new life as a denizen of London. Everybody congratulating us – old friends are true, new ones all agreeable.' She also congratulated herself in that entry on the improvement in her sight, and the fact that she had started work again on the book that she had been contemplating for a long time, *Woman and her Master*.

But first of all Sydney had to find somewhere to live, so that she could make full use of her other talent – that for entertaining. She wanted to transfer the old Kildare Street scene

31 William St, Belgravia, London home of Lady Morgan

into London terms. It was a period of great expansion in
London; the Victorian building boom had started; landowners
with estates bordering on to the metropolis were eager to
convert land into money, and there were plenty of builders
eager to cover fields and parklands with houses. The conversion
of Buckingham House into Buckingham Palace by George IV

made the adjoining estates of Belgravia and Pimlico, hitherto private land, very fashionable, and it was there that Sydney, with her unerring nose for fashion, started to look. She found her dream house before the rest of the terraced street that was to contain it was even built. This was in William Street, just off Lowndes Square, where Cubitt the contractor had just begun building in an open field. A survey of this prestigious development, 'The Metropolitan Improvements, 1827–1831', reported:

> This extensive area is now covering with mansions and handsome houses, laid out with beautiful plantations. This great undertaking, equal in extent and value to many cities, is destined to be the future residences of the highest classes of the fashionable world.

Sydney, as she had been in Kildare Street, was in 'a most desirable area'. She wrote:

> I was busy writing my article on Pimlico when Lady Arthur Lennox came to know what were my intentions. I told her of my search after a house in the new quarter of Belgrave Square. I wanted one which should be cheap and charming. She advised me to look in a new street containing one or two houses as yet built by the great builder Cubitt.

Soon she had the great builder under her thumb, and he would put things up and knock things down to her suggestion. There was an old brewery at the end of the road which spoilt her view of Hyde Park. After a long campaign of agitating on her part with the appropriate government department, Cubitt bought the brewery, demolished it, and built a gate into the park. Albert Gate, which stands to this day, is yet another memorial to the little Dublin busy-body's powers of persuasion. 'Hurrah', she wrote 'I have got my gate, just as we got Catholic Emancipation, by worrying for it!'

Sydney wanted to be to London what she had been to Dublin – the centre of a large circle of literary, scientic and aristocratic people, and she often crowded a hundred guests into her two small reception rooms managing, as Samuel Carter Hall reported, with 'admirable tact to bring together elements that never could socially mingle'. In the evenings she entertained, waving her large green fan which had now become her trademark, and in the day she worked away on large sheets of green paper, which she thought might help her eyes, on *Woman and her Master*.

Colburn, who ever since her arrival in London had been trying to win her back into his fold, gave her a beautiful mirror for the new drawing room, and made her promise to let him publish *Woman* when it was ready. In 1840 the first and only part came out. From her first book to her last, one message was constant: that women in every age, in spite of the systematic subordination in which they have been kept, have not only never been subjugated, but have been the real trustees of the vital and important ideas of their time. Through the characters of her heroines, she demonstrated her belief that women were of 'finer clay' than their so-called master, man, and in this, her last book, she spelt it out. With all her old industry and application she proves with historical examples taken from ancient Greece, Italy and the Bible, that 'wherever woman has been, there she has left the track of her humanity'. Madame de Staël would have been proud of her acolyte. The strong feminism of its seven hundred and fifty pages is presented, however, in a mood of such conciliatory charm that even the *Quarterly Review* found the work inoffensive, and conceded that 'Men are much more apprehensive of criticism than their fair fellows, and take it worse when administered.' The critic of the *Dublin Review*, however, was still in the old groove when he described it as 'a work without one claim to notice except the antiquity of the author'.

Colburn, anxious to establish his hold, then persuaded Sydney to collect essays that she had contributed with Sir Charles for various periodicals over the years. *The Book without a Name* came out in 1841, but now she had started to suffer from quite serious heart palpitations which coupled with her ever present eye trouble prevented her from doing any original work. In January 1843 she wrote:

> I enter on my third year's illness, which has interfered with my enjoyment of life, my worldly interests (for I cannot write without pain and palpitations), and all my social pleasures.

But her indomitable determination to make the best of things prevailed. In June of the same year she wrote:

> Is it possible that I am again restored to health and sight . . .
> soirées, opera, concerts, a discretion which we (old fools as we are) enjoy a l'indiscretion! Well, so here I am taking a new lease of life, available for any length of time, with a peppercorn fine . . . my life may be deemed a frivolity for one

of my age, but no, it is a philosophy, a profound and just
philosophy, founded on the wisdom of the principle to do
and enjoy all the good I can, while I submit to the penalty of
that mystery called life.

She needed all her philosophy and stoicism in the months to
come. From Ireland came the news of the death of her young
niece, Olivia. While she was overwhelmed with grief by this
news, Morgan said to her 'Oh, Sydney, if you grieve thus for a
niece whom you never see much of, what is to become of you if
I were to go?' As if acting under a premonition he died, a
fortnight later, of what had seemed a not very threatening
illness. She felt this death even more than that of her father
when she had written 'Nothing can fill the place he held in my
heart.' But her husband had done more than that. He had loved
her passionately; he had admired her inordinately; and he had
been her constant companion and support, subordinating his
own gifts and preferences to hers. She wrote 'Oh, my husband.
I cannot endure this. I was quite unprepared for this. So ends
my life.' She was sixty-eight years old – if one can ever estimate
her right age – and had been married for thirty-one years. She
wrote again in November of the same year:

> The winter fire kindles alone for me now. The chair, the
> table, the lamp, the very books and paper cutter, all *these* are
> here, this November – gloomy wretched November. How I
> used to long for November – social home-girt November;
> now I spend it wandering through this deserted house.

But what Sydney called her 'constitutional cheerfulness' helped
her through once more. In April of the next year she wrote:
'Time applied to grief is a worldly common place . . . it softens
sighs and dries tears . . . the loss of that which is, or was, part
of yourself remains forever.' Society still wanted her, and she
wanted society:

> Everybody makes a point of having me out, and I am
> beginning to be familiarised with my terrible loss. I go in and
> out of drawing rooms, and sit at good men's tables . . .
> London is the best place in the world for the happy and the
> unhappy, and there is a floating capital of sympathy for every
> human, good or evil. I am nobody, and yet what kindness I
> am daily receiving.

And then, in the midst of coming to terms with grief, there
occurred a piece of pure farce.

Sydney had become friendly with a wealthy widower who lived in neighbouring Hyde Park Place. The size of Mr McKinnon's reception rooms, the style of his decor, gave her the idea of amalgamating her evenings with his, and bringing together the top names in the social world with their equivalents in artistic circles, on a scale impossible in her bijou residence. She persuaded him to give a joint soirée, where he would send cards to guests of his order, and she would invite the aristocracy of talent. The cards carried both their names, and soon gossip was abroad that her ladyship was considering a second match. Captain Marryat, bluff author of boy's yarns like *Midshipman Ready* reacted typically. He wrote to a friend:

> Lady Morgan going to be married? I did not think she was such an Irish jackass. I'd as soon go to church with a paint-pot. Mercy on us . . . well, let her hear me or not, I will say it: 'There's no fool like an old fool!'

On the evening of the affair, more than two hundred of 'the aristocracy of rank' arrived in a state of lively curiosity, but apart from three or four invited personally by Lady Morgan there were no representatives of the arts. An incredibly dull evening was had by all, and she was furious and humiliated. Days later all was explained. McKinnon's butler, who was in charge of the invitations only posted the ones entrusted to him by his master, and whether motivated by snobbery or genuine forgetfulness put all those addressed to untitled guests in his desk. So ended the scheme to bring the titled and the talented together, and all talk of a second marriage stopped also.

She was not to take off her widow's weeds. Black crêpe became her habitual daily wear. Olivia, her junior by about ten years, had always been delicate and was now terminally ill. In 1845, at the age of sixty, she died. She had been only two when her own mother had died, and had looked to Sydney for maternal as well as sisterly affection – and Sydney had responded wholeheartedly. In her very first book of poems, published in 1801 she recorded their relationship:

> What, and no lines to thee addrest,
> Thou longest known, and loved the best
> Not one to thee?
> For whom I've oft wept, sighed and smiled,
> My sister, mother, friend and child . . .
> Thou all to me!

Now it was painful for her to write 'my noble minded and affectionate sister, my first friend and earliest companion, with whom I had struggled through a precarious youth – my beloved Olivia is no more'. She turned to the 'world' as an alcoholic turns to the bottle, and expressed her need in those terms: 'So I reel on! The "world" is my gin or opium. I take it for a few hours per diem, excitement, intoxication, absence. I return to my desolate home, and awaken to all the horrors of sobriety.'

She saw herself clearly as society saw her; 'the agreeable rattle of the great ladies' coterie', and continued to play her part when in company, with her rouge put on her cheeks like a red badge of courage. But she confessed that now she never more walked in the park adjacent to her house; 'that park so near to me that I worked so hard to get an entrance into. It seems to be covered in black crepe!' In that age of high memoralising of death, she remained true to her old rational self, and never turned to mawkish sentimentality or even to religion. Her friendly but Pecksniffian critic, the journalist Samuel Carter Hall, complained of this:

> She was essentially material; in not one of her letters, in no part of her journal can there be found the remotest reference to that High Power from which her genius was derived, which protected her wayward and perilous youth, her prosperous womanhood, and her popular if not honoured old age. There is no word of prayer or of thanksgiving in any of her written thoughts.

So Sydney remained a stoic, and paid no lipservice to the available consolations of any church. She trusted her own courage, even though she feared the lonely years ahead:

> I dare not trust myself to chronicle my feelings as to passing more years. To forget is my philosophy; to hope would be my insanity; to endure is my system – but it is only a system from which the dreary impulses of my state and condition revolt but too often. Still I am grateful for the good I yet enjoy – to be so is my religion.

Religion, the more orthodox form of religion that is, was, nevertheless to give her one more chance to come before the public and enjoy herself. In 1850, Father Nicholas Wiseman was made the Cardinal Archbishop of Westminster, the first Roman Catholic Cardinal in England since the Reformation.

This appointment raised a storm of outraged Protestantism, and a flood of protesting letters to the press. In one of these there was a reference to a pamphlet that Wiseman had written in 1830, when he was in Rome, attacking Lady Morgan's book on Italy. She had cast doubts on the authenticity of St Peter's Chair in the Vatican, saying that it dated only from the Crusades; that it had been looted from the Arabs; and that there was an inscription upon it in Arabic which said 'There is but one God, and Mahomet is his prophet.' Wiseman refuted this allegation as a wicked and foolish tale, dismissing her as a superficial 'writer of romances'. So vehement was his attack that her book was placed on the *Index Purgatorious*. But now, after nineteen years, the controversy was brought into the open again, and she took it up with all her old zest for a fight. She published her own pamphlet, *A Letter to Cardinal Wiseman*, in which she defended her original statement with her best display of erudition, and she mocked His Eminence and all authoritarianism with all her old, gay impudence. For once the English press, always ready for a swipe at Catholic triumphalism, was on her side. Her pamphlet was reprinted five times. *Punch* made it the theme of a full page cartoon, a poem, and a long dialogue between 'Lady Fan and Cardinal Crozier'. She was delighted with all the attention, and wrote to her diary: 'Lots of notes and notices of my letter to Cardinal Wisemen. It has had the run of all the newspapers. The little old woman still lives!' But of course she put the last phrase in French.

Sydney thought that she would never shed tears again, that no loss could move her. But the death of Tom Moore in 1852 struck home. She saw the announcement in *The Times* and was saddened to read that when he was buried in a small English churchyard, only one coach followed the funeral. This was the man who had been so lionised in his early life, and who had loved society as much as she did. He had also died practically penniless. The odious Croker, true to form, remembered him meanly, with the phrase 'his delirous tremens of vanity'. She, more generous, hoped that his memory would be honoured in Ireland, and resolved to do something about it. She wrote to the Dublin papers, and to influential friends, and as a result a monument to Moore was erected with great civic pride near College Green. Their lives had crossed many times since their first meeting in the little room above his parent's shop, when they were both young and promising. They had both been fêted in London and abroad; they had shared the same inspiration of patriotism and opportunism, taking popular sentiment and turning it into politics. The Wild Irish Girl and the Minstrel Boy – Ireland's ambassadors to the world – had both suffered the blows of time, that takes beauty, hope and friends away. Tom Moore's earliest songs had praised the faithful heart that remains true 'though all the world betrays thee', and Sydney had often struck the strings of her little Irish harp, and sung his sweet sentiments:

> The heart that has truly loved, never forgets,
> But as truly loves on till the close
> And the sunflower gives to her God when he sets
> The same look as she gave when he rose.

Other deaths moved her less. She recorded Lady Cork as having passed 'in a surfeit of bitterness and good dinners' and when Colburn died in 1855 she noted in her diary: 'Poor old Colburn . . . one who could not take tea without a strategem . . . I wish that we had parted friends.' But she was still capable of being moved. Ireland, the country that she had left in 1839, and to which she had never returned, was still able to trouble her. It was the aftermath of the terrible famine of 1848, when through bad government and mismanagement probably a million people died of hunger and disease, and another million emigrated. Then there had followed the political failure of the Young Ireland Movement, when yet another abortive rebellion had taken place, and the young men involved were all deported or imprisoned. Many of these were poets and writers who had been influenced by the romantic nationalism of such as herself and Thomas Moore. But Sydney was old now, and virtually an absentee. Catholic emancipation was the only issue on which she could claim real success in Irish politics. Everything else she had wanted for her country had now become impossible. O'Connell had replaced her dream of a reconciliation between liberal Protestant and romantic Gael with a sectarian demagogy, and his own policy had been overwhelmed by the famine. This was the watershed that had made patriotic sentiment, and 'oratory' redundant. Neither sad, sweet elegies nor rousing rhetoric could heal the wounds. Even in her comfortable old age, far away in fashionable Belgravia, she felt the reality of Ireland very sharply and wrote:

> Fiction has nothing more pathetic than that great
> melodramatic tragedy now performing on the shores of

Ireland – the Celtic Exodus. The Jews left a foreign country, 'a house of bondage' but the Celtic exodus is the departure of the Irish emigrant from the land of their love, their inheritance and their traditions, of their passions and their prejudices; with all the details of wild grief and heart-rending incidents, their ignorance of the strangers they are going to seek – their tenderness for the objects they are leaving behind. Their departure exceeds in deep pathos all the poetical tragedy that has ever been presented on the stage, or national novelists have ever depicted in their volumes.

Here she puts her own work into perspective. She had, in her national tales depicted many times the romance of ruins; wild thistles, brambles and clinging ivy prettily decorate her landscape; but now the reality was the roofless cabin, the deserted farmhouse, and the peasant in flight from the rotting, stinking land. This was not the material for her pen. All she could do was to send money to charities, and go on working away at whatever her poor sight would now allow. She made arrangements to revise first *The Wild Irish Girl* and then *Salvator Rosa* for republication. She was ill and almost blind, but she had plenty of loyal help. Her widowed niece Sydney lived with her and looked after her domestic affairs; the editor of the *Athenaeum*, Hepworth Dixon, was her literary counsellor, and now there was a new friend, Geraldine Jewsbury, constantly at her side. This young woman had come to London from Manchester to try her luck as a novelist. She had hero-worshipped women of letters, and for years she had corresponded with Elizabeth Barrett Browning, and Jane Welsh Carlyle, before she was invited by Lady Morgan to work for her, putting her papers and journals in order and arranging her memoirs with a view to publication.

The little house in William Street was busy in the daytime with them both working, sorting all the letters of a lifetime, kept in a trunk that had originally held her trousseau. Now it contained all the accumulated debris of a long life; nothing that had ever interested her had been thrown away, and the yellowing pages of the past were identified and dated in her old woman's handwriting. There were the letters from school to her father, written in a flowing copperplate, in extraordinary contrast to the frantic scribble of her nearly blind later state. There were the scraps of letters from Sir Charles Ormsby, quarrelsome with the familiarity of a lover; there were drawings for costumes for fancy dress balls for herself and Olivia; lists of subscribers to the Italian opera in Dublin; reviews of concerts; menus of meals given and received, recipes, lists of guests at formal dinners; there were hundreds of press cuttings, including Colburn's cruel advertisement for 'Lady Morgan's books at half price'. There were the book reviews, good and bad, and her letters to the papers. And there were obituaries, so many obituaries, of old friends and sometimes of enemies. What she thought was interesting she was sure would interest future readers of her memoirs.

In the evenings, as she could no longer go out at night herself, people came to her. She sent invitation cards out nearly every day, and when Geraldine Jewsbury had been sent home, exhausted from the day's work, Sydney dressed for the evening, sat on her small green sofa, and entertained. The Halls were regular visitors and have left records of her conversation at this time:

> I know I am vain [she once said to Mrs Hall] but I have a
> right to be so. It is not put off and on like my rouge, it is
> always with me; it sleeps with me, wakes with me,
> companions me in my solitude and arrays itself for publicity
> whenever I go abroad. I wrote books when your mothers
> worked samplers, and demanded freedom for Ireland when
> Dan O'Connell scrambled for gulls' eggs among the wild
> crags of Derrynane.

Sydney laughed at herself and her vanity, calling herself a mere 'pensioned scribbler', but was still impressed that she, a poor actor's daughter, should have had such a life. She had some sound advice for other young girls, bereft of fortune as she was:

> I desire to give every girl, no matter her rank, a trade –
> profession if the word pleases better. Cultivate one thing to
> perfection, no matter what it is, for which she has a talent –
> drawing, music, embroidery, housekeeping, even; give her a
> staff to lay hold of; let her feel 'That will carry me through
> life without dependence!' I was independent at fourteen, and
> never went into debt.

Her boast of 'independence at fourteen' is another example of her indomitable determination never – even at this stage – to give away her age. But she had her eighty-second birthday on Christmas Day 1858. A few friends came to dinner, and if her diary is to be believed she sang to the assembled group a comic and gruesome Irish song 'The Night before Larry was stretched', with all the appropriate gestures for execution by hanging. On 1 January 1859, *Passages from my Autobiography* put together by Geraldine from Lady Morgan's journals and letters relating to the second visit to France in 1818, was published by Bentley. In reviewing it the *Athenaeum* remarked that she had 'lived through the love, admiration and malignity of three generations of men. A literary Ninon, she seems as brisk and captivating now as when the author of "Kate Kearney" divided the laureateship of society and song with Tom Moore.' The comparison with Ninon de l'Enclos, a woman famous for her liaisons with some of the most distinguished men of her day in France, including Voltaire, must have been some compensation to her for the reference to her age.

Delving into the old trunk where she kept all the papers collected throughout her long life carried her back in memory until the early days of childhood were reached. During the long sleepless nights in which she was plagued with respiratory trouble, she passed the time singing the Irish songs that her father had taught her. On St Patrick's Day, 1859, she celebrated Ireland's national saint with a morning musical party, where she seemed as lively as ever. On being complimented on looking well, she replied 'Perhaps I am better rouged than ever.' A week later she caught a chill, and took to her bed.

On the morning of 16 April she felt better and got up, and began to write a letter, but collapsed again, and said to her niece who was supporting her 'Sydney, is this death?'. She died that evening.

So with a pen more or less in her hand, Sydney Morgan left the stage. With that pen she had earned and saved more than fifteen thousand pounds, which she left to her nieces. Honouring the influences of her early life, she left a hundred pounds for a marble tablet to be set up in St Patrick's Cathedral Dublin, to the memory of Turlough O'Carolan, the blind harper that her father had adored. She also left a hundred pounds to the Theatrical Fund for Actors, and two hundred pounds to the Governesses' Benevolent Association. She was buried in old Brompton Cemetery, and at her own request the funeral was private. She wanted no fashionable cortège: 'Let no such ghastly mockery accompany my poor remains to their last resting place . . . I desire that my funeral may be strictly private and limited to a hearse and one mourning coach.' Her tomb also seems to echo her wishes; a block of white polished marble records the date of her death, but not of her birth. Above the inscription is an ancient Irish harp resting on two volumes, one of which is *The Wild Irish Girl*, and the other *France*. So she wished to be remembered.

There were fulsome obituaries to her in all the leading papers, particularly the *Athenaeum* and the *Art Journal*. Julia Kavanagh, in *English Women of Letters* published in 1863 said 'In the years to come her name will hold no contemptible position in the political and literary history of her time.'

This solemn judgment did not prove prophetic. The paradox of Lady Morgan is that one who was so important in her lifetime should be almost completely forgotten today. The books that went into so many editions and caused so much political dissent are almost impossible to find, and only *The Wild Irish Girl* recently republished, raises an occasional gleam of recognition. In the history of the Anglo-Irish novel she is just a footnote. This dismissal of her is as unfair as the wild over-reaction shown in the hostile criticism that was vented in her lifetime. Today she is not read because long ago some critics thought her brand of literary patriotism outmoded, and the reasons why she seemed outstanding and original in her own time, and even dangerous, are no longer valid. In Ireland she is disregarded for yet another reason. Her literary images are rated as so much kitsch; the harp entwined with the shamrocks is strictly for the tourist trade, and anyone who dances a jig, metaphorically or otherwise, in English drawing rooms is an embarrassment. So she is put aside, precisely for the qualities that made her a bestseller in her lifetime.

She was read in her life time because she told people something about Ireland – and England – that they wanted to know, and in doing so she worked out her own journey through the thickets of national identity. She wrote always as a woman, claiming for women the right to be involved in the most important matters of their day, and for a while, in her pleas for justice and tolerance, she influenced liberal opinion in England. Because she was a woman she was dismissed as a purveyor of romantic nonsense, but she was really attacked because the political message beneath the nonsense was a persuasive and powerful one. The role of woman in society and the rights of small nations to independence were her themes, and in spite of archaic language, pedantry and story telling tricks her concept of these two major issues is relevant, modern – and valid.

BIBLIOGRAPHY

WORKS BY SYDNEY OWENSON, LADY MORGAN

Poems dedicated by permission to the Countess of Moira, Dublin, (Stewart); London (Phillips) 1801.

St. Clair, or First love, Dublin 1802, reissued as *St. Clair, or the Heiress of Desmond*, London (Harding and Highley); Dublin (Archer) 1803.

'Pamphlet in answer to "Familiar Epistles on the Present State of the Irish Stage", attributed to Miss Owenson', Dublin (Parry) 1804.

The Novice of St. Dominick, 4 vols, London (Phillips).

Twelve Original Hibernian Melodies, from the works of the ancient Irish Bards, London (Preston), 1805.

The Wild Irish Girl, 3 vols, London (Phillips) 1806.

The First Attempt, or Whim of a Moment, Dublin, 1807.

The Lay of an Irish Harp or Metrical Fragments, London (Phillips) 1807.

Patriotic Sketches of Ireland, 2 vols, London (Phillips) 1807.

Woman, or Ida of Athens, 4 vols, London (Longman) 1809.

The Missionary – an Indian Tale, 3 vols, London (Stockdale) 1811.

O'Donnel – a National Tale, 3 vols, London (Colburn) 1814.

France, 2 vols, London (Colburn) 1817.

Florence Macarthy, an Irish Tale, 4 vols, London (Colburn) 1818.

Italy, 2 vols, London (Colburn) 1821.

The Life and Times of Salvator Rosa, 2 vols, London (Colburn) 1824.

Absenteeism, London (Colburn) 1825.

The O'Briens and the O'Flahertys; a National Tale, 4 vols, London (Colburn) 1827.

The Book of the Boudoir, 2 vols, London (Colburn) 1829.

France in 1829–30, 2 vols, London (Saunders and Otley) 1830.

Dramatic Scenes from Real Life, 2 vols, London (Saunders and Otley) 1830.

The Princess or The Beguine, 3 vols, London (Bentley) 1834.

Woman and her Master, 2 vols, London (Colburn) 1840.

The Book without a Name, Articles jointly with Sir Charles Morgan, 2 vols, London (Colburn) 1841.

Letter to Cardinal Wiseman, London (Westerton) 1851.

Passages from my Autobiography, London (Bentley) 1859.
Luxima – a Tale of India, Revision of *The Missionary*, (Westerton) 1859.

BOOKS AND ARTICLES DEALING WITH LADY MORGAN

Lady Morgan's Memoirs, ed. W. Hepworth Dixon and Geraldine Jewsbury, London 1863.
Lady Morgan, her Career, Literary and Personal, W.J. Fitzpatrick, London, 1863.
The Wild Irish Girl. The life of Sydney Owenson, Lady Morgan, Lionel Stevenson, Chapman & Hall, 1936.
The Irish Novelists 1800–1850, Thomas Flanagan, Columbia University Press, 1959.
Lady Morgan – Generalisations and Errors, James Newcomer, *Etudes Irlandaises*, University of Lille, December 1978.
A Book of Memoirs, Samuel Carter Hall, London 1871.
English Women of Letters, Julia Kavanagh, Hurst and Blackett, London, 1863.
Lady Morgan in France, ed. Elizabeth Suddaby and P.J. Yarrow, Oriel Press, 1971.
Mss. of commonplace books, letters and notebooks in Dublin National Libary.

OTHER WORKS CONSULTED

Adburgham, Alison, *The Silver Fork Novelists*, London, Constable, 1983.
Adburgham, Alison, *Women in Print*, London, Allen & Unwin, 1972.
Austen, Jane, *Letters*, ed. R.W. Chapman, Oxford, 1932.
Barrington, Sir Jonah, *Personal Sketches and Recollections of his own Times*, London, 1827.
Bates, William (ed.), *The Maclise Portrait Gallery*, London, Chatto & Windus, 1898.
Byron: Letters and Journals, ed. Peter Gunn, Penguin Lives and Letters, 1984.
Clark, William, *The Irish Stage in the County Towns*, Oxford University Press, 1965.
Cloncurry, Lord, *Personal Recollections of his Life and Times*, Dublin, 1849.
Craig, Maurice J., *Georgian Dublin*, Cresset Press, 1952.
The Creevey Papers, ed. John Gore, Batsford, 1902.
The Croker Papers, ed. L.J. Jennings, London, 1884.
Davis, Thomas, *Collected Prose Writings*, ed. W. O'Donoghue, Dublin, 1891.
Dowden, Ernest, *The Life of Shelley*, London, Routledge & Kegan Paul, 1969.
Duggan, G.C., *The Stage Irishman*, London, 1937.

Edgeworth, Maria, *Life and Letters*, ed. Augustus Hare, London, 1875.

Genlis, Comtesse de, *Memoires inedits*, Paris, 1825.

Gerard, Frances, *Picturesque Dublin*, London, Hutchinson, 1898.

Gross, John, *Rise and Fall of the Man of Letters*, London, Weidenfeld & Nicolson, 1969.

Hennessy, Maurice, *The Wild Geese*, London, Sidgwick & Jackson, 1973.

Herold, Christopher, *Madame de Staël: Mistress to an Age*, London, Hamish Hamilton, 1959.

Lecky, W.E., *History of Ireland in the Eighteenth Century*, Longman, 1892.

Leinster, Emily Duchess of, *Diaries and Letters*. ed. Brian Fitzgerald, Irish Stationery Office, 1957.

Malone, Andrew F., *Irish Drama*, London, 1929.

Maturin, Charles, *The life of Niilo Idman*, London, Constable, 1923.

Mavor, Elizabeth, *The Ladies of Llangollen*, London, Penguin, 1973.

Maxwell, Constantia, *Dublin under the Georges*, London, Harrap, 1936.

Maxwell, Constantia, *Country and Town in Eighteenth-Century Ireland*, London, Harrap, 1940.

Maxwell, Constantia, *The Stranger in Ireland*, London, Jonathan Cape, 1954.

Moers, Ellen, *The Dandy*, London, Secker and Warburg, 1960.

Moore, T., *Journal of Thomas Moore*, ed. Peter Quennell, London, Batsford, 1964.

Moore, T., *Life of Lord Edward Fitzgerald*, London, Longman, 1831.

O'Connor, Frank, *Kings, Lords and Commons*, Translations from the Irish, Knopf, 1959.

O'Faolain, Sean, *King of the Beggars: The Life of Dan O'Connell*, London, Viking Press, 1938.

O'Keefe, John, *Recollections*, London, 1826.

Paston, George, *Mrs. Delany A Memoir*, Grant Richards, 1900.

Sadleir, Michael, *Blessington D'Orsay*, London, Constable, 1933.

Sadlier, Michael, *Bulwer and his wife*, London, Constable, 1931.

Thrall, Miriam, *Rebellious Frasers*, Columbia University Press, 1934.

Tomalin, C., *Life of Mary Wollstonecraft*, London, Weidenfeld & Nicolson, 1975.

Yeats, W.B., *Collected Poems*, Macmillan, 1950.

Young, Arthur, *A Tour of Ireland: 1776–1779*, Dublin.

JOURNALS
Anthropologica Hibernica; *Athenaeum*; *Blackwood's*; *Edinburgh Review*; *Fraser's*; *Freeman's Journal*; *Quarterly Review*; *The Art Journal*.

INDEX

Pandora Press
LIFE AND TIMES

Already published:

Women of Letters
A Life of Virginia Woolf
by Phyllis Rose

Phyllis Rose stimulates a new way of viewing Virginia Woolf and the shape of her career, striving to overcome the traditional emphasis on Woolf's illness and suicide by showing the extent to which she directed her own life.

'Phyllis Rose writes with considerable insight and feeling of Woolf's attitude to herself as a woman and of the possibility of being a woman writer.' – Margaret Drabble, *New Statesman*
0–86358–066–1   paperback

Jane and May Morris
A Biographical Story 1839-1938
by Jan Marsh

'What an excellent book! Calmly written, beautifully researched, responsible and highly readable – the story, if you like, behind the wallpaper, of Jane and May, wife and daughter to William Morris, master craftsman.' – Fay Weldon, *Mail on Sunday*
illustrated/0–86358–026–2   cloth and paperback

Ellen and Edy
A Biography of Ellen Terry and her daughter, Edith Craig 1847-1947
by Joy Melville

The story of the life of the great Victorian actress and her suffragette daughter concentrates not so much on the public life of Ellen Terry as on her relationships with her son Ted, with Henry Irving, Shaw, and most of the mutually possessive but ultimately strong relationship between mother and daughter.

'I recommend Joy Melville's book . . . it has a sure grasp of the social setting; it also has the blessed virtue of clarity.' – Claire Tomalin, *Observer*
0–86358–078–5   paperback

This Narrow Place: Sylvia Townsend Warner and Valentine Ackland Life, Letters and Politics, 1930-1951
by Wendy Mulford

A celebration of a poignant and unique partnership between two remarkable and unorthodox women, politically committed writers, Communist Party activists and peace campaigners, whose relationship spanned the heady period of left-wing cultural activity during the 1930s and 1940s, and survived the strain of Sylvia's increasing fame as a novelist as well as Valentine's search for consolation through drinking and her other relationships. Wendy Mulford draws on unpublished letters, journals and photographs to bring us a vivid and moving picture of their lives together.
0-86358-056-4/0-86358-262-1   cloth and paperback

Rosa Luxemburg: A Life
by Elżbieta Ettinger

'Ettinger's approach extends our understanding of this divided woman. . . . Her biography brings alive Polish history and the predicament of Polish Jews . . . and shows us a woman who was at once vulnerable and ruthless, who challenged the customary destiny of woman intellectually, politically and sexually.' – Sheila Robotham, *New Society*

'A superb account of an exceptional life, incorporating the results of fresh research and told with an admirable balance of sympathy and critical detachment.' – *New Statesman*
0-86358-261-3   paperback

Forthcoming in 1988 and 1989

Charlotte Despard
by Margaret Mulvihill

Charlotte Despard (1844–1939) was, with Mrs Pankhurst and Mrs Fawcett, one of the three great widow-leaders of the Votes for Women movement. She was also a friend of Kier Hardie, a parliamentary candidate in 1918 (the first General Election in which women could be considered as candidates) and Maud Gonne's companion in her IRA safe house. A popular novelist, feminist and Republican, she was simultaneously a Theosophist and a Catholic, a pacifist and a revolutionary, a philanthropist and a socialist, and, above all, a woman of extraordinary faith, optimism and sheer courage.
0–86358–213–3   paperback

The Parnell Sisters
Women in an Irish World
by Mary Fitz Gerald
A vivid biography of Fanny and Anna Parnell which uses new sources to explore their controversial role in the politics of nineteenth-century Ireland.
0–86358–215–X   paperback

Maud Gonne
by Margaret Ward

In popular memory Maud Gonne is but the beauty who spurned the love of W. B. Yeats. This political biography by the author of the acclaimed *Smashing Times*, shows Maud Gonne to have been a truly remarkable fighter, friend to many women, imprisoned, exiled and a lifelong campaigner for Ireland from the 1880s to her death in 1953.
0–86358–284–2   paperback

Eva Gore-Booth and Esther Roper
by Gifford Lewis

Dual biography of the couple who left their privileged backgrounds to work for the poor, and for the suffrage in England. Eva is Constance Markievicz's sister, Esther the daughter of a missionary. They have been largely erased from the records; this is the fascinating and largely untold story of their life together.
0-86358-159-5   paperback

Constance Markievicz
by Anne Haverty

A fresh feminist biography of probably the best-known woman in the history of Irish nationalism. Anne Haverty gives us new insights into an exceptional, brave, unconventional woman, whose life dramatised the remarkable events of her time.
0-86358-161-7   paperback

Kitty O'Shea
by Mary Rose Callaghan

In this biography of the woman who is known as 'she who enslaved Parnell, the uncrowned king of Ireland', Mary Rose Callaghan aclaims a staunch, intelligent political figure, who has unjustly been made the scapegoat of history.
0-86358-156-0   paperback

Suzanne Valadon
by Felicity Edholm

Suzanne Valadon is one of the great French painters. Yet it is as Renoir's model and Utrillo's mother that she has been portrayed. Felicity Edholm tells her story – from peasant background to the last years as grande dame in Montmartre with verve and affection and with great sensitivity to Suzanne Valadon's art.
0–86358–241–9   cloth

Gluck
A Biography of Hannah Gluckstein
by Diana Souhami

The first, and authorised biography of the painter Gluck. Gluck broke convention in both her life and her art. In the 1930s she achieved her best work, dressed always as a man, 'a beautiful boy'. Diana Souhami gives us the remarkable life of a remarkable figure.
0–86358–236–2   cloth

Also available from Pandora Press

Local Heroines
A Women's History Gazetter to England, Scotland and Wales
by Jane Legget

A comprehensive guide to the places in mainland Britain associated with individuals and feminist achievements. *Local Heroines* puts women's history firmly on the map by seeking out the birthplaces, former homes, schools, places of work, sources of inspiration, graves and memorials of artists and actors, suffragettes and politicians, trade union activists and welfare workers. It covers pioneers in every field – from medicine to the military. A book for everyone interested in British women's history – from the earnest explorer and researcher to the laziest of armchair travellers.
0–86358–037–8/0–86358–193–5   cloth and paperback

Discovering Women's History
A Practical Manual
by Deirdre Beddoe

'An invaluable, fascinating guide to the raw material for anyone approaching this underexplored territory. – Sean French, *Sunday Times*
   'Deirdre Beddoe's book does exactly what it sets out to: it offers a clear, detailed and well-conceived guide to anyone who is interested, or thinks they could be interested, in digging into the past . . . She encourages us to begin from where we are now, to find out about our own family or school or street or workplace; to reappropriate our past as a way of understanding what we are and what we could be.' – Margaret Walters, *City Limits*
   '. . . a feminist history, a researcher's bible and a fascinating glimpse into the lives of our forebears.' – Katie Campbell, *Spare Rib*
0–86358–008–4   paperback

Order Form

Discovering Women's History Deirdre Beddoe	£4.95 ☐
Kitty O'Shea Mary Rose Callaghan	£7.95 ☐
Gluck: A Biography of Hannah Gluckstein Diana Souhami	£17.95 ☐
Rosa Luxemburg: A Life Elzbieta Ettinger	£5.95 ☐
The Parnell Sisters Mary Fitz Gerald	£7.95 ☐
Local Heroines: A Women's History Gazetteer to England,	
Scotland and Wales Jane Legget	£8.95 ☐
Eva Gore-Boothe and Esther Roper Gifford Lewis	£7.95 ☐
Jane and May Morris Jan Marsh	£4.95 ☐
Ellen and Edy Joy Melville	£5.95 ☐
This Narrow Place: Sylvia Townsend Warner and Valentine	
Ackland Wendy Mulford	£5.95 ☐
Charlotte Despard Margaret Mulvihill	£7.95 ☐
Women of Letters Phyllis Rose	£3.95 ☐
Constance Markiewicz Anne Haverty	£7.95 ☐
Maud Gonne Margaret Ward	£7.95 ☐
Suzanne Valadon Felicity Edholm	£17.95 ☐

All these books are available at your local bookshop or newsagent or can be ordered direct by post. Just tick the titles you want and fill in the form below.

_____

Name _____

Address _____

_____

_____

Send to: Unwin Hyman Cash Sales, PO Box 11, Falmouth, Cornwall TR10 9EN

Please enclose remittance to the value of the cover price plus:

UK: 60p for the first book plus 25p for the second book, thereafter 15p for each additional book ordered to a maximum charge of £1.90.

BFPO and EIRE: 60p for the first book plus 25p for the second book and 15p for the next 7 books and thereafter 9p per book.

OVERSEAS INCLUDING EIRE: £1.25 for the first book plus 75p for the second book and 28p for each additional book.

Unwin Paperbacks reserve the right to show new retail prices on covers which may differ from those previously advertised in the text or elsewhere. Postage rates are also subject to revision.